PRAISE FOR

The Myth of the A.D.D. Child

"Armstrong does more than just tell the reader what is wrong with the A.D.D. diagnosis. He provides innovative solutions to behavioral problems, none of which require medication. This is must reading for parents who seek safe, alternative solutions for managing a difficult child."

—Diane McGuinness, professor of psychology, University of Florida, author of *When Children Don't Learn*

"Provides parents and professionals with information and tools in helping children to develop positive behaviors at home and at school."

—Bettie B. Youngs, Ph.D., Ed.D., author of *Stress and Your Child* and *How to Develop Self-Esteem in Your Child*

"Full of good ideas that are inexpensive and without side-effects. A can't-lose investment for parents of distractible children."

—Richard Bromfield, Ph.D., Harvard Medical School, author of *Playing for Real: The World of Play Therapy*

(More .·. .)

THOMAS ARMSTRONG, Ph.D., is the author of seven books, including *Seven Kinds of Smart* (Plume), *In Their Own Way*, and *Awakening Your Child's Natural Genius*. A former special education teacher, he has written frequently on parenting and education issues for publications such as *Ladies' Home Journal* and *Family Circle*. He lives in Sonoma County, California.

"This is the book that many of us have been waiting for. It questions the all too pervasive A.D.D. label, and offers practical and sensible ways of dealing with the children so labeled."
— Louise Bates Ames, Ph.D., director, Gessell Institute

"Clarifying and demystifying . . . practical recommendations concerning the discipline of *all* children, not just ones with labels."
— John K. Rosemond, author of *John Rosemond's Six-Point Plan for Raising Happy, Healthy, Children*

"Superb information. . . . Dr. Armstrong brings new insights to the hyper child."
— Lendon H. Smith, M.D., author of *Feed Your Body Right*

"Authoritative, comprehensive, easy to read and understand. I highly recommend it."
— William G. Crook, M.D., author of *Solving the Puzzle of Your Hard-to-Raise Child*

The Myth of the A.D.D. Child

◆

50 Ways to Improve Your Child's
Behavior and Attention Span
Without Drugs, Labels, or Coercion

Thomas Armstrong, Ph.D.

A PLUME BOOK

PLUME
Published by the Penguin Group
Penguin Putnam Inc., 375 Hudson Street, New York, New York 10014, U.S.A.
Penguin Books Ltd, 27 Wrights Lane, London W8 5TZ, England
Penguin Books Australia Ltd, Ringwood, Victoria, Australia
Penguin Books Canada Ltd, 10 Alcorn Avenue, Toronto, Ontario, Canada M4V 3B2
Penguin Books (N.Z.) Ltd, 182–190 Wairau Road, Auckland 10, New Zealand

Penguin Books Ltd, Registered Offices: Harmondsworth, Middlesex, England

Published by Plume, an imprint of Dutton Signet,
a member of Penguin Putnam Inc.
Previously published in a Dutton edition.

First Plume Printing, September, 1997
20 19 18 17 16

 REGISTERED TRADEMARK—MARCA REGISTRADA

The Library of Congress has catalogued the Dutton edition as follows:
Armstrong, Thomas.
    The myth of the A.D.D. child: 50 ways to improve your child's behavior and attention
span without drugs, labels, or coercion / Thomas Armstrong.
        p.   cm.
    Includes bibliographical references.
    ISBN 0-525-93841-9 (hc.)
    ISBN 0-452-27547-4 (pbk.)
    1. Attention-deficit hyperactivity disorder—Diagnosis—Moral and ethical aspects.
2. Behavior disorders in children—Treatment.   3. Child rearing.   4. Attention-deficit
hyperactivity disorder—Treatment—Moral and ethical aspects.   5. Problem children—
Behavior modification.   I. Title.
RJ506.H9A76   1995
618.92'8589—dc20   95-9877
                                                                                                                              CIP

Printed in the United States of America
Original hardcover design by Eve L. Kirch

BOOKS ARE AVAILABLE AT QUANTITY DISCOUNTS WHEN USED TO PROMOTE PRODUCTS
OR SERVICES. FOR INFORMATION PLEASE WRITE TO PREMIUM MARKETING DIVISION,
PENGUIN PUTNAM INC., 375 HUDSON STREET, NEW YORK, NEW YORK 10014.

This book is dedicated to my father,
Dr. William B. Armstrong

Contents

Preface to the Paperback Edition

Since the publication of the hardcover edition of *The Myth of the A.D.D. Child* in 1995, A.D.D. has continued to gather momentum and shows no signs of slowing down. As a recent *Washington Post Magazine* article put it: "An entire subculture has grown up around A.D.D. . . . a world where science and medicine have mingled so thoroughly with capitalism and 12-step revivalism that it's hard to tell where the boundaries are anymore." Indeed, with its A.D.D. cyberspace chat rooms on Prodigy and other on-line services, with its nationwide network of support groups and "coaches" (people hired by A.D.D.ers to help them remember appointments, organize schedules, and the like), and with its proliferation of new books, systems, programs, drugs, and machines to treat A.D.D., this movement has developed a rich technomythology that rivals anything Steven Spielberg or George Lucas has ever put on the silver screen.

Science continues to feed this mythology with a number of studies suggesting that A.D.D. is a medical disorder having a genetic basis. Recently, headlines reported that A.D.D. was linked to the "thrill-seeking" gene, a gene that is related to the neurotransmitter dopamine (a brain chemical that, among other things, regulates the need for rewards). A few months later, however, in the same journal that reported the A.D.D. link, scientists failed to find any significant association between the dopamine gene and novelty seeking among groups of subjects in Finland, calling into question the validity of the "thrill-seeking" gene in the first place. The study brings up a larger issue, that is, the attempt by science and the media to reduce the complex personality behaviors of a human being to a single gene, or even a set of genes. This trend to geneticize human behavior all too often ignores the crucial impact that experience itself can have on genetic structure. Research at McGill University suggests that the genes for certain brain receptors in newborn rats can be altered simply by separating the babies from their mothers for six stressful hours a day. While studies of this kind cannot be carried out in humans for obvious ethical reasons, there is research showing a positive correlation between A.D.D. diagnoses and adversity in the home environment (including factors such as marital discord, parental mental disorder, foster care placement, and large family size). Such findings fit well with the perspective that a child's biochemical patterns might be significantly impaired by early trauma at home. To simply say that A.D.D. is genetic in origin lets environmental factors off the hook and might lead parents and professionals to neglect important environmental interventions that may positively impact biochemical and genetic structures.

Another problem with genetic studies are the interpretations given to them. The gene in question above has been variously called the "risk-taking" gene, the "thrill-seeking" gene, and the "novelty-seeking" gene. Each of these terms comes with a different set of attitudes. Risk taking sounds dangerous, but novelty seeking may actually be a good thing. In fact, novelty seeking is a trait closely linked to creativity. So, even if the A.D.D.-gene study cited above were correct, perhaps we'd be looking here at a "creativity" gene in kids who are labeled A.D.D. Bonnie Cramond, a researcher at the University of Georgia, has examined the similarities between the "symptoms" of A.D.D. and the traits of the creative person. Both the so-called A.D.D. individual and the creative person are highly active, tend to get easily "distracted" by ideas considered unimportant to others, and are willing to take chances. I'm alarmed to think that modern science may be turning creativity into a medical disorder having a genetic basis. Underlying the A.D.D. point of view is a severe bioreductionism that views reality as nothing but a collection of genes, neurons, and chemicals. The tremendous vitality of many children who are labeled A.D.D. should remind us that we're dealing with more than genes and chemicals here—we're talking about real human beings who have rich inner worlds that respond in myriad ways to the vagaries of the complex world into which they've been cast.

The A.D.D. world view also pathologizes these children by attempting to show that they have abnormal brains. One study, for example, suggested that certain parts of the corpus collosum (the structure that links the right and left hemispheres of the neocortex) were smaller in children identified as having A.D.D. than in so-called "normals." However, even one of this study's own researchers commented: "It's only slightly better than phrenology. Now we're just measuring the bumps on the inside of the brain." Moreover, even if there are subtle differences in the brains of some children labeled A.D.D., we may be looking at just that: differences, not abnormalities.

Perhaps these neurological differences add something *positive* to human diversity. I'm concerned about the way the medical model seems to be taking up so much of our lives and turning them into problems and even disorders. I was playing around with this idea the other day and fantasized about what the world would be like if everyone were a flower. I could see the Rose psychiatrist looking at every flower-patient as some kind of abnormality. His comments on the daisy might sound like this: "Clearly there are structural abnormalities—witness, for example, the large lobe that appears in the center and the perseverative regularity in the radiating petal structure." His diagnosis for the lily might be the following: "Here, the absence of unfolding petals in its core suggests a petal-deficit disorder." And finally, his research on the pansy might reveal the following: "This flower is quite obviously disordered in the way its pathologically flat petals persist through the frosts of winter—it is structurally incapable of withdrawing its petals when it quite obviously should do so." In each case, the Rose psychiatrist fails to appreciate the natural beauty of each flower, seeing instead its failure to measure up to his own standards of normality.

I suggest that we need to apply more of a naturalistic perspective to children labeled A.D.D. and to seek to become less labelers of what might be missing in their gene structure or outer brain matter and more acknowledgers and gardeners of what's positive and fertile within children's rich inner lives. I challenge the A.D.D. field to devote a sizeable portion of its multimillion-dollar research budget to studying the strengths, talents, abilities, and multiple intelligences of children labeled A.D.D. So far, they've done nothing at all in this area.

These idealistic visions of mine seem to be swimming against the tide of a more pragmatic time. A.D.D. thrives because it delivers more than it appears to take away from its hungry consumers. The A.D.D. label actually provides many material benefits to those who know how to work the system. *Forbes* magazine reports that parents seek to get their children classified as having A.D.D. to help them maintain a competitive edge in school and life. A diagnosis of A.D.D. qualifies students for more time to take the SAT, LSAT (law school entrance exam), and MCAT (medical school exam). It also enables individuals to receive special protections at work and school under the Americans with Disabilities Act. Parents can even receive Social Security (S.S.I.) monies for every child identified as A.D.D. The use of medications like Ritalin seems to be on the upswing for similar reasons. Many upper-middle-class parents see them almost as "cognitive steroids" that can be used to help their kids focus on their schoolwork better than the next kid, thus helping to ensure better performance on tests and a greater chance of admission into the college of their choice.

Before I get any deeper into the Ritalin controversy, however, I feel that I need to "come out of the medicine cabinet," so to speak, and describe a little of the personal conflict that has caused me to spend so many years focused on nonmedical alternatives to behavioral difficulties. When I was about six years old, my father started experiencing severe anxiety and depression. He began taking psychoactive medications, which seemed only to make the problems worse. He eventually stopped working and remained at home for seventeen years, dutifully taking his medications as prescribed by his psychiatrists. Finally, one day he decided to stop the medications on his own and began feeling better almost immediately. He eventually resumed his career as a pediatrician and retired at the age of seventy-eight. In my mind, psychiatric medication was partially responsible for diminishing the quality of a good part of my father's and our family's life.

About five years ago, as I was beginning to write this book, I was prepared to pour out my rage from this experience into a chronicle of the evils of Ritalin and other psychiatric drugs. Right around that time, I was teaching in Holland and under a great deal of stress from overwork, when I suddenly stopped sleeping for five days. I'd experienced chronic insomnia before (with accompanying depression and anxiety), but this was so severe that on my return to the United States I began taking an antidepressant. I found that it helped me sleep better than I had in years, and I also felt better about life in general. I discovered the personal benefits of medication in my own life even as I'd seen it disrupt a major part of my father's life.

It's really been the conflict between these two experiences—my own and my father's—that has provided much of the friction and its accompanying "heat" to fuel the writing of *The Myth of the A.D.D. Child.* I've seen in my father's case what can happen when medication is relied upon as the sole solution to complex problems. I've also personally experienced the benefits of medication in my own life, which is why I am put off by those who are attracted to my book because they feel Ritalin is poisoning our children's minds (like fluoride in the water system!). Medication is a tool, only one of many, that can be helpful to some when used with nonmedical approaches. (I also meditate, do yoga, exercise, keep a journal, go to psychotherapy, and practice other stress-reduction strategies.) And even though medication has helped me, I continue to be wary of the tremendous increase in the use of psychoactive medications to control children's behavior. I'm dismayed that more hasn't been made of a recent DEA report suggesting that methylphenidate use may be a risk factor for later substance abuse. While medications can be helpful, they can also be traps that keep us from searching for deeper and better solutions to the troubles in children's lives. I hope that this paperback edition of *The Myth of the A.D.D. Child* will help to further this quest by putting a wide range of practical nonmedical strategies into the hands of more and more parents and professionals, so that every child with behavioral or attentional difficulties may have the opportunity to reach his or her fullest potential.

Preface

In C. S. Lewis's wonderful children's classic *The Chronicles of Narnia*, there is a chilling scene in which the Queen of Underland seeks to enchant Prince Rilian and his traveling companions by throwing a green powder on a fire and then playing a monotonous tune on a mandolin-like instrument. These enchantments make it hard for the prisoners to think. The Prince starts to forget his real identity as head of Narnia. His friend Jill's memory of her life in England grows dim. They all begin to believe the Emerald Witch's story that their true home is there in the underworld prison where they find themselves incarcerated. Fortunately, a Narnian Marsh-wiggle named Puddleglum refuses to submit to this enchantment and helps the others clear their heads and remember their true identities. And thus, the spell is broken.

I often think of this scene when contemplating the growth over the past fifteen years of America's new learning disease: attention deficit disorder (A.D.D.). Through an aggressive public relations campaign, solid support from the medical community, and scores of well-meaning books and tapes for parents on helping "the A.D.D. child," millions of parents and teachers have been enchanted into believing in the existence of a discrete psychiatric illness called "attention deficit disorder" that supposedly afflicts millions of American children. I find that when I begin reading these books, listening to experts on the subject, and reviewing extensive scientific studies in the field of A.D.D., I too feel the greenish musk of the Queen's magic powder begin to lull me into acquiescence, and a little voice speaks in me saying: "You know, Thomas, there really *are* kids who have A.D.D.!"

But then the wise and woolly Marsh-wiggle inside of me rouses into action and speaks a more fundamental truth echoing my deepest feelings about children, growth, and learning: "A.D.D. *does not exist;* these children are *not* disordered. They may have a different style of thinking, attending, and behaving, but it's the broader social and educational influences that create the disorder, not the children." At such times I realize that I am actually speaking for the children when I present more positive ways of looking at those who struggle with attention and behavior problems. And so, it is in honor of Puddleglum, the children of the world, and all those who strive to remember the true nature of things, that I present to you this book.

This is a book based on a *wellness* model of children and learning. It suggests that children who experience attention or behavior problems are themselves at core fully intact, whole, and *healthy* human beings— not kids suffering from a medical disorder. It proposes that the best way of helping these kids is not by saddling them with a medical label and then applying a cautiously selected group of specialized treatments, but by providing them with the kinds of nurturing, stimulating, and encouraging interventions that are good for *all* kids!

The Myth of the A.D.D. Child is divided into two main sections. In the first, my objective is to help clear the reader's mind of the enchanting effects of what I call "the A.D.D. myth." Chapter 1 looks at the A.D.D. phenomenon for what it really is: a recent historical development that represents a confluence of parent advocacy groups, legislative efforts, psychological studies, pharmaceutical advances, and psychiatric endorsements. A.D.D. isn't an educational "virus" that's been lurking in the brains of our children for centuries waiting for a chance to spring into action. Instead, A.D.D. is a construct that was essentially invented in the cognitive psychology laboratories of our nation's (and Canada's) universities, and then given life by the American Psychiatric Association, the U.S. Department of Education, and the chemical laboratories of the world's pharmaceutical corporations.

Chapter 2 examines the specious nature of this so-called disorder— how, like a UFO, it makes appearances here and there to its circle of believers but never really materializes into a full-fledged disorder that can be authoritatively identified in the same way as polio, heart disease, or other legitimate illnesses.

Chapter 3 provides a number of alternative explanations for why children might have the behavior or attention problems that experts currently link to A.D.D. One of the biggest difficulties with the A.D.D. myth is that its holy trinity of symptoms—hyperactivity, distractibility, and impulsivity—are sufficiently global as to be likely to result from any of a wide number of potential causes. A child can have trouble paying attention or behaving, for example, because his schoolwork is boring, because his family is going through a crisis, because his way of learning doesn't match the school's way of teaching, because he's allergic to milk, because his temperament doesn't match that of his parents, or because he's anxious or depressed. In Chapter 3, I look at these and other alternative explanations for A.D.D. symptoms and explain why the A.D.D. experts don't do a sufficiently effective job of telling us where these factors leave off and A.D.D. begins.

Chapter 4 looks at the use of medication to control A.D.D.: what's good about it and what some of its problem are. Contrary to what people may think, I don't advocate the elimination of medication as a treatment strategy for kids with attention and behavior problems. I've heard too many medication success stories from parents and teachers and I've come to realize that some children can really benefit from its judicious use. But I'm alarmed at the way psychoactive medications have become the treatment of choice for behavior and attention problems in our society. The more parents focus on drugs as solutions for their children's behavior problems, the less likely it will be that they'll look at important non-drug interventions. In fact, that's how this book was born. I was practically booed off the stage of a high school auditorium in upstate New York in 1989 when I made the comment "I'm not sure parents are aware of all the different non-drug approaches that are out there!" It was at that moment of running for cover that I realized there needed to be a book that laid out the wide range of alternative strategies to improve attention and behavior.

Chapter 5 examines the non-drug alternatives recommended by the A.D.D. community. In looking over the short list, I am now able to understand why those New York parents reacted so strongly to my statement. It was because their understanding of treatment alternatives was formed from reading A.D.D.-community sponsored literature, in which relatively few treatment approaches are promoted. I am struck by the general level of poverty when it comes to A.D.D.-community-sanctioned interventions. Apparently, if a treatment method can't be scientifically "proven" through a double-blind placebo-controlled study, then it is discarded by many in the A.D.D. community. That's one reason why *only two treatments* are consistently recommended by A.D.D. experts: medications and behavior modification.

I was originally going to include behavior modification in my book because, after all, it represented a drug-free approach. However, I remembered reading about a spokesperson with Canines for Independence—a group that trains dogs to help individuals with disabilities—who said that she never uses treats as rewards when training her dogs, because then "they'll always be expecting them in the future." I figured that if rewards weren't good enough for dogs, then they weren't going to be good enough for children either. Then I ran into Alfie Kohn's wonderful book *Punished by Rewards.* In this well-researched work, Kohn demonstrates that using rewards to make children behave subverts initiative, cooperation, creativity, and the desire to learn for its own sake. His book provided me with enough solid evidence demonstrating the many drawbacks of behavior modification to support my intuition and justify my keeping it out of this book.

In the second part of this book, I present fifty practical strategies to help your child discover his true nature and achieve success in life. I was inspired to choose fifty ways by the popular ecology handbook *50 Things You Can Do to Save the Earth.* I believe that children are the earth's most valuable natural resource and in particular that kids who have been labeled hyperactive or A.D.D. are sitting on a storehouse of creative energy that hasn't yet been effectively tapped. I'd like to think of my book as an ecology guide for conserving and channeling this precious energy source. Rather than viewing your child as a disordered individual who at best can learn to live with his handicap, I choose instead to value and to celebrate the dynamic energy, creativity, spontaneity, vitality, and uniqueness that lives within every child regardless of label.

The Myth of the A.D.D. Child is an antidote to the inherent conservativism that runs through the A.D.D. worldview. Inside you'll discover a rich and diverse collection of strategies, resources, activities, and exercises to deal with the wide variety of issues that come up in the lives of those with behavior and attention problems. This is a book for awakening that incredible person inside your child and for learning how to channel his creative energies into productive pathways. I'm not saying that he doesn't currently have some major obstacles in his way. But I would suggest that one of the biggest roadblocks he may currently confront is the limiting set of beliefs the A.D.D. myth engenders about who he really is and what he's capable of achieving.

I've designed each of the fifty strategies to be of maximum benefit to you as a parent or teacher. For each strategy, I supply practical guidelines, present current research and other support, and finally include a listing of resources to help you go more deeply into the subject. Because I believe that there is no single way to help children with attention and behavior problems, I've provided a wide range of interventions touching upon educational, cognitive, psychological, behavioral, biological, and even cultural issues. Some of these strategies, such as the Feingold diet or psychotherapy, I've simply asked you to consider— since only a certain group of children may specifically benefit from them. But most of the approaches can help any child. That's why I feel this book can be valuable for almost any parent. But in particular, this book may be useful to you if:

♦ Your child is currently on medication and you're looking for non-drug supplementary activities as part of a total treatment plan

♦ Your child is currently on medication and you'd like to work with your child's physician on implementing non-drug strategies so that his dosage can be decreased or even eliminated

♦ Your child is about to be tested and considered for medication and/or special education and you'd like to get a different perspective on him than the one provided by the A.D.D. community or the school

♦ Your child is highly active, possibly a candidate for labeling as A.D.D., but you'd like to explore some ideas and activities first before getting involved in the process of diagnosis and treatment

♦ Your child isn't a candidate for labeling as A.D.D. but he seems like he would benefit from many of the suggestions made in this book

There is a questionaire on pages 63–66 to guide you in selecting those approaches that might be of special benefit to your child. Finally, I've provided a comprehensive Notes section to show you that what I say in this book is not merely my opinion but represents as well some of the best cutting-edge research in the fields of child development, human learning, and educational psychology (including many sources from the A.D.D. community itself).

I'd like to thank several people who helped immeasurably in the development of this book, including Peter Schrag and Diane Divoky (whose 1975 book *The Myth of the Hyperactive Child* provided the inspiration for the title of this book), Gerald Coles, John George, Diane McGuinness, and the editors of *Parenting* and *Mothering* magazines for providing me with support over the years in offering an alternative perspective with regard to A.D.D. I want to thank my editor at Dutton, Deb Brody, for her enthusiasm for the project and her apt comments on early drafts of the book, Eivind Allan Boe, for his meticulous care in even the smallest detail of the manuscript, and my literary agent, Linda Allen. I'd like to thank my wife, Barbara Turner, for all her patience and encouragement during the writing of this book. And a special thanks to the hundreds of teachers and parents who wrote to me, called me, communicated with me through online computer services, or spoke with me in person and shared their stories. Many of these stories were filled with pain and spoke of journeys through educational bureaucracies and medical mazes, family conflicts, and school troubles. I want to say that I feel the heartache of many of you and hope that this book offers some degree of support, guidance, hope, and inspiration in your very important work of guiding our generation of creative and energetic kids into the next millennium.

◆ PART ONE ◆

Uncovering the
A.D.D. Myth

Chapter 1

America's New Learning Disease

I'll never forget Manny. This remarkable twelve-year-old son of a Portuguese immigrant worker was a student of mine in the mid-1970s in a special education class I taught at a junior high school in Montreal, Canada. Manny actually looked like a miniature Robin Williams, and the resemblance didn't end there. Frequently cracking jokes and hamming it up in the middle of class, Manny was the class clown. Yet Manny could also be deadly serious and even philosophical. I remember some of our best times together were spent outside of the classroom, in the walks we took in a nearby park discussing life, the world, and our futures. He always functioned better when he was on the move. Seeming so mature at times, Manny was also like a toddler in the way that he was attracted to new things. He could really irritate me when he would burst out of his seat with no warning during class and walk toward an object of interest—a book, a poster on the wall, a new game—completely oblivious to the rules of the class, my astonishment, or the titters of his classmates. Manny was truly an enigma, a delight, a burden, a perpetual motion machine, and a test of my patience, all wrapped up in one fascinating package.

Today, Manny would probably be labeled attention deficit disordered (A.D.D.) and medicated to help control his impulsive, distractible, and hyperactive behaviors. No doubt this might have helped him immeasurably. Possibly, too, it could even have allowed him to return to a regular classroom from my special education program. But I wonder what such labeling and medication might have done to Manny's uniqueness, to his "Manny-ness." Somehow I would almost prefer my uneven memories of Manny to a more sanitized version such as "that hyperactive kid we successfully treated back in '76."

It seems as if the past fifteen or twenty years has witnessed a kind of takeover by the medical establishment of certain domains that were once the province of the educator and the parent. Children who were once seen as "bundles of energy," "daydreamers," or "fireballs," are now considered "hyperactive," "distractible," and "impulsive": the three classic warning signs of attention deficit disorder. Kids who in times past might have needed to "blow off a little steam" or "kick up a little dust" now have their medication dosages carefully measured out and monitored to control dysfunctional behavior.

I'm not necessarily arguing that medication is a bad thing for some kids. I feel certain that thousands of children have been helped by the use of psychoactive medication used in conjunction with non-drug interventions. However, I wonder whether there aren't hundreds of thousands of kids out there who may be done a disservice by having their uniqueness reduced to a disorder and by having their creative spirit controlled by a drug. This, then, is the essential motivation behind my writing *The Myth of the A.D.D. Child:* to question America's new learning disease (A.D.D.) and the primary treatment for this "disorder" (Ritalin), and to provide parents and professionals with some alternative ways of thinking about and helping kids with behavior and attention problems.

The A.D.D. Myth

If you should pick up any of the many recent popular books on attention deficit disorder written by physicians, psychologists, or concerned parents, you will probably be indoctrinated into the "A.D.D. myth," a certain set of beliefs offered up as basic truths about why some children won't behave or pay attention. I'd like to present this myth to you before going on to explore some of the problems that are inherent in such a perspective. Here, then, is the A.D.D. myth:

A.D.D. is a neurologically based disorder, most probably of genetic origin, that afflicts from 3 to 5 percent of America's children (roughly two million children in all). Significantly more boys appear to have this disorder than girls, although girls who have evaded detection for years are increasingly being identified. A.D.D. is characterized by three main features: hyperactivity (e.g., fidgeting, excessive running and climbing, leaving one's classroom seat), impulsivity (e.g., blurting out answers in class, interrupting others, having problems waiting turns), and inattention (e.g., forgetfulness, disorganization, losing things, careless mistakes). Current thinking has identified three major groups of A.D.D. children, one group that appears more hyperactive-impulsive, another that seems more inattentive, and a third that combines all three traits. There is no lab test available to diagnose this condition. Assessment methods include parent, child, and teacher interviews, a thorough medical examination, and the use of specially designed behavior rating scales and performance tests.

There is no known "cure" for A.D.D., but it can be successfully treated in most instances using psychoactive medication (usually methylphenidate hydrochloride, commonly known as Ritalin, but also other drugs, including psychostimulants, antidepressants, and anticonvulsants), as well as behavior modification, a structured classroom setting, parent training, and counseling as needed. There is no known cause of A.D.D., but current thinking sees it as involving biochemical imbalances in areas of the brain that are responsible for attention, planning, and motor activity.

Children who suffer from A.D.D. can experience significant school problems, suffer from low self-esteem, have difficulty relating to peers, and encounter problems in complying with rules at home leading to conflict with parents. Some kids with A.D.D. also have learning disabilities, conduct disorders (destructive and/or antisocial behaviors), Tourette's syndrome (a disorder characterized by uncontrollable motor or verbal "tics"), and/or mood disorders including depression and anxiety. While A.D.D. seems to disappear for some children around puberty, it can represent a lifelong disorder for up to half of all those initially diagnosed.

This represents a quick overview of the A.D.D. myth. While it may neglect certain fine points in the overall picture, there is little in the above summary that most A.D.D. experts would seriously disagree with. And for the most part, it represents a coherently organized system of beliefs—an orthodoxy, so to speak—that helps contextualize the concerns parents, teachers, and other professionals have about children who won't behave or pay attention despite appearing normal in other ways. The problem with the above canon is not so much that it is wrong—for within its little universe it makes perfect sense, as most myths do. The problem, rather, lies in the fact that it omits, or gives scant attention to, the broader social, political, economic, psychological, and educational issues that have surrounded this term—and others like it—from its inception. To begin to shed light on this wider context, let's look at the history of A.D.D.

The Birth of a Learning Disease

Restless children who don't mind their parents and who ignore their teachers have probably been around since the dawn of humanity—and even earlier, if evidence of impudent tykes from the animal kingdom give us any indication. However, the roots of modern-day attention and behavior problems—and their control—might very well be found in a nineteenth-century children's tale written by German doctor Heinrich Hoffmann for the benefit of his son. Among the characters represented, there is one Fidgety Phil:

> Fidgety Phil,
> He won't sit still,
> He wriggles,
> And giggles
> And then, I declare,
> Swings backwards and forwards
> And tilts up his chair . . .

This tale stresses a Teutonic ideal of discipline and control, virtues that appear to quietly but firmly underline the modern-day A.D.D. myth.

The medicalization of attention and behavior problems seems to have taken place around the turn of the century, with the 1902 lectures of George Frederic Still to the Royal College of Physicians in England that were published in the British journal *Lancet*. Still described twenty children in his clinical practice who were often aggressive, defiant, resistant to discipline, excessively emotional or "passionate," showed little "inhibitory volition," and displayed lawlessness, spitefulness, cruelty, and dishonesty. Still believed that these children shared a basic "defect in moral control," which was probably hereditary in some children, and due to pre- or postbirth injury in others.

This linking of children's troublesome behaviors to biological causes received a big boost during a major epidemic of encephalitis that affected large numbers of children during and after World War I. Doctors noticed that children with this disease often developed a postencephalitic syndrome with symptoms that included impaired memory and attention, poor motor control, irritability, personal untidiness, and general hyperactivity. Other researchers during the 1920s and 1930s investigated the relationship between behavior problems and birth trauma or postbirth head injuries in children. The 1930s also saw the first use of psychoactive drugs to control hyperactivity. A Portland, Oregon, physician, Charles Bradley, reported that the use of benzedrine—a stimulant drug—helped to calm the behavior of hyperactive children.

A further milestone in the development of A.D.D. occurred in the 1940s, when several researchers at the Wayne County Training School in Northville, Michigan, studied the psychological effects of brain injury in a group of mentally retarded children. Among the symptoms observed were distractibility and hyperactivity. Their work culminated in the 1947 publication of *Psychopathology and Education of the Brain-Injured Child*, and led the way in the 1950s and 1960s to the use of such terms as "minimal brain damage," "minimal brain dysfunction," or simply "MBD," to describe children who displayed these characteristics. The term *MDB*, however, fell out of favor during the 1960s, when little evidence was produced to show that brain damage actually existed in these kids. The 1960s also saw the first use of Ritalin (in 1961) in the treatment of hyperactivity and the first official "consecration," in 1968, of A.D.D.-precursor "hyperkinetic reaction of childhood" as a disorder by the American Psychiatric Association (APA).

In the 1970s, psychologists and psychiatrists turned the focus of their research regarding behavior problems in children to the study of *attention problems*. Canadian researcher Virginia Douglas may have helped to initiate this new focus in 1970, when she delivered her presidential address to the Canadian Psychological Association, arguing that deficits in attention were more likely to be the real culprit in many children's behavioral difficulties rather than hyperactivity. By the end of the 1970s, there were over two thousand published studies on attention deficits. The APA sanctioned this new disease in 1980 by listing "attention deficit disorder" in the third edition of its influential *Diagnostic and Statistical Manual (DSM-III)*.

The 1980s witnessed an even greater surge in research on A.D.D., and the founding in 1987 of the parent advocacy group Children with Attention Deficit Disorder (CH.A.D.D.), which mushroomed in size from twenty-nine chapters in 1988 to over six hundred chapters in forty-nine states by 1994. In 1994, the best-selling book *Driven to Distraction* and a cover story in *Time* magazine on attention deficit disorder put A.D.D.

on the lips and in the minds of millions of Americans. One commentator in the *Time* article even suggested that President Bill Clinton had A.D.D. and was "only a pill away from greatness." By the mid-1990s, A.D.D. had come into its own as the learning disease *du jour* of American culture.

The Hidden History of A.D.D.

It should be apparent from reading the brief history above that A.D.D. has had a rather bumpy ride on its way to its current popularity. The syndrome itself has gone through at least twenty-five different name changes in the past century, including:

- ◆ organic drivenness
- ◆ restlessness syndrome
- ◆ postencephalitic behavior disorder
- ◆ Strauss syndrome
- ◆ brain-injured child
- ◆ minimal brain dysfunction
- ◆ minimal brain damage
- ◆ hyperactive child syndrome
- ◆ hyperkinetic reaction of childhood
- ◆ developmental hyperactivity
- ◆ attention deficit disorder (A.D.D.)
- ◆ attention deficit hyperactivity disorder (ADHD)

The history of this disorder, then, is not like the stories of how other diseases, like polio, diabetes, or AIDS, were discovered. This is not the tale of a hidden disorder carefully unmasked by scientists through years of patient research. It appears more closely to resemble the errant wanderings of a pinball through the mazes of an arcade machine. And the discovery of "attention deficit disorder" represents not so much the unveiling of a malady that has been waiting for decades to be discovered, as it does the confluence of complex social, political, economic, medical, and psychological factors coming together at just the right time.

It seems improbable, for example, that A.D.D. would have received such widespread support as a learning disease had not the powerful American Psychiatric Association officially named it as a disorder in 1980. Yet it should be remembered that psychiatric illnesses tend to go in and out of fashion with the social and political climate of the times.

Before 1974, for example, homosexuality was considered by the APA to be a disease. During the 1930s, individuals scoring low enough on standardized intelligence tests could be diagnosed by psychiatrists as "idiots," "imbeciles," or "morons."

Similarly, over the past forty years, the APA has shifted dramatically in its classification of restless and inattentive children. In the early 1950s, the APA had no category for restless and inattentive children. Children who showed these problems would be listed in the *Diagnostic and Statistical Manual (DSM)* under "organic brain syndromes," and comparatively few children qualified. With each new edition of the *DSM*, however, psychiatrists created categories for hyperactivity and inattention that included more and more children. As University of Houston psychologists Gay Goodman and Mary Jo Poillion put it: "The field [of A.D.D.] has shifted from a very narrow, medically based category to a much broader, more inclusive and more subjective category ... In part, this could be because the characteristics for A.D.D. have been subjectively defined by a committee rather than having been developed on the basis of empirical evidence."

A.D.D.'s growth and development also benefited greatly from governmental support. The parent advocacy group CH.A.D.D. lobbied Congress in 1990 to have A.D.D. officially declared a handicapping condition eligible for special services under federal law. It encountered massive opposition, however, from several national educational and civil rights groups which argued, among other things, that the A.D.D. label could be used to stigmatize minority children. As a result, Congress refused to certify A.D.D. as a handicapping condition under the new law. Yet in 1991, a letter from the U.S. Department of Education to state school superintendents outlined three ways in which children labeled A.D.D. could qualify for special education services in public schools under existing laws. Having been stopped by Congress, A.D.D. essentially came into the schools quietly through the back door.

There is an economic side to A.D.D., as well, that serves to drive its popularity. Many people have something to gain financially from the continued existence of this "disease." Pharmaceutical companies collect hundreds of millions of dollars annually from the drugs that are sold to treat the estimated one million children who are currently being medicated for A.D.D. Physicians, psychologists, and learning specialists have new markets opened up for them in treating the needs of children with A.D.D. It costs, for example, an estimated $1,200 for the medical diagnosis of a child suspected of having A.D.D. and $1,270 for a school system evaluation to determine eligibility for special education. One brochure for psychologists that I received in the mail advertised "How to Effectively Market the ADHD and Other Sub-Specialty Segments of Your Practice." Another brochure advertised a Caribbean cruise to learn more about A.D.D. Hundreds of tests, learning programs, and other educational materials have been created over the past five years, the makers of which in each case are seeking to get at least a piece of the A.D.D. market. It appears, then, that those individuals with a robust capitalistic instinct in America know when they see a good thing and have responded by turning A.D.D. into a veritable growth industry likely to remain in existence into the foreseeable future.

Finally, it seems unlikely that A.D.D. would have become a popular and respectable idea in this country if our nation's psychological and psychiatric research institutions had not embraced cognitive and psychopharmaceutical perspectives from the 1960s until the present. Previous to that time, the psychology departments of our nation's universities were ruled largely by the behaviorists, and the psychiatric training institutes were fundamentally psychoanalytic in their theoretical orientation. Consequently, a child's hyperactive or inattentive behaviors were more likely to be chalked up to poor conditioning or the absence of a father figure in the house.

During the 1950s and 1960s, however, a revolution occurred in psychiatry, as a whole host of psychoactive medications were discovered that could be used to treat a wide range of mental illnesses. Drug treatment began to replace psychoanalysis as the treatment of choice for many psychiatrists. Similarly, at about the same time, research psychologists began to focus their attention less on the external behaviors of human beings and more on the internal workings of the mind, including such factors as memory, perception, and, significantly, *attention*. The shifts that occurred in professional priorities over the past three decades were tailor-made for the creation of a cognitive problem (attention deficit disorder) that could be treated primarily through psychopharmaceutical intervention (medications).

Essentially, then, A.D.D. appears to exist largely because of a unique coming together of the interests of frustrated activist parents, a highly developed psychopharmacological technology, a new cognitive research paradigm, a growth industry in new educational products, and a group of professionals (teachers, doctors, and psychologists) eager to introduce them to each other—all of this taking place under the beneficent influence of governmental approval. Of course, such a coordination of efforts would hardly be a problem if A.D.D. really existed as a discrete clinical entity. Then the governmental, psychiatric, social, and economic factors described above could be positively viewed as the logical outcome of a concerted attempt to meet the needs of children who have this disorder. However, as we'll see in the next chapter, no one really can be certain what A.D.D. is, how prevalent it is, or what causes it. While there are thousands of studies that have been done in the past three decades using some version of the A.D.D. myth as a governing paradigm, once we begin to peel away the artifice, layer by layer, we discover that—as with the disappearing Cheshire cat in Lewis Carroll's classic children's tale—all we're really left with in the end is the smile, if that.

Chapter 2

A.D.D.: Now You See It,
Now You Don't

Several years ago I worked for an organization that assisted teachers in using the arts in their classrooms. We were located in a large warehouse in Cambridge, Massachusetts, and several children in the surrounding lower-working-class neighborhood volunteered to help with routine jobs. I recall one child, Eddie, a nine-year-old African American youngster possessed of great vitality and energy who was particularly valuable in helping out with many tasks. These jobs included going around the city with an adult supervisor and finding recycled materials that could be used by teachers in developing arts programs, then organizing the materials, and even field-testing them back at the headquarters. In the context of this arts organization, Eddie was a definite asset.

A few months after this experience, I became involved in a special program through Lesley College, where I was getting my masters degree in special education. This project involved studying "resource rooms" (special education programs designed to help students who were having problems learning or behaving in the regular classroom) in several Boston-area school districts. During one visit to a Cambridge resource room, I unexpectedly ran into Eddie. Eddie was a real problem in this classroom. He couldn't stay in his seat, wandered around the room, talked out of turn, and basically made the teacher's life miserable. Eddie seemed like a fish out of water. In the context of this school's special education program, Eddie was anything but an asset. In retrospect, he appeared to fit the definition of a child with attention deficit disorder.

A.D.D.: The Disorder That Goes "Poof!"

The gap that existed between Eddie in the arts organization and Eddie in the special education classroom underscores what I feel is a primary difficulty with the definition of attention deficit disorder. By stating that A.D.D. is a *medical disorder*, experts are placing the source of the problem *inside of* the child. Yet, unlike other medical diseases, such as diabetes or pneumonia, this is a disorder that pops up in one setting, only to disappear in another. A physician mother with wiggly kids of her own wrote to me not long ago about her frustration with this protean diagnosis: "When I ... began pointing out to people that my child is capable of long periods of concentration when he is watching his favorite sci-fi video or examining the inner workings of a pin-tumbler lock, I notice that the next year's definition states that some kids with A.D.D. are capable of normal attention in certain specific circumstances. Poof! A few thousand more kids instantly fall into the definition."

There is in fact substantial evidence to suggest that children labeled A.D.D. do not show symptoms of this disorder in several different real-life contexts. First, up to 80 percent of them don't appear to be A.D.D. when in the physician's office. They also seem to behave normally in other unfamiliar settings where there is a one-to-one interaction with an adult (and this is especially true when the adult happens to be their father). Second, they appear to be indistinguishable from so-called normals when they are in classrooms or other learning environments where children can choose their learning activities and pace themselves through those experiences. Third, they seem to perform quite normally when they are *paid* to do specific activities designed to assess attention. Fourth, and perhaps most significantly, children labeled A.D.D. behave and attend quite normally when they are involved in activities that *interest* them, that are *novel* in some way, or that involve high levels of *stimulation*. Finally, about 50 percent of these children reach adulthood and discover that the A.D.D. apparently just goes away. Poof!

It's understandable, then, that prevalence figures for A.D.D. vary widely, far more widely than the standard 3 to 5 percent figure that popular books and articles use as a standard. As Russell Barkley points out in his classic work on attention deficits, *Attention Deficit Hyperac-*

tivity Disorder: A Handbook for Diagnosis and Treatment, the 3 to 5 percent figure "hinges on how one chooses to define ADHD, the population studied, the geographic locale of the survey, and even the degree of agreement required among parents, teachers and professionals.... Estimates vary between 1–20 percent." In fact, estimates fluctuate even more than Barkley suggests. In one epidemiological survey conducted in England, only 2 children out of 2,199 were diagnosed as hyperactive (0.09 percent). Conversely, in a study in Israel, 28 percent of children were rated as hyperactive by their teachers. And in an earlier study conducted in the United States, teachers rated 49.7 percent of boys as restless, 43.5 percent of boys as having "short attention span," and 43.5 percent of boys as "inattentive to what others say."

The Rating Game

These wildly divergent statistics call into question the assessments used to decide who is A.D.D. and who is not. Among the most widely used tools for this purpose are behavior rating scales. These are typically checklists consisting of items that relate to the child's attention and behavior at home or school. In one widely used scale, teachers are asked to rate the child on a scale from 1 (almost never) to 5 (almost always) in terms of behavioral statements such as "Fidgety (hands always busy)," "Restless (squirms in seat)," and "Follows a sequence of instructions." The problem with these scales is that they depend upon *subjective judgments* by teachers and parents who may have a deep, and often subconscious, emotional investment in the outcome. After all, a diagnosis of A.D.D. may lead to medication to keep a child compliant at home or may result in special education placement in the school to relieve a regular classroom teacher of having to teach a troublesome child. To put it more bluntly, How would you like your *own* psychiatric status to be determined by your relatives and teachers?

Moreover, since these behavior rating scales depend upon opinion rather than fact, there is no objective criteria through which to decide *how much* a child is demonstrating symptoms of A.D.D.. What is the difference in terms of hard data, for example, between a child who scores a 5 on being fidgety, and a child who scores a 4? Does that mean that the first child is one point more fidgety than the second? Of course not. The idea of assigning a number to a behavior trait raises the additional problem, addressed above, of context. The child may be a 5 on "fidgetiness" in some contexts (during worksheet time, for example) and a 1 at other times (during recess, motivating activities, and at other highly stimulating times of the day). Who is to decide what the final number should be based on? If a teacher places more importance upon workbook learning than on hands-on activities such as building with blocks, the rating may be biased toward academic tasks, yet this would hardly paint an accurate picture of the child's total experience in school, let alone in life.

It's not surprising, then, to discover that there is often disagreement among parents, teachers, and professionals using these behavior rating scales as to who exactly is hyperactive or A.D.D. In one study, parent, teacher, and physician groups were asked to identify hyperactive children in a sample of five thousand elementary school children. Approximately 5 percent were considered hyperactive by at least one of the groups, while only 1 percent were considered hyperactive by all three groups. In another study using a well-known behavior rating scale, mothers and fathers agreed only about 32 percent of the time on whether a child of theirs was hyperactive, and parent-versus-teacher ratings were even worse: they agreed only about 13 percent of the time.

These behavior rating scales implicitly ask parents and teachers to compare a potential A.D.D. child's attention and behavior to that of a "normal" child. But this raises the question, What is normal behavior? Do normal children fidget? Of course they do. Do normal children have trouble paying attention? Yes, under certain circumstances. So exactly when does normal fidgeting turn into A.D.D. fidgeting, and when does normal difficulty in paying attention become A.D.D. difficulty?

These questions have not been adequately addressed by professionals in the field; indeed, they cast serious doubt over the legitimacy of behavior rating scales. Curiously, with all the focus being placed on children who score at the *high* end of the hyperactivity and distractibility continuum, virtually no one in the field talks about the kids who must statistically exist at the low end of the behavioral bell curve: children who are *too* focused, *too* compliant, *too* still; children who are *hypo*active. Why don't we have special classes, medications, and treatments for these kids as well?

A Brave New World of Soulless Tests

Besides behavior rating scales, special "continuous performance tasks" (CPTs) are used to diagnose children as A.D.D.. These tasks usually involve repetitive actions that require the examinee to remain alert and attentive throughout the test. The earliest versions of these tasks were developed to select candidates for radar operations during World War II. Their use with children in today's world is highly questionable. One of the most popular of the current CPT instruments is the Gordon Diagnostic System (GDS). This Orwellian device consists of a plastic box with a large button on the front and an electronic display above it that flashes a series of random digits. The child is told to press the button every time a "1" is followed by a "9." The box then records the number of "hits" and "misses" made by the child. More complex versions, involving multiple digits, are used with older children and adults.

Quite apart from the fact that this task bears no resemblance to anything else that the child will ever do in his life, the GDS creates an "objective" score that is taken as an important measure of his ability to attend. In reality, it only tells us how a child will perform when attending to a repetitive series of meaningless numbers on a soulless task. Yet A.D.D. expert Russell Barkley writes: "[The GDS] is the only CPT that has enough available evidence . . . to be adopted for clinical practice." As a result, the GDS is used not only to assess children for A.D.D., but also to determine and adjust medication doses for children with the label.

Other diagnostic tools used to test for A.D.D. in children include the following:

♦ *The Matching Familiar Figures Test (MFFT):* The child is shown a picture of a common object; the child must then choose the identical matching picture from among a group of six pictures that look very similar to each other.

♦ *The Wechsler Intelligence Scale for Children:* Certain tasks on this test (including remembering random digits, solving arithmetic problems, and working with a code) are said to be indicators of a child's freedom from or inclination toward distractibility—one aspect of A.D.D.

♦ *The Wisconsin Card Sort Test:* The child must sort cards that have different-colored geometric shapes and numbers of shapes on them according to a rule known only to the examiner; the child must guess this rule in as few trials as possible using feedback from the examiner on whether the child has sorted the cards correctly.

Again, these tasks bear little resemblance to real life. More importantly, these tests, while appropriate for other psychological purposes, have not generally been useful in helping to identify A.D.D. in children, and are not even recommended by many professionals within the A.D.D. community itself.

There is a broader difficulty with the use of *any* standardized assessment to identify children as A.D.D. Most of the approaches discussed above (including behavior rating scales and continuous performance tasks) have themselves been assessed as indicators of A.D.D. through a process that involves testing groups of children who have been previously labeled A.D.D. and comparing the results with groups of children who have been judged to be "normal." If the assessment shows that it can discriminate between these two groups to a significant degree, it is then touted as a valid indicator of A.D.D. However, one must ask how the initial group of A.D.D. children came to be originally identified as A.D.D. The answer would have to be through an earlier test. And how do we know that the earlier test was a valid indicator of A.D.D.? Because it was validated using two groups: A.D.D. and normal. How do we know that *this* group of A.D.D. children was in fact A.D.D.? Through an even earlier test . . . and so on ad infinitum. There is no prime mover in this chain of tests; no First Test for A.D.D. that has been declared self-referential and infallible. Consequently, the validity of these tests must always remain in doubt.

Even if we admit that such tests *could* tell the difference between A.D.D. and "normal" children, recent evidence suggests that there really aren't any significant differences between these two groups. A group of researchers at the Hospital for Sick Children in Toronto, for example, discovered that children who had been labeled A.D.D. did not deteriorate in performance over time on a continuous performance task any more than did a group of so-called normal children. The researchers concluded that these "A.D.D. children" did not appear to have a unique sustained attention deficit. In another study, conducted at the University of Groningen in the Netherlands, children were presented with irrelevant information on a task to see if they would become distracted from their central task involving identification of groups of dots on a piece of paper (focusing on groups of four dots and ignoring groups of three or five dots). So-called hyperactive children did not become distracted any more than so-called normal children, leading the researchers to conclude that there did not seem to be a focused-attention deficit in these kids. Other studies have suggested that A.D.D. children don't appear to have problems with short-term memory or other factors that are important in paying attention. Where, then, is the attention deficit?

The Perils of Obedience

This difficulty in finding any real attention deficit in "A.D.D. kids" has led some researchers in the field to propose that maybe these kids don't have attention deficits at all! In addition, some researchers are proposing new ways of helping to explain the "A.D.D. child's" often puzzling behavior. Russell Barkley, for example suggests that these kids may have specific deficits in what he calls "rule-governed behavior." In this view, A.D.D. children are considered to be less responsive to rules established by authorities, and less sensitive to the positive or negative consequences that authorities set down for them in advance. They're less likely, for example, to respond positively to statements like "If you get out of your seat, then I will keep you in during recess" or "If you stay in your seat, then I will give you a prize at the end of the day." In other words, kids labeled A.D.D. will not play the game set down by the rule-making parents and teachers.

While a certain amount of rule-following is necessary to maintain the social order, it's not always advantageous to be a rule-follower. Witness the classic example of superobedience in Nazi Germany. Closer to home, Yale psychologist Stanley Milgram's experiments in obedience suggest that human beings have a frightening capacity to follow orders when given by a respected authority. Milgram had volunteers administer "electric shocks" to a subject in a control room every time the subject made an error on a learning task. With each subsequent error, the "voltage level" was increased. Despite protests from the subject, the volunteers were ordered to proceed to higher levels of voltage. Statements like "It is absolutely essential that you continue," and "You have no other choice: you *must* go on," were used by the experimenter in charge to pressure the volunteers into continuing to shock the subjects. In actuality, no real shock was given. The subject only pretended to be in pain. But the volunteers didn't know that, and fully 65 percent of them showed total obedience in administering the full range of shocks. One wonders, then, why there isn't a parent advocacy group or professional organization designed to treat *overly compliant children.* These children would seem to be a far greater threat to civilization than children who have problems with "rule-governed behavior."

A Model of Machines and Disease

The A.D.D. myth is essentially a *paradigm*, a worldview, that has certain assumptions about human beings at its core. Unfortunately, the beliefs about human capacity addressed in the A.D.D. paradigm are not terribly positive ones. It appears as if the A.D.D. myth tacitly endorses the view that human beings function very much like *machines*. A.D.D., in this perspective, represents something very much like a mechanical breakdown. This underlying belief shows up most clearly in the kinds of explanations that parents, teachers, and professionals give to children labeled A.D.D. about their problems. In one book for children entitled *Otto Learns About His Medicine*, a red car named Otto goes to a mechanic after experiencing difficulties in car school. The mechanic says to Otto: "Your motor does go too fast" and recommends a special car medicine.

While attending the CH.A.D.D. national conference, I heard A.D.D. experts share similar ways of explaining A.D.D. to kids, including comparisons to planes ("Your mind is like a big jet plane. . . . You're having trouble in the cockpit"), a car radio ("You have trouble filtering out noise"), and television ("You're experiencing difficulty with the channel selector"). These simplistic metaphors seem to imply that human beings really aren't very complex organisms and that one simply needs to find the right wrench, the proper gas, or the appropriate circuit box—and all will be well. They are also just a short hop away from more insulting mechanical metaphors (e.g., "your elevator doesn't go all the way to the top floor").

The other feature that strikes me as being at the heart of the A.D.D. myth is the focus on *disease* and *disability*. I was particularly struck by this while attending a workshop with a leading authority on A.D.D., who started out his lecture by saying that he would treat A.D.D. as a medical disorder with its own etiology (causes), pathogenesis (development), clinical features (symptoms), and epidemiology (prevalence). Proponents talk about the fact that there is "no cure" for A.D.D., and that parents need to go through a "grieving process" once they receive the "diagnosis." A.D.D. guru Russell Barkley commented, in a recent address, that "although these children do not look physically disabled, they are neurologically handicapped nonetheless. . . . Remember, this is a disabled child." Absent from this perspective is any mention of a child's potentials, strengths, talents, abilities, gifts, and other manifestations of health: traits that are crucial in helping a child achieve success in life.

In Search of the A.D.D. Brain

Naturally, in order to make the claim that A.D.D. is a disease, there must be a medical or biological cause. Yet like everything else with A.D.D., no one is exactly sure what causes it. Possible biological causes that have been proposed include genetic factors, biochemical abnormalities (imbalances of such brain chemicals as serotonin, dopamine, and norepinephrine), neurological damage, lead poisoning, thyroid problems, prenatal exposure to adverse drugs and environmental agents, and delayed myelinization (insulation) of the nerve pathways in the brain.

In its search for a physical cause, the A.D.D. movement reached another milestone in its development with the 1990 publication in *The New England Journal of Medicine* of a study by A. J. Zametkin and his colleagues at the National Institute of Mental Health. This study appeared to link hyperactivity in adults with reduced metabolism of glucose (a prime energy source) in the premotor cortex and the superior prefrontal cortex—areas in the brain that are involved in the control of attention, planning, and motor activity. In other words, these areas of the brain were not working as hard as they should have been, according to Zametkin. The media picked up on Zametkin's research and reported it nationally. A.D.D. proponents latched on to this study as "proof" of the medical basis for A.D.D. Pictures depicting the spread of glucose through a "normal" brain compared to a "hyperactive" brain began showing up in CH.A.D.D. literature, and at CH.A.D.D. conventions and meetings. One A.D.D. advocate seemed to speak for many in the A.D.D. movement when she wrote: "In November, 1990, parents of children with A.D.D. heaved a collective sigh of relief when Dr. Alan Zametkin released a report that hyperactivity (which is closely linked to A.D.D.) results from an insufficient rate of glucose metabolism in the brain. Finally, commented a supporter, we have an answer to skeptics who pass this off as bratty behavior caused by poor parenting."

What was *not* reported by the media, or cheered by the A.D.D. community, was the report that came out three years later by Zametkin and others in the *Archives of General Psychiatry*, attempting to repeat the 1990 study with adolescents. In that study, no significant differences were found between the brains of so-called hyperactive adolescents and the brains of so-called normal adolescents. And in retrospect, the results of the first study didn't look so good either. For example, a recent critique of Zametkin's research by faculty members at the University of Nebraska also pointed out that the study did not make clear whether the lower glucose-metabolism rates found in "hyperactive brains" were a cause or a result of attention problems. They pointed out that if a group of subjects were startled and then had their levels of adrenaline monitored, adrenaline levels would probably be quite high. We would not say, however, that these individuals have an adrenaline disorder. Rather, we'd look at the underlying conditions that led to the finding of abnormal adrenaline levels. Similarly, even if biochemical differences did exist in the so-called hyperactive brain, it may be that such differences become disorders only when combined with specific environmental factors. Thus, instead of searching for "the A.D.D. brain," researchers ought to be more concerned about describing the interaction of different kinds of brains to stress, parenting style, classroom structure, and other environmental influences (see Chapter 3 for a discussion of some of these factors).

Why We Label Children

You may be wondering at this point how A.D.D. has come to gain such wide respect in the past few years when there is so little evidence to support it. The fact is, A.D.D. fulfills a number of important needs among parents, teachers, and professionals. Perhaps most significantly, the term *attention deficit disorder* gives parents and teachers a relatively simple way of explaining troublesome behaviors. Many parents of kids who've been labeled A.D.D. speak gloomily about the years preceding diagnosis. These stories often reveal long periods of personal turmoil during which parents took their children from one specialist to another, only to be given different opinions about the nature of the problems involved. "He'll grow out of it," says one professional. "It's a vitamin deficiency," declares another. "He needs to buckle down in school," counsels an administrator. "You're being too soft on him at home," advises a mother-in-law. Parents who have floundered for years in trying to cope with their child's difficult and puzzling behaviors now have a simple term to use in describing their child's difficulties. As one mother recently related to me: "Once my son was diagnosed as A.D.D., it was like a giant burden was lifted off of me, and we finally knew what was going on with him."

The A.D.D. label serves as a neutral term that helps to organize all the contradictory elements in these children's lives. Moreover, it does this without blaming anyone. Like its older cousin—*learning disabilities (LD)*—"A.D.D." comes to us dressed in the cloak of scientific respectability. A report by a federal commission on the needs of children in the 1970s could have substituted "A.D.D." for "LD" in its own assessment of the user-friendliness of the label when it concluded: "The term learning disabilities [read: A.D.D.] has appeal because it implies a specific neurological condition for which no one can be held particularly responsible.... There is no implication of neglect, emotional disturbance, or improper training or education.... For these cosmetic reasons, it is a rather nice term to have around."

The A.D.D. label also provides a central point around which parents, teachers, and professionals can rally for political and economic support. We've already seen in the last chapter how a lobbying effort by an A.D.D. advocacy group helped to secure an informal place for A.D.D. in existing laws regarding disabled children. Teachers who are disturbed by a child's behavior can now petition to have him removed to a special classroom. Parents can press to have their A.D.D. children taught in expensive private schools at public school expense and sue if they feel their children aren't being given an appropriate education.

Bearing the Stigma of A.D.D.

The danger in all of this is that children may be stigmatized by a label that could haunt them for the rest of their lives. Attention deficit disorder, after all, is a psychiatric disorder. In times past, mental illnesses such as schizophrenia were reserved for the extremes in human behavior. With prevalence statistics for A.D.D. running from 1 to 20 percent and higher, however, millions of kids could be threatened with the prospect of joining the ranks of the psychiatrically disturbed.

The A.D.D. label creates unintended side effects that are anything but positive. Research over the past twenty-five years has consistently supported the existence of what has been called "the self-fulfilling prophecy." That is, what you expect from a child, you often get as a result of your expectations. Thus, if you expect a child to do well, then the child will tend to rise to your high expectations. On the other hand, if a parent or teacher sees a child as "disordered," (e.g., A.D.D.) then the child will tend to modify his behavior to that expectation. Studies reveal that teachers may not teach as effectively to children perceived as having learning problems, even when those children are actually "normal." Recent research suggests that the self-fulfilling prophecy may work in peer relationships as well. In one study, children were paired and given instructions to work with Lego building blocks and drawing materials. When a normal child was told in advance that his partner had a "behavior problem," his interaction with the partner was disturbed, even when the so-called problem child was actually normal.

Major educational and civic groups opposing A.D.D. as a new school label have underscored these concerns about stigmatizing children. Former president of the National Association of School Psychologists Peg Dawson commented, "We don't think that a proliferation of labels is the best way to address the A.D.D. issue. It's in the best interest to all children that we stop creating categories of exclusion and start responding to the needs of individual children." Similarly, in response to a 1991 request by the federal government for more information about the A.D.D. controversy, Debra DeLee, a spokesperson for the National Education Association, the largest organization in the country for teachers, wrote: "Establishing a new category [A.D.D.] based on behavioral characteristics alone, such as overactivity, impulsiveness, and inattentiveness, increases the likelihood of inappropriate labeling for racial, ethnic, and linguistic minority students."

A.D.D.: One Big PR Campaign

Proponents of A.D.D. are aware of the many criticisms leveled against it, and have engaged in what I'd like to call "definition management," in response. As part of a 1993 fund-raising letter to members of the parent advocacy organization CH.A.D.D., then-president Bonnie Fell made reference to a professor who had questioned the existence of A.D.D. in *The Wall Street Journal* as if such a criticism could hardly be conceivable in a person of intelligence (Fell writes: "Yes, he's a university professor! In the *Wall Street Journal!*"). Later on in the letter, she writes: "I'm going to stop writing now, but I know I won't be able to stop worrying—not when press reports of two recent court cases have highlighted the attempts of defense attorneys to blame convicted murderers' actions on A.D.D...."

A.D.D. proponents like Ms. Fell seem to be steering a middle course for A.D.D. between the Scylla of normality (A.D.D. is something that everybody has to one extent or another) and the Charybdis of extreme pathology (A.D.D. can lead people to Satan worship, animal mutilation, and even murder). Such a strategy seems to be based on the belief that if A.D.D. is seen as too much a part of normal behavior, then it could run the danger of losing its tenuous disability status as well as the substantial financial support that comes from donors wishing to help the handicapped. On the other hand, if A.D.D. is seen as linked to *too much* pathology, then parents won't want to have their children associated with the label. Ultimately, then, when we look deep into the heart of the A.D.D. movement, what we discover at its core is that A.D.D. is as much a public relations effort as anything else. That the lives of millions of children should be guided by such a flimsy notion certainly should give us cause for great concern.

Chapter 3

Why A.D.D. Is a Simplistic Answer to the Problems of a Complex World

While attending the third annual CH.A.D.D. conference in Chicago in October 1992, I happened to sit next to a mother of an "A.D.D. child." After learning of her background, I told her a little bit about my own work, and then explained: "I don't believe in A.D.D." She didn't blink an eye but responded softly and with determination: "I *know* my child is A.D.D." She then went on to describe some of his behaviors and a little of the anguish she had gone through in getting others to understand her child. I tried to explain to her what I meant in saying that there is no such thing as A.D.D., but I could see that I wasn't making a dent in her perspective. In fact, as we parted, I could tell there was an underlying sense of anger toward my position.

During talks I've given around the country, I've similarly noticed among some parents a strong negative reaction to my statement that "A.D.D. doesn't exist." I think these parents believe I'm saying that their children's difficulties with behavior and attention don't exist. This isn't what I'm saying at all. In fact, I empathize deeply with the struggles of parents who for years have tried to get others to understand and accept their puzzling children. I recognize that many of these kids have had tremendous difficulties at home and in school. Most of these children *do* have the kinds of behaviors described in the diagnostic and statistical manuals: fidgeting, not following through on work, disorganization, daydreaming, blurting out, restlessness, and so forth. The issue is whether or not the A.D.D. myth described in Chapter 1 is the best way of understanding and helping these youngsters.

Clearly, I'm saying in this book that it isn't the best way. A.D.D. proponents would have you believe that A.D.D. is a medical disorder. In fact, the causes of A.D.D.-type behaviors are complex and many-faceted. Some of these causes are cultural or social in nature. Other causes are more specific to the individual. Ultimately, there may be as many explanations for A.D.D. behavior as there are children with the label. However, in this chapter, I'd like to present a few of what I consider are some plausible non-biological explanations for A.D.D.-type behaviors such as hyperactivity, distractibility, and impulsivity.

A.D.D. as a Social Invention

The first explanation I'd like to give suggests that society has actually invented A.D.D. to help preserve its social order. To close one's eyes to the important role society has in defining deviance risks falling into the same kind of trap as Samuel A. Cartwright, a well-respected Louisiana physician and American Medical Association member who felt he had discovered a new "disease" during the 1850s in pre–Civil War America. After conducting a study on runaway slaves who had been caught and returned to their Southern owners, Cartwright concluded that the slaves suffered from *drapetomania (drapeto,* to flee; *mania,* craze), a disease that caused them to flee. In a written report to the Louisiana Medical Society, Cartwright wrote: "With the advantages of proper medical advice, strictly followed, this troublesome practice that many negroes have of running away can be almost entirely prevented." As social theorist Ivan Illich pointed out in his devastating critique of the medical model, "Each civilization defines its own diseases. What is sickness in one might be chromosomal abnormality, crime, holiness or sin in another. For the same symptom of compulsive stealing one might be executed, tortured to death, exiled, hospitalized, or given alms or tax money."

A.D.D. may exist, then, because the values of our society demand that it exist. What are those values? A look at the roots of American culture from colonial days on suggests that the Protestant work ethic, for one example, has played an important role in defining standards for appropriate conduct. As former American Psychological Association president Nicholas Hobbs pointed out, "According to this doctrine . . . God's chosen ones are inspired to attain to positions of wealth and power through the rational and efficient use of their time and energy, through their willingness to control distracting impulses, and to delay gratification in the service of productivity, and through their thriftiness and ambition." Such a society might well be expected to define deviance in terms of distractibility, impulsiveness, and lack of motivation—the same traits frequently used to describe children suffering from A.D.D. Labeling children A.D.D., then, may represent a means through which our society attempts to preserve its underlying value system. For as Nicholas Hobbs noted, "A good case can be made for the position that protection of the community is a primary function of classifying and labeling children who are different or deviant."

Other cultures appear to have very different expectations toward children's behavior and attention levels. Children with A.D.D. behaviors in cultures with more relaxed behavioral standards may be considered entirely healthy. Educator Terry Orlick, for example, compares parental attitudes in North America with those held half a world away in Papua New Guinea: "If I take my daughter out to eat in North America, she is expected to sit quietly and wait (like an adult) even if there are all kinds of interesting objects and areas and people to explore. . . . Now if I take her out to a village feast in Papua New Guinea, none of these restrictions are placed on her. The villagers don't expect children to sit quietly for an hour while orders are taken and adults chat. Children are free to do what is natural for them, thus eliminating potential hassle for everyone." On the other hand, for societies with stricter behavioral norms than those of the United States—including China and Indonesia—research suggests that mental health clinicians are more likely to identify "normal" children (by U.S. standards) as hyperactive.

A.D.D. as a Symptom of Societal Breakdown

Our culture may also be creating A.D.D. in quite a different way. Children's A.D.D. behaviors may actually be reflections of the very deterioration of those values described above. Harvard professor Lester Grinspoon and Susan B. Singer observed twenty years ago that "our society has been undergoing a critical upheaval in values. Children growing up in the past decade have seen claims to authority and existing institutions questioned as an everyday occurrence. . . . Teachers no longer have the unquestioned authority they once had in the classroom.... The child, on the other side, is no longer so intimidated by whatever authority the teacher has." Grinspoon and Singer go on to say: " 'Hyperkinesis' [a term used to describe A.D.D. symptoms in the 1960s], whatever organic condition it may legitimately refer to, has become a convenient label with which to dismiss this phenomenon as a physical 'disease' rather than treating it as the social problem it is."

Grinspoon and Singer might also have referred to the breakdown of the American *family* in their assessment of the deterioration of authority. There are twice as many single-parent households—8 million—as there were in 1970. The number of working mothers has risen 65 percent from 10.2 million in 1970 to 16.8 million in 1990. Some parents simply aren't around as much these days to provide the kind of guidance and support that is essential to a child's emotional development. As a result, children are experiencing an epidemic of stress-related and mental health difficulties. Nearly 1 million reports of child abuse or neglect are recorded each year. An estimated 15 to 19 percent of the nation's 63 million children and youth suffer from emotional or other problems warranting mental health treatment. Having less support to deal with an increasing number of societal pressures, many children simply buckle under the stress. As Antoinette Saunders and Bonnie Remsberg point out in their book *The Stress-Proof Child*, "Our children experience the stress of illness, divorce, financial problems, living with single parents, death, school, remarriage, jealousy, achievement, vacations, step brothers and sisters, sex, drugs, sensory bombardment, violence, the threat of nuclear war—a long, long list. The effect can be overwhelming."

Among the most frequent symptoms of child stress that Saunders and Remsberg include in their book are restlessness, difficulty concentrating, and irritating behavior. In other words, the same behaviors that make up attention deficit disorder. At the same time, researchers are increasingly recognizing the presence of even more serious problems in many children who've been identified as A.D.D. Recent studies have suggested, for example, that as many as 25 percent of children labeled A.D.D. suffer from severe anxiety, and that up to 75 percent of "A.D.D. children" have some form of depression. As one pair of researchers noted, "Our results suggest that ... treatable childhood depression may be *the* major underlying disorder with hyperactive school problems." It could be, then, that many children who are hyperactive or inattentive are not A.D.D. but rather are anxious or depressed due to any number of family, school, or other problems.

A.D.D. as a Product of a Short-Attention-Span Culture

Not all children labeled A.D.D., however, are hyperactive or distractible because of stress-related anxiety or depression. For the past couple of years, the Comedy Central Network on cable television has broadcast a show entitled *Short Attention Span Theater* consisting of short comedy sketches and clips. I have to chuckle when I hear this title because it serves as a kind of reminder of the times in which we live. A hundred years ago, it was common for a group of farmers to stand in a wheat field for two or three hours listening to a traveling politician. These days, the attention span of the average American has been shortened considerably by mass media. In one instance, a CBS experiment to use 30-second sound bites in its news shows during the 1992 presidential election was stopped because of the slow pace (the industry average was 7.3 seconds).

This suggests to me that our culture may be producing a whole new generation of "short-attention-span kids." In fact, over thirty years ago, media prophet Marshall McLuhan suggested this when he referred to a new generation of kids whose worldview was no longer based on plodding one-step-at-a-time thinking but rather on instantaneous flashes of immediate sensory data. Film critic Arthur Knight addressed this phenomenon when he wrote: "One has only to view an old movie with a young audience to realize that the kids have gotten the message of a shot almost at the first flash; when it remains on the screen, they giggle because the protraction seems to underline what is, for them, the obvious. As a result, editing tempos have had to be stepped up."

Today's fast-paced media—MTV, video software, multimedia computer programs, Nintendo games, and other electronic marvels—shower children with an ever more rapid succession of images and bits of information. As a result, many kids seem to have evolved attentional strategies based on grasping information in quick and rapid chunks. As media expert Tony Schwartz points out in his book *The Responsive Chord*, "Today's child is a scanner. His experience with electronic media has taught him to scan life the way his eye scans a television set or his ears scan auditory signals from a radio or stereo speaker." Many of these fast-paced, media-fed kids may be labeled A.D.D. by adults who live life in the slow lane. What is considered a disease or disorder by parents or professionals may in fact be, for some kids at least, an entirely normal and healthy response to a faster cultural tempo.

A.D.D. as a Response to Boring Classrooms

The collision between short-attention-span kids and life-in-the-slow-lane adults is particularly evident in our schools. Here, students must often sit at desks for hours at a time, listening to monotone lectures, and going over textbook and worksheet material that is presented—not like MTV—but like MTB (Material That's Boring). Kids who are labeled A.D.D. have a particularly rough time in such environments. Studies suggest that "A.D.D. students" do most poorly in environments that are boring and repetitive, externally controlled, lack immediate feedback, or are presided over by a familiar, maternal-like authority. This sounds like a typical American classroom. As A.D.D. researcher Russell Barkley puts it: "The classroom is their Waterloo." Yet Barkley is talking here about the *traditional* classroom model; one that has as its chief features an emphasis upon rote drill, externally controlled tasks ("Do the work on pages 143 to 145"), and lots of sitting in one place.

Unfortunately, this kind of classroom is deadly not only for the so-called A.D.D. child but for all kids. In a monumental study of one thousand U.S. classrooms funded by over a dozen foundations, John Goodlad, professor of education at the University of Washington and director of the study, concluded that America's students spent by far the greatest amount of time in school being lectured to and working on written assignments—especially workbooks and worksheets. The study criticized the lack of exciting learning activities in our nation's schools: "Students reported that they liked to do activities that involved them actively or in which they worked with others. These included going on field trips, making films, building or drawing things, making collections, interviewing people, acting things out, and carrying out projects. These are the things which students reported doing least and which we observed infrequently." Goodlad lamented this educational poverty by commenting: "Part of the brain, known as Magoun's brain, is stimulated by novelty. It appears to me that students spending twelve years in the schools we studied would be unlikely to experience much novelty. Does part of the brain just sleep, then?"

Some students do in fact sleep, but many others respond with hyperactivity, distractibility, and other symptoms of A.D.D. For it is this kind of classroom that students labeled A.D.D. are having trouble fitting into and this sort of school that many students are being medicated into accepting. I'm reminded here of the canaries that were kept by coal miners deep in the mines. If the level of oxygen fell below a certain level, the canaries would fall over on their perches and die, warning the miners to get out fast. It's possible that children who have been labeled A.D.D. are the canaries of modern-day education: they are signaling us to reform our worksheet wastelands and transform classrooms into more dynamic, novel, and exciting learning environments. A.D.D. may be more accurately termed A.D.D.D., or attention-to-ditto deficit disorder.

A.D.D. as a Reflection of Normal Gender Differences

There have always been more boys than girls in programs for A.D.D. children, with ratios ranging from two to one (boys to girls) at the low end to ten to one at the high. Former Stanford researcher Diane McGuinness suggests that many of the features typically attributed to hyperactivity in children can in fact be accounted for by *normal differences* between boys and girls. In one study she conducted with a group of normal preschoolers where children were observed over a long period of time during free play sessions, boys spent less time on any given activity than did girls (eight minutes for boys, twelve minutes for girls), and interrupted their play three times more often than girls. She also cites research indicating that boys tend to be more interested in *objects* (e.g., blocks, manipulatives, toys), while girls show a greater preference for *people*, and that girls are more sensitive to *verbal* sounds, while boys' attention is grabbed more by non-verbal or *environmental* sounds (e.g., fire engines on the street, loud noises in the hall, the sound of a clock ticking).

This research suggests that girls may have an easier time (or appear at least to adapt well) to a traditional classroom environment that involves listening to teacher's instructions, sticking with an assignment, and relating well to peers and adults. Boys, on the other hand, are likely to be at a disadvantage. They may appear, by comparison, to be more distractible—picking up less of teacher's voice and more of other interesting noises in and outside of class—and more restless with their limited focus on any one activity. Essentially, then, some boys may be at risk to be identified as hyperactive or A.D.D. simply because their gender-appropriate activities clash with the expectations of a highly verbal, highly schedule-oriented, and usually female-dominated classroom environment.

A.D.D. as a "Bad Fit" Between Parent and Child

Psychologists have known for decades that children are born with personality styles or temperaments that influence them throughout their lives. The most highly regarded theory of temperament, developed by Alexander Thomas, Stella Chess, and Herbert Birch at New York University, suggests that children can be divided into three major temperament groups: the easy child, the slow-to-warm-up child, and the difficult child. According to New York psychiatrist Stanley Turecki, difficult children have any combination of the following nine characteristics: high activity level, distractibility, and high intensity, irregularity, negative persistence, low sensory threshold, initial withdrawal, poor adaptability, and or negative mood. While Thomas and his colleagues suggest that 10 percent of all children are difficult, Turecki estimates that 20 percent of all kids fit into this category. Significantly, Turecki points out that difficult children are normal: "I strongly believe that you don't have to be average in order to be normal. Nor are you abnormal simply because you are difficult. . . . Human beings are all different, and a great variety of characteristics and behaviors falls well into the range of normality."

Whether a difficult child will develop serious behavioral problems (including symptoms of A.D.D.) depends at least in part upon how the environment responds to his temperamental nature. If there is what temperament theorists call a "goodness of fit" between child and environment, where the parent responds to a child's difficult nature with facilitating responses, then there often won't be a behavior problem. However, if there is a "poorness of fit" between the child's temperament and parental expectations and behaviors, this can result in behavioral disturbances. A child with a difficult temperament, for example, would be likely to have more behavioral problems in a family with a rigid or authoritarian parenting style than in a family that provides structure within an accepting and loving framework. Psychologist James Cameron concluded that "behavioral problems resembled metaphorically the origins of earthquakes, with children's temperament analogous to the fault lines, and environment events, particularly parenting styles, analogous to strain." In the context of temperament theory, then, A.D.D. may not be a "disease" that the child "has"; rather, it would be, at least for some children, a "poor fit" between the child's inborn temperament and the quality of the environment surrounding him. This does not mean that parents are to blame for a child's A.D.D. symptoms. The problem is neither in the child nor in the parent, but rather in the "chemistry" (or lack of chemistry) between the two.

A.D.D. as a Different Way of Learning

Some children may be labeled A.D.D. simply because they learn differently from the way most students learn. As we saw earlier in this chapter, the traditional classroom is set up for children who are good at sitting for long periods of time, listening to verbal instructions, and completing endless pages of worksheets. Most of this kind of instruction consists of what we might call "central-task" learning. In order to succeed in this type of setting, students have to be able to selectively attend to very specific features of the classroom environment: the teacher's voice, the words on the blackboard, the word problems on pages 142 and 156 of the textbook, items 1 through 15 on the worksheet, and so forth. Studies suggest, however, that certain students identified as A.D.D. may have a cognitive style that clashes with this particular teaching approach. Cornell University researchers, for example, discovered that so-called hyperactive students have a particular strength in "incidental" learning and may possess a wide or diffused attentional style. This suggests that they take in information from several different sources at the same time and may be expected to do better in learning environments that involve creating projects or going on field trips— settings where multiple sources of information are internalized and processed. Another study, at Purdue University, showed that hyperactive children were more spontaneously talkative than "normal" classmates and told stories that were more "novel" or creative.

What this means is that many A.D.D. students who attend schools that are based on "central-task," verbal, non-spontaneous learning will be at a distinct disadvantage compared to other students and may have learning difficulties and/or attentional or behavioral problems. That, in fact, is what the research reveals: that as many as 90 percent of students labeled A.D.D. have learning problems. The boundary line between learning difficulties and behavior problems is rather fuzzy for these kids. Because they have trouble learning in traditional ways, they become inattentive, restless, and disruptive. These behaviors make it even more difficult for them to learn material covered in class. If these students were provided with opportunities to learn in environments that embraced their personal learning style, they might well experience success. This is what the research shows. A.D.D. students are often indistinguishable from so-called normal students in classroom environments that use activity centers, hands-on learning, self-paced projects, films, games, and other highly stimulating curricula (in other words, the kinds of activities that *all* children enjoy).

A.D.D.: A Mixed Bag of Kids

After reading this far into the book, I hope that you have begun to seriously question the existence of A.D.D. as a distinct medical disorder. I also hope that you've started to sense the complexity of the issues involved and understand that, in fact, there is no "A.D.D. child," but many different kinds of children who are hyperactive and inattentive for many different reasons. For some kids who suffer from lead poisoning or distinct brain illness or injury (e.g., as was seen in postencephalitic children), the emphasis is undoubtedly on the biological side of the ledger. However, for kids with difficult temperaments or those suffering from depression or anxiety, psychological factors may be most important. For students with cognitive or learning style differences in traditional classrooms, educational issues may predominate. And in the case of certain Nintendo-crazed, television-addicted youngsters, broader cultural issues could become primary. Even where biological issues appear to predominate, I'd prefer to think of these as "biological predispositions" that need to interact with cultural, social, educational, and/or psychological factors in order to give birth to A.D.D. symptoms. In the same way, parents, teachers, and mental health professionals have the opportunity to create optimal educational, social, and psychological environments for these kids so that their "biological predispositions" don't erupt into A.D.D. symptoms.

Most A.D.D. proponents are acutely aware of these non-biological factors. However, they have found a place for them in their paradigm so that the basic tenants of the A.D.D. myth, particularly its existence as a discrete medical disorder, can be preserved. These other factors, especially the psychological and educational ones, are reduced to what they refer to, appropriately enough in this medical model, as "co-morbid" factors. In other words, a child can have A.D.D., *and/or* learning disabilities (LD), *and/or* mood disorders (depression, anxiety), *and/or* a range of other clinical disorders. What are in reality confounding factors (where does A.D.D. begin and depression or learning problems leave off?) are transformed into these co-morbid factors and the essential nature of the A.D.D. myth remains intact.

This artful process of piling on the categories reminds me of what the Alexandrian scientist Ptolemy did when confronted with data that contradicted his view that the sun and planets revolved around the earth. He created "epicycles" in the orbits of planets to account for the discrepancies in planetary motion. These epicycles were fictions, but they allowed Ptolemy and his followers to hold on to their illusions for a few more centuries. How many years of adding co-morbid "epicycles" will it take before social scientists recognize that there are too many complex influences in today's world creating hyperactivity and inattention in children to be able to speak credibly of A.D.D. as a unitary medical disorder?

Chapter 4

What's Good (and Not So Good) About the Good Pill

I walked into a small classroom in a northern California community center and sat down in one of the twenty-five or so chairs set up for the
CH.A.D.D. support group meeting. The talk for the evening was on
medication for A.D.D. kids and was to be delivered by a local pediatrician. In the front of the room was a large piece of newsprint taped to
the chalkboard with the words "A.D.D. Kids and Drugs" at the top. Un-
derneath this inscription, there was a hand-drawn picture of a "sad
face" (a circle with dots for the eyes and nose and a drooping line for
the mouth), and next to it, a "happy face." Below the title and faces was
a list of several brand names of drugs, including central nervous system
stimulants (Ritalin, Dexedrine, Cylert), antidepressants (Desipramine,
Imipramine), antipsychotics (Haldol, Orap), anticonvulsants (Tegre-
tol), anti-anxiety agents (Buspar), and blood-pressure medications (In-
deral, Clonidine). A line with an arrow on the end of it connected the
sad face to the happy face. The implication seemed to be that these
drugs would turn a sad kid into a glad kid.

The physician soon appeared and spent the next hour and a half talking with a group of twenty parents and myself about the pros and cons
of using each of the above drugs to control hyperactivity and attention
problems. The talk was peppered with frequent questions from the audience. One parent asked: "I've heard Ritalin improves organizational
problems, but I haven't seen it in my kid. Is there another drug that

can?" Another mentioned that her son had been on Ritalin a month and now cries easily. One mother of twins shared her own story: "I have twins that have been on Ritalin for six years. I've heard Ritalin is the first choice, but it's short-acting. Brad's one way, then another, and I find it hard to deal with his roller-coaster behavior."

After the physician discussed research about how certain drugs can actually stimulate children to seek the approval of adults, a parent spoke up: "I'm always telling my kid to follow his own decisions. He's very popular. I can't imagine stressing that he do all these things just to get approval. What about individual choice?" The physician's response was curious. He replied: "How much free choice do we really have in life?"

How much free choice, indeed. For this brave new world of drugs has now made it possible for parents and professionals to encourage compliance in children through purely biological means. All the messiness involved in growing up—the battle of the child's will against the adult's will, the endless restless curiosity, the sudden bursts of anger, excitement, or jealousy—all this unpleasantness can now be avoided. One simply needs to classify the unruly child in a soundly scientific framework, give him a diagnostic label—attention deficit disorder—and control him through a psychopharmaceutical cornucopia of state-of-the-art medications. No longer do parents have to ask so many of the difficult questions: "Why is my son so angry at life?" "How can I learn to communicate with my daughter?" "Why is my child not excited by school?" Instead, they can consult with the doctor: "This drug isn't working so well. Do you have one that won't make his migraines worse?" "The stimulant you prescribed is helping him focus, but he's still aggressive—what have you got to control that?" "My child's medication wears off during math class. What should I do?"

A History of Chemical Compliance

The use of "medicines" to control children's behavior is certainly not new. The second-century Greek physician Galen prescribed opium for restless, colicky infants. During the heyday of the Industrial Revolution, working moms and dads used to soak their crying infants' teething rags with liquor to create a soporific effect. In the late 1800s, overwhelmed parents flocked to Winslow's Soothing Syrup, an opium-based elixir that was then available without a prescription. But it wasn't until the 1930s that the use of behavior-controlling drugs took on an air of sophistication by being administered under the supervision of a licensed physician. It was in 1937 that a Providence, Rhode Island, physician, Charles Bradley, observed how regular doses of Benzedrine, an amphetamine, calmed down a group of children with behavior problems and helped them focus more effectively on schoolwork. His discovery went unheeded for the most part during the 1940s and 1950s, when tranquilizers seemed to be the primary means of subduing difficult children. However, in the early 1960s, researchers at Johns Hopkins University discredited the use of tranquilizers in pacifying unruly kids, and saw promise in a new group of psychostimulants, including dextroamphetamine sulfate (known by its brand name, Dexedrine) and methylphenidate hydrochloride (Ritalin), an amphetamine-like drug originally approved by the Food and Drug Administration (FDA) in 1955 to control mild depression and senility in adults.

Ritalin soon became the drug of choice for controlling hyperactivity. According to a survey conducted by Daniel Safer and John Krager for the Baltimore County Health Department, 40 percent of all prescriptions for behavior problems in 1971 were for Ritalin and 36 percent for Dexedrine. By 1987, the situation had dramatically altered, with Dexedrine accounting for only 3 percent of all prescriptions and Ritalin taking the lion's share—93 percent—of the behavior-control drug market. While these figures represent only Baltimore County, there is evidence that the trend is national.

The 1990s has seen a continued rise in the use of Ritalin. In 1990, the DEA quota for Ritalin production was set at 1,768 kilograms. In 1994, that figure had increased more than 400 percent to 8,189 kilograms. In the fall of 1993, when demand for Ritalin appeared to outstrip supply, the parent group CH.A.D.D. declared a "nationwide Ritalin shortage" and encouraged its members to contact Congress to pressure the DEA to increase its production ceiling to make Ritalin more available to physicians. There has been, as well, a trend toward the use of drugs other than psychostimulants, including antidepressants, anticonvulsants, and even antipsychotic medications to control hyperactivity and attention problems. A 1991 issue of the American Psychological Association's newspaper, *The APA Monitor*, announced: "In the past 10 years, there has been an enormous surge in the amount of and variety of psychotropic drugs given children in the U.S., accompanied by greater societal acceptance of such treatment." Statistics vary widely, but the most current figures suggest the number of children receiving psychoactive medications for attention and behavior problems to be around one million.

The Positive Impact of Drugs on Kids

The popularity of these drugs, especially psychostimulants, is easy to understand when one considers their efficiency and low cost. As Carol Whalen and Barbara Henker, two University of California researchers, point out: "Psychostimulant medication is relatively inexpensive, readily available, and easily administered. No nonchemical intervention can be applied at a cost of approximately 20 cents and 5 or 10 minutes per day, and no other intervention can claim documented success rates ranging from 60 to 90 percent." Side effects of Ritalin in particular are generally considered to be minimal, especially when compared to other psychoactive drugs, such as the psychostimulant Cylert (which can cause liver damage) and antidepressants (which can cause heart problems that have resulted in the sudden death of a few children).

There is a vast research literature supporting the effectiveness of psychostimulants across a broad range of behavioral skills. Studies suggest that psychostimulants reduce both large and small motor movements and increase attentiveness, especially in structured task-oriented settings such as traditional classrooms. Psychostimulant medication also improves compliance with parent or teacher directives, and reduces aggressive, interfering, or other oppositional behaviors toward both adults and peers. There is also some evidence that such medications improve children's short-term academic performance in spelling and arithmetic, in reading comprehension workbooks, and on certain memory and writing tasks (although, as we'll see later in this chapter, there is little evidence that these improvements carry over into long-term academic achievement).

More recently, psychostimulant medications have been observed to produce a positive effect on "A.D.D. children's" social interactions. Mothers decrease their controlling and negative behaviors toward their medicated children. Teachers appear to be less intense and controlling toward medicated children than they are with hyperactive kids taking placebos. And when medicated kids interact with peers on structured tasks as well as games, they appear to be less controlling and off-task, which in turn results in their "normal" peers becoming less controlling and off-task. Psychostimulant medications appear to favorably influence each of these social settings, helping to reverse a vicious cycle of negative interaction and plummeting self-esteem.

In my own discussions with parents and teachers around the country, I've heard numerous accounts of Ritalin producing a positive turn-around in the lives of children. Teachers have told me that their medicated students are calmer than they were before medication, better focused, socially accepted, have fewer temper tantrums, stay on task, complete assignments, and feel a sense of control over themselves, often for the first time. Parents report similar results. One mother commented: "Take it from a parent that has a ten-year-old son that has been labeled a troublemaker, lazy, fidgety, loudmouth, and more that would take up another six pages.... Medication has done wonders for him. I am so sorry that we waited so long before we put him on it."

The Dark Side of Psychostimulants

Looking at this long list of positive effects, you might wonder what all the fuss is about concerning whether to medicate children for A.D.D. In fact, the thought might have occurred to you: "If this stuff produces all these wonderful effects, why don't we give it to normal kids?" Since research suggests that so-called normal children *do* in fact reap many of the same benefits as so-called A.D.D. children, one might argue that these children could benefit from psychostimulant medication to help them with their studies, their social life, and their relationships with teachers and parents. Why not spread the wealth around?

The reason psychostimulants aren't available at your local drugstore as a "study aid" has to do with the fact that these drugs are a mixed blessing. By any measure, psychostimulants such as Ritalin are potent drugs. The DEA lists Ritalin as a Schedule II drug, which means that among all legal drugs, it has the highest potential for abuse (other Schedule II drugs include morphine and barbiturates). The National Collegiate Athletic Association (NCAA) and the U.S. Olympic Committee ban the use of Ritalin, Cylert, and Dexedrine by their athletes. In some countries, such as Britain, stimulants are rarely or never used in treating children with attention and behavior problems.

Ritalin can produce a wide range of side effects. Although most of these are minor and disappear over time or with the proper adjustment of dosage, they nevertheless prove to be a troublesome factor for the days, weeks, or months that they last. The most common ones include nervousness, decreased appetite, insomnia, stomachaches, headaches, dizziness, and drowsiness. Ritalin appears to influence mood and can cause some children to cry more easily, to have "dysphoria" (a generalized ill-feeling), and to be more socially isolated. As one researcher commented, "In contrast to unmedicated hyperactive boys, medicated children were observed to be more sad/depressed, nervous/withdrawn, and lacking in positive affect."

There are even reports that Ritalin may restrict an individual's creativity. As self-described A.D.D. adult Thom Hartmann reports, "I've spoken with numerous A.D.D.-diagnosed writers, artists, and public speakers about their experience with Ritalin.... Many report that, while their lives became more organized and their workdays easier when taking the drug, their creativity seems to dry up." One novelist used Ritalin when proofreading but not when writing. He noted: "Ritalin brings me to a single point of concentration, which is useless when I'm trying to find that random spark of inspiration about how my character is going to extricate himself from a snake pit in India, or escape a horde of Mongols."

Ritalin is a short-acting drug that is often administered in the morning. It wears off after about four hours, leading to a "rebound" effect in the late afternoon or evening for some kids that consists of changes in mood, irritability, and increases in the behavior and attention problems that were there before the drug was taken. Less common side effects include skin rash, nausea, abdominal pain, weight loss, visual problems, and changes in heart rate, heart rhythm, and blood pressure. At one time it was thought that psychostimulants could stunt a child's growth, but recent studies indicate that reduction in growth is temporary and is generally made up after the drug is discontinued.

There are a number of more serious side effects that are comparatively rare. Drugs like Ritalin can aggravate or even trigger latent conditions in children, including seizures, Tourette's syndrome (a condition characterized by unpredictable physical movements and unusual—sometimes obscene—vocal eruptions), glaucoma, and severe emotional problems. Cases of "methylphenidate-induced delusional disorder," and "methylphenidate-induced mania" have been documented in the medical literature, and have also been highlighted by the media. Unfortunately, it appears as if these rare occurrences have been allowed to occupy center stage in the media controversy surrounding the use of psychostimulants with children and even have had an impact on the sale of these drugs. While these negative events are indeed significant to those whose lives have been affected, they have often served to take the focus off other more subtle shortcomings of psychostimulant use.

Little attention, for example, is placed on the fact that many children simply don't like taking these drugs. Montreal Children's Hospital researcher Gabrielle Weiss and her colleagues found in one study that "children on the whole preferred being without the pills"; in another, follow-up study of adults who'd been on psychostimulants as children, they discovered that a majority regarded medication as a hindrance rather than a help to them. University of Illinois pediatrician Eleanor Sleator was more blunt on the results of her own project, which was reported in the journal *Clinical Pediatrics*: "Above all else, we found a pervasive dislike among hyperactive children for taking stimulants." Comments by children in the research included the following: "It makes me sad and I like to eat" (referring to the appetite suppression effect of the drug) "It takes over of me [sic]; it takes control." "It numbed me." "It makes me feel like a baby." And one child's comment seemed to sum up all the others: "I don't know how to explain. I just don't want to take it anymore."

Even children who *said* they didn't mind taking the medications showed, by their actions, a very different attitude. Sleator reports: "A ten-year-old boy denied that he ever tried to avoid taking his medicine. In fact, this child was known to hate taking it, and his mother fought with him about it daily. The physician actually witnessed a scene during which the mother was trying to persuade the child to go back on medication and she alternately pleaded, begged, demanded, and threatened. Tears were shed and voices raised in the doctor's office. Yet this same child, when interviewed a year later by the physician, said the medicine was helpful and denied that he had ever objected or tried to avoid taking it." Sleator mentions several methods children use to avoid taking the medications, including deliberately failing to remind a parent or teacher who forgot to give it, arguing with parents, and "cheeking" the pill and/or throwing it away when no one was looking.

Drugs, Damage, and Dependency

Ominously, the *Physicians' Desk Reference* section on Ritalin reports that "sufficient data on safety and efficacy of long-term use of Ritalin in children are not yet available." Since amphetamines create changes in brain chemistry, University of South Florida psychology professor Diane McGuinness warns, "The amphetamines interact with dopamine and norepinephrine. The consequences of a prolonged use of amphetamines could produce subsequent changes in the production and action of these two neurotransmitters." The consequences of this are unknown at present. However, one study appearing in the journal *Psychiatry Research* reported a significantly greater frequency of cerebral atrophy (abnormalities in the brain) in young adult males who had taken stimulant drugs like Ritalin during childhood, speculating that their drug treatments *may* have been a possible cause.

The *Physicians' Desk Reference* product description for Ritalin has a black box midway through the listing. The box is labeled "Drug Dependence" and states that "Ritalin should be given cautiously to emotionally unstable patients, such as those with a history of drug dependence or alcoholism." Recall that Ritalin is a Schedule II drug with a high potential for such abuse. In fact, Ritalin is already used illicitly on the streets in Canada and the United States. According to an article in the Canadian newsmagazine *Maclean's*, "Ritalin has become one of the more popular street drugs in major western Canadian cities. Vancouver police detective Gordon Spencer ... called it 'a poor man's substitute for heroin.' ... According to Detective Spencer, Ritalin ranks fourth behind marijuana, cocaine, and heroin as the drug used most on the streets of Vancouver (a [ten-milligram] Ritalin tablet sells for $20, compared to $35 for a capsule of heroin)." (For some reason, methylphenidate appears to produce euphoria in adults and dysphoria in children.) There are even reports in the United States that adolescents and their parents are hoarding their legal prescriptions and giving them to friends or selling them to pushers for a tidy profit.

No scientific evidence exists, as yet, to suggest that Ritalin actually *turns* children into drug addicts. However, there are some disturbing data that leave one wondering whether Ritalin and other potent psychoactive drugs are the best things to expose troubled children to during the most vulnerable years of their lives. A recent follow-up study of ninety-one men who had been diagnosed as "hyperactive" in childhood and ninety-five "normals" indicated that the "hyperactive" group (most of whom had been medicated in childhood) had significantly higher rates of drug abuse (16 percent versus 4 percent). And Carol Whalen and Barbara Henker have reported that "... evidence of a familial tendency toward alcoholism in families with hyperactive children raises the possibility that hyperactive children may be particularly prone to drug dependence, and that the medical use of psychostimulants with these youngsters may potentiate substance abuse." The late author and film actress Jill Ireland suggested that her son Jason's battles with heroin addiction during young adulthood were actually triggered in his elementary school years, when he was prescribed Ritalin for hyperactivity. Stories such as this one raise troubling questions. What kind of message do we send to kids when we tell them "Just say no to drugs. But don't forget to take your behavior-controlling, consciousness-altering drug after lunch"?

Pills Rather Than Skills

There may be an even deeper message we're sending to children when we use medication instead of mediation to improve behavior and attention span: "To be successful—to be an okay person—you need to take a drug." Studies indicate that children taking Ritalin may have a tendency to attribute their improved behaviors and academic performances to the drug and not to their own internal efforts. Peter S. Jensen of the Eisenhower Army Medical Center in Fort Gordon, Georgia, studied the attitudes of children toward the medications they were taking to control hyperactivity. He concluded that "children often disavowed any responsibility for their behavior and claimed they needed a 'good pill' to control themselves." Carol Whalen and Barbara Henker similarly reported, "We have heard children credit their pills when they complete their schoolwork, are kind to their pets, clean their rooms, and get invited to parties. They report that the medication prevents them from acting crazy, picking fights, getting kicked out of school, spending all of their money in a single day, and killing frogs! Analogously, forgetting to take medication is blamed for poor grades, temper tantrums, rule infractions, social squabbles, breaking or burying other people's toys, and even rolling toilet paper down the stairs while parents are entertaining!"

Psychostimulant treatment also exerts a subtle but significant force upon the expectations of *others* toward a child's ability to behave and pay attention. Carol Whalen and Barbara Henker observed that "once a child, his parents, and his teachers begin to ascribe positive behaviors to potent chemicals (external agents), it may be quite difficult to effect reattribution to an internal agent, such as a child's developing competencies." The number of parents, teachers, peers, and acquaintances involved in attributing the child's performance to drugs can take in quite a wide social network. In one study, a girl reported, "One girl, like Rhonda, knows about my medicine. [She found out from] her grandma—because my mom told her grandmom. Well, she spread it to a girl named

Karla and now if she notices that I'm not acting calm she goes, 'Did you take your hyper pills?' "

The effect of all this is that drugs begin to supplant life as the child's real teacher. So instead of using good behavioral and communication strategies with a child in conflict, a parent might well ask, "Did you take your pill?" And rather than changing the curriculum to one that's more appropriate for a child's individual academic needs, a teacher might be more likely to attribute the child's problems to A.D.D. and refer him to a physician for possible medication. In fact, some researchers have suggested that once a child starts medication and his behavior begins to improve in school, efforts to work on underlying learning problems may actually be curtailed, leaving these difficulties to continue to fester beneath the surface. "There's no doubt in my mind that Ritalin is prescribed sometimes for the wrong reason," says Jerry Weiner, chairman of psychiatry at George Washington University and former president of the American Academy of Child and Adolescent Psychiatry. "There's no question that it's going to be used sometimes because a teacher or a parent finds a child's behavior distressing."

These troubling developments raise an issue of broader social concern. By using drugs to treat behavior and attention span problems, we may be substituting chemistry for coping in coming to grips with life's difficulties. Turn on any television set and see the evidence for yourself in the string of commercials that promote pharmaceutical interventions for everyday problems. How do you spell relief? D-R-U-G-S. Have nervous tension? Take a pill. Can't sleep? Take a drug. Consumers now spend over $1 billion a year for nervous system drugs alone. The use of Ritalin and other psychoactive drugs to control behavior and attention span in children represents only another wave in this tide of chemical convenience that's swept over the land. Yet it may be among the most serious forms of pollution, because it could be eroding our nation's most precious natural resource: our children.

Who's Minding the Drugs?

Proponents of psychostimulants and other drugs for hyperactive children argue that the kinds of problems mentioned above have been overemphasized at the expense of the advantages to be gained from drug use, including success in the classroom and better relations with others. Side effects, they are apt to point out, can be easily controlled by a responsible physician through changes in dosage levels, "drug-holidays" during weekends and summers, and by switching to other drugs should one or another prove troublesome to a child's sensitive bio-chemical system. This is all true. The problem with this argument, how-ever, is that it assumes all children around the country are receiving careful and regular monitoring of medication effects from physicians who treat these drugs with the respect that their potency deserves.

A look at the evidence, however, suggests otherwise. An informal survey by a Georgia parent advocacy group found that only 2 out of 102 children underwent a complete battery of tests that manufacturers recommend before any child is put on the drug. The American Academy of Pediatrics (AAP) issued a statement on medication for hyperactive children in which it asserted that "unfortunately, some children are treated with a stimulant drug for prolonged periods of time without an adequate diagnostic evaluation or follow-up." One of the statement's authors, Julian Haber, in an interview with *NEA Today*, a publica-tion of the National Education Association, said, "It's my personal opinion that the drug [Ritalin] is overprescribed due to inadequate diag-nostic workups and, at times, due to undue pressure by both parents and teachers."

Statistics on the distribution of Ritalin prescriptions around the country support these disturbing findings. Georgia, for example, was us-ing nearly three times as much Ritalin as New York during the mid-1980s. A zip code check of drug shipments showed that certain pharmacies in a few rich Atlanta suburbs accounted for 45 percent of all sales in the state! *NEA Today* points out that "Utah's rate—the highest in the nation—has fueled speculation that widespread Ritalin use may be associated with large family size [in a state with a substantial Mor-mon population], overcrowded classrooms, and strict behavior norms." Here Ritalin may function more as a quick and easy child-control strat-egy than as a means of helping individual children with special behav-ioral difficulties.

Furthermore, while even the most ardent expert on psychostimulant medication indicates that it should not be the only treatment for a child's hyperactivity or attention problems but must be supplemented with behavioral, cognitive, and psychological interventions, many physi-cians nevertheless appear to flout this consensus and rely *solely* on the drug to effect change. "The majority of hyperactive kids today are treated only with Ritalin—the *vast* majority," says L. Alan Sroufe, pro-fessor of child psychology at the University of Minnesota.

Finally, although proponents of "the good pill" are quick to tout its salutary qualities in improving classroom performance—perhaps its major use with hyperactive kids—the evidence tells another story. Most studies, in fact, have shown no significant improvement in a child's long-term learning ability or academic achievement. University of South Florida professor Diane McGuinness reports that "although stimulant medication does improve performance on repetitive and boring tasks, most research indicates that drugs will not make it possible for a child to develop or expand academic skills, especially those he or she does not already possess." A.D.D. researchers Charles Cunningham and Russell Barkley reviewed a large number of short- and long-term studies on the impact of medication in a wide range of academic skills and found no improvement in 82 percent of the studies, and inconsistent results in the rest. Judith Rapoport and her colleagues at the National Institute of Mental Health did a two-year follow-up study of hyperactive boys between the ages of eight and ten, divided into two groups, one that received medication, and one that took a placebo. At the end of two years, there was no evidence of any difference between the two groups on tests of reading, spelling, or math. Other studies have looked at groups over even longer follow-up periods (four or five years) and discovered the same thing: no effect of medication on long-range academic achievement.

In fact, for some children, Ritalin and other drugs serve to *impair* thinking abilities and make it *harder* for them to succeed in school. Some studies have shown that certain children require a dosage level of around one milligram per kilogram of body weight per day in order for their behavior to improve substantially. However, at that dosage level, many children's cognitive skills—their ability to attend, remember, and engage in other mental actions—tend to be negatively affected. There are also specific groups of children—termed "non-responders"—who will be impaired cognitively at even lower dosage levels.

When to Just Say Yes

Readers may wonder whether I am suggesting—after such a long litany of negatives—that parents and professionals just say no to these drugs forever. I do not join in sympathy with psychiatrists such as Sydney Walker, who boldly states, "In my medical practice I see many hyperactive children. I have never prescribed stimulants for these patients and I never will." I am not a Christian Scientist nor a Scientologist who has a religious or moral revulsion to the use of psychoactive medications. Such drugs, used in the right way with the right individuals by responsible physicians, can significantly enhance the quality of life for many children.

There are at least three situations where the use of psychostimulants or related drugs may be appropriate and useful in helping children. First, it may be successfully used with children who have severe and unremitting hyperactivity due to identified neurological problems resulting from lead or chemical poisoning, brain damage, parkinsonism, or other clearly biological causes. Diane McGuinness estimates this group of individuals at less than 1 percent of the population—far less than the 3 to 5 percent (or greater) figure usually used to indicate the total number of children with attention deficit disorder.

Second, it can be successfully used on a *short-term* basis with children who are experiencing severe crises in their lives. According to New York psychiatrist Stanley Turecki, when "A.D.D. children" are under pressure, they move toward the extremes on the spectrum of behavior and temperament. Ritalin can serve to reverse this process. He says in his book *The Difficult Child*, "If the child's family and school are in a state of crisis, the temporary use of Ritalin can reverse the situation and create an atmosphere of greater calm, which in turn will allow the parents and the teacher to institute a program of improved management. Once things are going better, the medication can often be discontinued."

Finally, and perhaps most importantly, medication can be used *as a last resort*, after a sincere attempt to employ a number of appropriate non-drug interventions has failed to produce significant results. This last criterion is fully in keeping with the position taken by the American Academy of Pediatrics (AAP). In a position paper developed by the Committee on Children with Disabilities and the Committee on Drugs, the AAP stated clearly that "medication for children with attention deficit disorder should never be used as an isolated treatment. Proper classroom placement, physical education programs, behavior modification, counseling, and provision of structure should be used *before* a trial of pharmacotherapy is attempted" (italics mine).

Beyond these three criteria, parents and professionals need to weigh carefully the pros and cons of stimulant drug use in each individual case and decide whether a child is better served with or without medication. If your child is currently on medication, *do not* take him off the drug without first consulting a physician. Abrupt termination of many of these drugs, including Ritalin, can cause severe reactions, including depression, anxiety, irritability, sleep problems, fatigue, agitation, or serious emotional difficulties. And if you are thinking of putting your child on medications, select a physician who will carefully monitor drug use. Pediatrician Martin Baren suggests that Ritalin dosage start at low levels (five milligrams once a day) and gradually be increased as side effects are monitored. He also recommends that the child be given frequent drug holidays unless there are major impulse-control problems. In addition to these suggestions, make sure that your physician is aware of non-drug alternatives that can be used in conjunction with medication. As William Pelham, professor of psychiatry at the University of Pittsburgh and a leading authority on A.D.D., commented, "Ritalin was never supposed to be the only form of intervention, but people relied on it as the only treatment." In the next chapter, we'll explore some of the controversies surrounding the use of non-drug interventions.

Chapter 5

To Control or to Empower:
That Is the Question!

Several years ago, I taught a group of ten boys in northern California who had been referred to my "special day class" because their behavior and learning problems had made it difficult for them to remain in a traditional classroom. The centerpiece of my special education program was a "behavior chipboard," which was prominently displayed on a wall at the front of the room. It consisted of a large sheet of plywood to which I'd affixed ten horizontal rows of pegs, six pegs to a row. On the left side of each row of pegs was a student's name. On each peg was a round "chip" (actually a round piece of tagboard with a hole cut in the middle so it could slide easily onto the peg).

Each morning, the students would come in and see that they all had six chips next to their name. During the day, however, they knew that if they broke any of the posted class rules (no fighting, no throwing things, no bad language, and so on), they would have chips removed from the board. A chart next to the chipboard explained that if a student had six chips left at the end of the day, he was entitled to thirty minutes of "choice time" during the next day (time to read, relax, listen to music, or do a number of other activities). Five chips would result in twenty minutes of choice time, four chips was worth ten minutes of choice time, three chips no choice time, two chips would mean they would have to stay after to complete work for ten minutes, one chip they'd have to stay after twenty minutes, and no chips would earn them a call home to their parents.

I was proud of my chipboard, not only because I had crafted it myself, but because it represented in my mind the quintessence of classroom control—a virtue that had been impressed upon me many times by my administrative superiors during my special education career. However, problems began to arise with it almost from the beginning. If some of the boys lost chips early in the day, it would create an emotional pall over the rest of the morning and afternoon, since they had no hope of getting them back until the next day. This would cause them to act up, resulting in further loss of chips and more emotional turmoil, and so on down the line in a vicious behavioral spiral. After a time, I decided to change things a bit, so that a student could "earn his chips back" through positive behavior. This helped for a while. However, the boys eventually began to complain about why they weren't getting chips back on the board when so-and-so got his back up. And they continued to spin out of control when chips were taken off for various offenses. As the weeks passed, the chipboard became the focal point of a battle that raged between wills—mine and the students'.

Eventually, I decided to discard the chipboard. But before I did so, I shared with the class the reasons for my dissatisfaction and heard their complaints as well. I also told them that before I could throw the board away, we needed to develop some ground rules for being together in the classroom. So we talked, for days, about rules and the consequences of breaking them. Some students wanted to institute much more severe consequences than the ones we had (including being paddled, starved, isolated, and beaten). But after a couple of weeks we developed a list of rules and contingencies that both I and my class could live with, and these we posted on the wall.

I remember vividly the day we stopped using the chipboard. By some strange twist of fate, the most authoritarian parent of the class showed up unexpectedly just as we started to march toward the dumpster with the chipboard held high in our hands like a sacrificial lamb. As she looked on with horror, we tossed the board into the garbage and unleashed a collective yell of joy up to the heavens. Free at last! We returned to the classroom to face ourselves and the system we had fashioned together. It was quite refreshing to see students almost immediately start breaking the rules that they had themselves made. It was even more liberating to see them submitting to the consequences they had agreed to. The weeks and months that followed were not always easy, but they were free of the sapping of energy that came from trying to control children's lives. We all worked together now and we all felt an underlying sense of commitment to our collaborative classroom.

Compliance at All Costs

The reason I've gone on at some length to describe this experience to you is that I feel it strikes right at the heart of the problem with A.D.D. treatment methods. Put simply, A.D.D. proponents have focused most of their attention on developing ways to externally control the behavior of children (the "chipboard approach"), when what these kids really need are adults who will help internally empower them (the "respect, listen, collaborate, and problem-solve" approach). A review of the A.D.D. literature will quickly reveal that the word "compliance" is golden. Behavior guides enjoin parents to use effective "commands," "pick your battles," "stick to your guns," and "enforce compliance" in their behaviorally disordered children. When reading this type of literature, I have at times wondered whether I was reading material more suitable for a course in military strategy than for raising a child.

A look at the list of products available through A.D.D. sources further reveals this penchant for control. Behavior modification programs abound, including those that use token economy systems, behavior charts, reward stickers, and other methods of "child training." A whole new breed of electronic devices has been developed for "treating" the A.D.D. child. There is, for example, a high-tech version of my behavior chipboard: a machine called the Attention Training System. This machine sits on a child's school desk and automatically awards the child a "point" every sixty seconds. If the student's attention wanders, the teacher uses a remote control device to deduct a point from the machine and activate a small warning light on the student's module. Points can be exchanged for rewards. Another device, called a "MotivAider," creates a "gentle vibration," reminding the student to pay attention, keep on working, raise his hand before talking, and so forth. Yet another machine (remember what I said in Chapter 3 about how the image of "machinery" pervades the A.D.D. myth?), called a "good-behavior clock," runs whenever a child is on-task, but is stopped when the child is disruptive or "off-task."

Some of the approaches used to control the child appear downright cruel. A popular A.D.D. book counsels teachers on how to deal with problem behavior: "For fairly minor offenses, creative techniques may be used, like removing the child's apple, pumpkin, snowman, or Easter bunny from the collection on the bulletin board." At other times, the advice seems merely thoughtless. One handbook for A.D.D. in the schools advises that children who have been non-compliant be "asked to perform an unpleasant task (e.g., a simple writing assignment)." Here it seems more likely that the child will learn to associate pain with academic performance than with his misbehavior, and thus be dissuaded from developing an interest in one of the most important skills taught in school.

The entire picture of the classroom that emerges from a survey of A.D.D. training methods is of an assembly line where students must complete "tasks" with a close attention to external detail but with less attention to the ideas and meanings of the material being taught. For example, in one handbook on A.D.D. teachers are advised to provide clear guidelines for neatness: "*a.* proper heading should be on all work, *b.* papers should not be crumpled, *c.* ink should not be smeared, *d.* writing should be done in one style, not part cursive and part printing, *e.* mistakes should be erased if done in pencil and crossed out once if done in ink, *f.* letters should be sized and spaced evenly, *g.* handwriting should be slanted in one, consistent direction...." Students are told to hold their pencil correctly, sit properly, place the paper in a certain way on the desk, and conform to a number of other behavioral standards. To interject some "excitement" into the learning process, A.D.D. proponents advocate such "active" methods as giving students a chance to "turn over flash cards." Wow! It shouldn't be surprising, then, if students have some difficulty "complying" with the rules in this type of coffin classroom. I sometimes wonder how parents and teachers would feel if they had to function in their work lives under similar conditions, with reward charts, smiley stickers, "response costs" (taking away privileges), and behavior-controlling machines dictating every minute of their day.

There also seems to be a certain condescending quality to many of the suggestions for helping so-called A.D.D. children. One guide tells teachers, "Use short, simple sentences when speaking to the students." This reminds me of how some people shout at blind individuals thinking them somehow deficient in hearing. Blind people can hear, and kids who've been labeled A.D.D. can understand complex sentences if they are meaningful and relevant to their lives. Other A.D.D. educators advise teachers to keep lessons short so that the "A.D.D." student has frequent experiences of completion. But what if a child gets absorbed in a project of great interest? When the bell rings, he has to move on to another task or risk being non-compliant. There's actually very little in the entire A.D.D. repertoire of teaching/parenting methods that is exciting, involving, relevant to a child's personal world, or *worthy of much attention.* Consequently, the child who really becomes passionate about something is likely to have points taken off for being "off-task," seeing as how passion rarely conforms itself to "tasks" and behavior charts.

A Movement with Its Head in the Sand

Many of the strategies and interventions that constitute the meat and potatoes of the A.D.D. movement simply don't reflect current knowledge about how children learn and what truly motivates them. While behavior modification programs based on the use of rewards, for example, make up a significant part of the A.D.D. child-control "arsenal," a growing body of research suggests that such extrinsic reinforcements can actually have a detrimental impact on the lives of children. In his book *Punished by Rewards: The Trouble with Gold Stars, Incentive Plans, A's, Praise, and Other Bribes,* writer-educator Alfie Kohn points out that rewards motivate people, but only to continue getting more rewards, not to actually learn or behave better. They also set people up as rivals (competing for rewards), discourage risk-taking, and impair creativity. Moreover, research studies have shown that reward systems can actually impair the behavioral and academic performances of kids labeled hyperactive or A.D.D. Perhaps most significantly, a child's desire for rewards all too often replaces his passion for learning in the classroom. As Kohn aptly points out, "Extrinsic rewards reduce intrinsic motivation. People's interest in what they are doing typically declines when they are rewarded for doing it."

And while the A.D.D. myth tacitly approves of a teacher-centered, worksheet- and textbook-driven model of education (almost all of its educational suggestions are based on this kind of classroom), current research suggests that all students benefit more from project-based environments in which they actively construct new meanings based upon their existing knowledge of a subject. That means that instead of spending hours a day listening to lectures and answering questions at the back of the book, students need to be questioning, hypothesizing, experimenting, interviewing, collaborating, problem-solving, and more.

Harvard psychologist Howard Gardner suggests that today's classrooms are too heavily focused on words and numbers to the detriment of other ways of knowing and proposes that schools embrace a more multidimensional approach to learning, an approach that includes greater emphasis on music, the arts, physical education, cooperative learning, and the use of journals and portfolios to help students reflect on their studies. Very little of this perspective has been allowed to filter into the A.D.D. corridors, despite the fact that some of its own researchers, most notably Sydney Zentall, professor of special education at Purdue University, have argued persuasively that children labeled A.D.D. need high levels of stimulation, novelty, and interest in their educational programs.

Finally, the stress that A.D.D. proponents have placed on external control of children stands in stark contrast to the observations of researchers who have noted that many children labeled A.D.D. do best when they are in environments where they can exert some control over their lives. Nowhere in the literature on A.D.D. have I seen any reference to programs in which children have any say about the use of medications, behavior modification, and other treatment options in their lives. These things are all done *to* the child. This set of circumstances led one group of researchers to declare, "One possible reason why various treatments are less than maximally effective with hyperkinetic children is that [the children] may resent being excluded from decision-making, and as a consequence resist intervention attempts."

Limiting the Options

Rather than expanding its thinking to incorporate these wider views of growth and learning, A.D.D. proponents seem more intent upon closing ranks and limiting the number of "acceptable treatments" that can be used in helping children labeled A.D.D. In their recent book *Attention Deficit Disorder and Learning Disabilities: Realities, Myths, and Controversial Treatments*, psychologists Barbara Ingersoll and Sam Goldstein list the following as "effective treatments" for A.D.D.: stimulant medication, tricyclic antidepressants, Clonidine (a blood pressure medication), behavior modification, and a few classroom suggestions (including the "turning flash cards" intervention mentioned earlier). That's it! Everything else is "out of the mainstream." They spend most of the book debunking a wide range of "controversial" treatments. While I'd

agree that several of the approaches they criticize, including megavitamin therapy, sugar-free diets, and oil of evening primrose, do lack empirical support (and have been left out of this book), others, such as cognitive therapy, EEG biofeedback, and additive-free diets, have been
shown to be effective at least with certain groups of kids and deserve
to be considered as options for parents and professionals. Moreover, the
Ingersoll-Goldstein book doesn't even mention a wide range of other options (including most of the strategies covered in Part Two of this book),
suggesting that they either don't know about them or consider them too
insignificant to either debunk or support.

In their book and in other writings, Ingersoll and Goldstein have established a set of standards that, they claim, need to be met in order for
a treatment to be judged as effective for A.D.D. According to Ingersoll
and Goldstein, treatments for A.D.D. must be scientifically verified using a placebo-controlled, double-blind experimental design. A placebo is
something that *looks* like the real treatment but in reality is not. The
reason for using a placebo is to determine whether other factors—
including the expectations researchers and subjects have for a treatment to succeed—might account for any improvements observed under
that treatment. "Double-blind" means that neither the researchers nor
the subjects can know when the subjects are receiving the actual treatment and when they are receiving the placebo treatment. According to
Ingersoll and Goldstein, "this process can take years but it allows us to
make sound decisions about new treatments."

This type of research makes sense for testing medications like
Ritalin. But it breaks down when considering more complex treatments.
For if placebo-controlled double-blind research of the kind envisaged
by Ingersoll and Goldstein had been the "gold standard" for the development of all treatments used by psychiatrists, psychologists, and
educators over the past one hundred years, we would not have psychoanalysis, stress-reduction programs, cooperative learning, and hundreds
of other therapeutic tools. Psychoanalysis, for example, was developed
largely through clinical case studies of single individuals. Stress-
reduction and cooperative learning programs have been evaluated by
looking at *outcomes* (e.g., a student going through a cooperative learning program scores higher on a self-esteem inventory than a similarly
matched student going through a program of individualized study).
There are in fact many different kinds of research tools, including epis-
temological approaches, participant observation, ethnographic studies,
clinical models, structuralist methods, narrative analysis, phenomeno-

logical research, and hermeneutic analysis. To limit A.D.D. treatment methods to those research approaches that survive the Ingersoll-Goldstein "gold-test" runs the risk that parents and professionals will be denied access to many potentially useful approaches for helping kids with attention and behavior difficulties. When told about how certain hyperactive children's problems cleared up after removal of sensitive foods, for example, two-time Nobel Prize–winning scientist Linus Pauling remarked, "It is from individual experiences of this sort that a great deal of progress has been made, rather than through double-blind controlled trials."

Beyond the Medical Model

It's precisely because the A.D.D. label encompasses such a heterogeneous group of kids that we need a wide range of interventions and strategies to help them become successful people. However, many A.D.D. proponents want to exert control over interventions (just as they maintain control over the behavior of children) by invoking the medical model. This tactic makes it "dangerous" to go beyond the realm of medically approved treatments. Researchers fear losing funding sources if they stray too far from the accepted treatments. As Beverly Rubik, director of the Center for Frontier Sciences at Temple University, points out, "There's a code of behavior in the scientific community that almost prohibits people from looking too far from the mainstream. If they do, they suffer extraordinary obstacles—they can't publish in peer-reviewed journals, funding is reduced or eliminated, they're ostracized. They're regarded as kooks, and they may even lose their jobs if they're not tenured."

Parents are also traumatized by this pressure to conform. Many who are seeking broader and richer solutions for their kids' problems are left feeling like they could do irreparable harm to their children if they seek treatments outside of the "official" ones—much as a parent would be considered cruel to withhold insulin from a diabetic child. However, the reality is that the most successful approaches for kids who've been labeled A.D.D. are in fact strategies that have been effective for *all* kids. I was reminded of this when reading a guide for A.D.D. kids that stated, "ADHD children typically function best in settings with clearly defined expectations that are realistic and appropriate to their developmental stages." Isn't this true for all kids?

That doesn't mean that parents should throw caution to the wind when looking for ways to help improve their children's attention span and behavior. As with any human need, there are opportunists who will seek to capitalize on children's problems by touting their own approach as "the answer." I would caution parents to steer clear of any individual or group that claims to have a "miracle cure" for A.D.D. There is no cure for A.D.D., because there is no such thing as A.D.D. There are only individual children with unique needs. And since every child is different, with his own pattern of likes and dislikes, temperament, learning style, cultural background, family affiliation, school setting, peer interactions, and hopes and aspirations, every child requires a different approach. The greater number of sensible options that parents have to choose from, the better able those parents will be in developing strategies that suit the needs of their special kids. Part Two of this book provides fifty sensible options to consider that go beyond medication, labels, and coercion in helping to nourish the life of your child.

• PART TWO •

---

50 Strategies to Improve Your Child's Behavior and Attention Span

---

Introduction

Over the past seven years, I've heard from hundreds of parents and teachers who have written, telephoned, or spoken with me in person concerning practical ideas for helping their "A.D.D." children and students. And like remedies for the common cold, strategies abound for calming and/or focusing these kids. Among the interventions mentioned are some of the following: Rolfing, token systems, Bach flower remedies, vitamin supplements, a sugar-free diet, love, an allergy-free diet, learning centers, change of lifestyle (from urban to rural), shiatsu, naturopathy, homeopathy, the Feingold diet, physical education, control of systemic yeast overgrowth, television, computers, Lego blocks, counseling, biofeedback, kinesiology, chiropracty, amino acid therapy, natural light, "Isis machines," homeschooling, self-esteem enhancement, Nintendo, visual imagery, relaxation therapy, and color therapy. I've also learned about additional approaches through my survey of the growing professional literature on this subject, including various forms of cognitive therapy, parent training, family therapy, special education, behavior management, and of course different sorts of medications.

Out of this diversity, I've had to make some decisions about which approaches to highlight in this book. In selecting the fifty ways to improve attention span and behavior presented in this book, I've been guided by several criteria. First, I've tried to leave out methods that are based primarily on external control of children (medications and behavior modification programs being the two major examples). However, I should point out that there are ways of turning externally controlling methods into internally empowering approaches. For example, if a parent uses "time out" as a strategy for sending a child to his room, it's externally controlling. However, if the parent helps a child use a time-out strategy to go to a quiet place of his own volition to "cool off," then it becomes internally empowering. By the same principle, it's possible to turn an internally empowering method into an externally driven one. This can happen with diet programs in which parents end up controlling everything a child eats. Where possible throughout the book, I've made suggestions so that this kind of subtle coercion might be avoided.

Second, I've left out strategies that involve the introduction of special substances into the child's body. This meant leaving out medications, megavitamin therapy, amino acid therapy, and homeopathy, among other treatments.

Third, I've generally kept off the list methods that seem to lack a convincing body of supporting research, including sugar-free diets, megavitamin therapy, and elimination of fluorescent lighting. Finally, I've attempted to present a broad range of approaches, a range that spans the totality of a child's life, including emotional, cognitive, educational, behavioral, physical, creative, social, and biological dimensions.

While the primary biological interventions for attention and behavior are omitted (medications), there are other approaches that have, at least in part, a biological component. These include diet interventions (strategies #1, #2, and #12) as well as self-control methods that may influence biochemical changes in the brain (including strategies #11, #18, and #34). Recent studies in biofeedback, meditation, psychoneuroimmunology, imagery research, and other self-regulation therapies have pointed to the role that the mind has in influencing the body. As the distinguished psychologist Robert Zajonc has said, "People should be their own pharmacists" by engaging in non-drug-related self-regulation activities that positively affect neurochemical functions.

Guidelines in Deciding Which Strategies to Use

Parents may feel bewildered when presented with as diverse a collection of ideas and strategies as that contained in this book. I'd like to suggest several guidelines in helping to sort things out. First, I suggest that parents read through all fifty of the strategies before making any decisions about which ones to try out. You might want to make a list of those ideas you've already tried (indicating those which have worked and those which haven't), ideas you could implement easily with little expense of time or money, and any other strategies you feel might be effective. Second, I recommend that you involve your child as much as possible in the selection of interventions. As author-physician T. Berry Brazelton points out, "Whether your child is using Ritalin, a self-comforting pattern [shared later in this book] or both, include him in decisions about his treatment. The more you empower him to take control of his disorder, the more progress you are likely to see." Third, to help guide you in the selection of the most appropriate interventions to meet the needs of *your unique child,* I've included a questionnaire about your child's life (below). Finally, I'd like to suggest that you not attempt to do everything at once. Select a strategy, try it out for two or three weeks, evaluate its effects, and then incorporate it or discard it before moving on to another approach. There are no miracle cures in this book. However, you may find ideas that can over time create positive changes in the life of your child.

QUESTIONNAIRE

This questionnaire will help direct you to the strategies most relevant to you and your child's situation. In parentheses after each item are the numbers of the strategies that relate to each question. Place a mark next to all items that apply to your child.

Does your child . . .

_____ watch two or more hours of television a day? (#3)

_____ become fidgety, unfocused, or uncooperative a half hour to an hour after a meal? (#1, #2, #12)

_____ have a chronically runny nose, red or swollen eyes, itching, stomachache, or other ongoing minor physical symptoms? (#2, #12)

_____ play Nintendo or other video games for two or more hours a day? (#3, #36)

_____ seem to do his best thinking when he's moving around at home or school? (#13, #28)

_____ have a good imagination? (#11)

_____ enjoy working with his hands? (#26)

_____ receive little or no physical education at school? (#6)

_____ talk a lot? (#4)

_____ have a favorite color? (#10)

_____ seem to calm down or focus when certain types of music are played? (#9)

_____ have difficulty getting along with his peers? (#38, #41)

_____ like to engage in outdoor activities? (#13, #28)

_____ seem to calm down or focus when he is hugged or touched? (#30)

_____ have a label in school like "attention deficit disorder" or "learning disabled"? (#50, #22)

_____ skip breakfasts or eat only high-carbohydrate foods (e.g., cereal, pastry, toast, pancakes) in the morning? (#1)

_____ seem to have a negative view of his future? (#19)

_____ appear to be anxious or depressed? (#29, #37)

_____ enjoy information when it is presented in a graphic way through images or pictures? (#8)

_____ like working with computers? (#36)

_____ have a negative self-image? (#50, #14)

_____ blame others or circumstances outside of himself for his successes and failures? (#32)

_____ have special hobbies or interests? (#5, #8, #17)

_____ seem to learn new things by absorbing information that's all around him? (#21)

_____ spend little or no positive time with you on a regular basis? (#27)

_____ have cravings for certain kinds of foods? (#12)

____ enjoy hanging around children who are younger than he is? (#48)

____ lack a special place at home for studying? (#28)

____ frequently drive you up the wall? (#33)

____ appear to be physically tense much of the time? (#20)

____ have nowhere at home to be "hyperactively creative"? (#25)

____ seem to have certain times of the day when he's particularly restless or inattentive? (#15)

____ appear to have been exposed to one or more serious stresses during the past year (e.g., family divorce, illness of self or family member, financial difficulties in family, fights with siblings, violence at school)? (#29, #37)

____ have few opportunities to make choices that affect his life? (#44)

____ have difficulty paying attention to things you ask him to do around the house? (#16)

____ have problems organizing his personal belongings and/or school assignments and materials? (#31)

____ have the ability to picture things in his head? (#11)

____ seem to learn more around the house than he does at school? (#24)

____ appear not to know what the rules are for appropriate conduct around the house and/or at school? (#46)

____ lack a special place he can go to when he feels upset or out of control? (#40)

____ get frequently locked up in power struggles with you or your spouse? (#45)

____ appear to benefit from receiving clear and immediate feedback about his behavior? (#35)

____ have difficulty thinking through a problem or solving a practical situation (e.g., a conflict with a friend)? (#38)

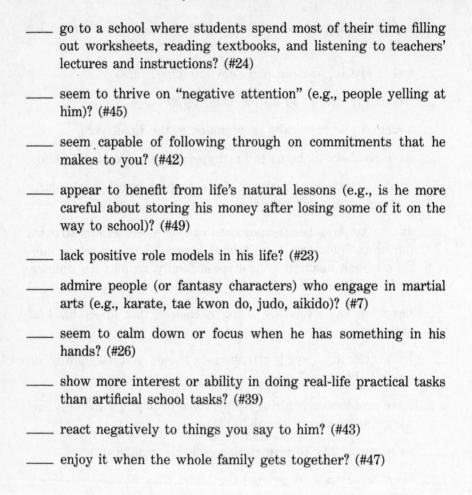

____ go to a school where students spend most of their time filling out worksheets, reading textbooks, and listening to teachers' lectures and instructions? (#24)

____ seem to thrive on "negative attention" (e.g., people yelling at him)? (#45)

____ seem capable of following through on commitments that he makes to you? (#42)

____ appear to benefit from life's natural lessons (e.g., is he more careful about storing his money after losing some of it on the way to school)? (#49)

____ lack positive role models in his life? (#23)

____ admire people (or fantasy characters) who engage in martial arts (e.g., karate, tae kwon do, judo, aikido)? (#7)

____ seem to calm down or focus when he has something in his hands? (#26)

____ show more interest or ability in doing real-life practical tasks than artificial school tasks? (#39)

____ react negatively to things you say to him? (#43)

____ enjoy it when the whole family gets together? (#47)

Strategies Categorized by Type of Approach

As an additional help in tailoring strategies to your child's needs, I've organized the 50 strategies in this book according to which broad aspects of a child's life are addressed (some strategies are listed in more than one category).

Cognitive Approaches—strategies to help your child *think* in new ways: #4, #11, #18, #31, #32, #34, #38

Educational Approaches—strategies to help your child succeed in the classroom: #6, #8, #17, #21, #22, #24, #26, #28

Social Approaches—strategies to help your child develop more positive relationships: #27, #30, #37, #41, #43, #47, #48

Behavioral Approaches—strategies to help your child learn more appropriate ways of behaving: #16, #35, #40, #42, #45, #46, #49

Psychological Approaches—strategies to help strengthen your child's emotional life and self-esteem: #5, #14, #19, #23, #25, #27, #29, #33, #37, #39, #44, #50

Ecological Approaches—strategies to provide a healthy and supportive environment: #1, #2, #3, #9, #10, #12, #15, #28

Physical Approaches—strategies to positively engage your child's physical energies: #6, #7, #13, #20, #26, #30

#1

Provide a Balanced Breakfast

When I was a child, Sunday morning breakfast usually consisted of some devilishly delicious sweet rolls my mother had gotten up early to bake. Sunday afternoons were spent sleeping them off (sometimes in church) or just feeling vaguely restless or irritable. It turns out that the effects of a sugar-laden high-carbohydrate breakfast of sweet rolls, or syrupy pancakes, or waffles dripping with jam, or even toast and butter, are particularly fierce on some biologically sensitive kids with attention and/or behavior problems.

Researchers at the George Washington University School of Medicine in Washington, D.C., gave high-carbohydrate breakfasts (two slices of toasted and buttered white bread) and high-protein breakfasts (two eggs scrambled in butter) to groups of "hyperactive and non-hyperactive children" between the ages of eight and thirteen. Children in each group were given, on alternate days, a non-nutritive orange drink sweetened with either aspartame or sucrose. Blood samples were taken just before and up to four hours after the meals. Also, subjects took a brief test involving attention span at one-half hour, two hours, and four hours after breakfast.

Results indicated that "hyperactive kids" who ate the carbohydrate breakfast and sugar drink did more poorly on the attention span test than any of the other kids in the study (they also had the highest blood-sugar levels). However, when "hyperactive kids" ate the protein meal and the sugar drink, they actually did better at the attention task than even the non-hyperactive groups. The researchers speculated that these "hyperactive children" may be more sensitive to increases in serotonin—a neurotransmitter in the brain—brought about by the consumption of sugar and carbohydrates.

Serotonin is the brain chemical that causes us to feel sleepy after a big meal (especially a meal that has a lot of carbohydrates in it). However, during the day it can also result in our feeling restless, irritable, or inattentive. Sudden surges of serotonin can also throw off levels of other neurotransmitters such as dopamine and norepinephrine. Protein, however, increases the level of amino acids, and these serve to block many of the effects of serotonin.

The upshot of this research is that parents should provide their "hyperactive and inattentive kids" with a breakfast that has a good balance of complex carbohydrates (e.g., cereals, bread, pasta), protein (e.g., milk, yogurt, cheese, eggs, lean meat, fish, poultry), and fruit (e.g., juice, fresh fruit, canned fruit). Here are some examples of poor breakfasts and good breakfasts:

Poor Breakfasts:

- white toast and butter
- hash browns and ketchup
- sugary cereals without milk
- pancakes with syrup
- waffles with butter and marmalade
- candy
- sweet rolls and/or danish
- muffins and orange juice

Good Breakfasts:

- granola and milk
- scrambled eggs and toast
- boiled egg and a muffin
- waffles and ham
- oatmeal with nuts and raisins
- potatoes and eggs
- pancakes with flavored yogurt
- bean burrito

For kids who are resistant to the good food items listed above, try jazzing up the meal by varying the appearance and ingredients of the breakfast. To serve oatmeal, for example, you might put some grapes on the top for eyes, the end of a banana for the nose, and a few walnuts (or a dribble of yogurt) for the mouth to create "Oatmeal Man." If your child loves pizza (and most kids do), try topping a packaged pizza crust with some scrambled eggs, sausage, tomato, and low-fat cheese. If your child is a dessert fiend, make a banana split from bananas, two or three different flavors of yogurt, granola, and some berries and pineapple. If you've got an "on the go" child who wants to zoom out the door before you've got breakfast on the table, try a quick breakfast shake made from some fruit, yogurt, nuts, dry milk, juice concentrate, and ice cubes thrown into a blender.

School psychologist Richard Morriss suggests that parents try out the balanced breakfast with their kids for at least two weeks, keeping records on a calendar of what was served for breakfast each morning. Then, each Thursday, Morriss recommends that parents call the school to find out whether their child's behavior has improved (they should also, of course, be monitoring changes at home). If there seems to be a positive effect, then keep the breakfasts going. Even if there doesn't seem to be an immediate effect, you might enjoy the more nutritious meals (and creative recipes) so much that you want to continue them indefinitely.

If your child *refuses* to eat breakfast, don't despair. Nutrition expert and family physician Lendon Smith says, "When kids refuse to eat in the morning, I would not coerce them, but I would slip a bag of peanuts or almonds along with some raisins in a convenient pocket so they have something to nibble when they do get hungry." A recent study from *The New England Journal of Medicine*, in fact, reports that children have a pretty good capacity to adjust their own eating habits over time, so that if they don't eat much at one meal, they often make up for it at the next. The important thing is to provide appropriate foods once they do eat. One thing that can help is if you set a good example by eating a healthy breakfast yourself. Another way to encourage your child is by allowing him to make choices about what *he* wants for breakfast. If he's old enough, get him involved in preparing his own meals. You might find that he begins to channel some of his frenetic energies into cooking. He might even become the "galloping gourmet" of the household!

RESOURCES

C. Keith Conners, *Feeding the Brain: How Foods Affect Children* (New York: Plenum, 1989).

Marion Cunningham, *The Breakfast Book* (New York: Knopf, 1987).

Phyllis Scully and Annie Gillian, *The Ultimate Breakfast Cookbook* (New York: Grove Weidenfield, 1988).

Sunset Ideas and Recipes for Breakfast and Brunch (Menlo Park, CA: Lane, 1982).

#2

Consider the Feingold Diet

Not too long ago, I received a letter from a New Jersey mother who wrote saying: "Please do not write a book on hyperactivity without discussing the Feingold Diet." She went on to describe her daughter, whose aggressiveness, tantrums, and sleep problems turned their family's life into a living nightmare. "We were thrown out of our La Leche League chapter," she writes, "... asked to leave synagogue, not invited to anything, told we were obviously abusive parents, accused of spoiling etc." One day a friend of the family suggested that they try the Feingold diet. "Within 3 days," says the mother, "Julie spoke completely intelligibly, slept the night, and stopped hitting."

This kind of success story has made the Feingold diet perhaps the nation's most popular non-drug alternative in treating hyperactivity. The diet was developed during the 1960s by Ben Feingold, a San Francisco allergist, who believed that up to 50 percent of the hyperactive children he saw in his practice improved when placed on a diet that was free of artificial flavorings, preservatives, dyes, and other additives, as well as foods containing naturally occurring salicylates (such as oranges, apples, apricots, berries, and grapes). His 1974 book *Why Your Child Is Hyperactive* went on to become a best-seller and led to the founding of the Feingold Association of the United States (FAUS), an organization that has helped thousands of families deal with hyperactive behavior. Feingold pointed out before his death in 1982 that children who benefited from the diet weren't allergic to these ingredients in the classic sense, but instead had what he termed "chemical sensitivities."

The Feingold diet has come under fire during the past fifteen years from critics who suggest that its successes are primarily anecdotal and fail to meet the rigorous standards of scientific research. In this view, any improvements under the diet could be attributed to the positive expectations that parents or teachers may have for the success of the diet, or to the positive changes in the family toward the child that occur during the diet (focusing less attention on blaming the child for misbehavior and more attention on reorganizing the diet). One double-blind placebo-controlled study commissioned by the Food Research Institute, a food industry group, yielded no support for the Feingold hypothesis, although the parents of ten preschoolers in the study saw improvements in their children's behavior when their children were put on the additive-free diet.

Other studies have shown that a number of children seem to consistently benefit from the Feingold diet. A study that appeared in the same issue of *Pediatrics* as the Food Research Institute study concluded that the behavior of 3 to 8 children out of 26 hyperactive kids improved because of the diet. Another study saw 2 children out of 22 showing mild to dramatic negative reactions to the reintroduction of specific food additives to their diet. A 1982 report drafted by a panel of experts assembled by the National Institute of Allergy and Infectious Diseases and the National Institute of Child Health and Human Development said that the behavior of some hyperactive children improved when placed on diets like the Feingold diet, though they pointed out that it is difficult to tell in advance which kids will specifically benefit. They recommended that such diets not be universally used as a treatment for hyperactivity but that "initiation of a trial of dietary treatment or continuation of a diet in patients whose families and physicians perceive benefits may be warranted."

If you choose to follow the Feingold diet, you have to be prepared to make some major changes in the way you cook, shop, eat out, and manage your child's entire food intake over a long period of time. You need to limit your child's exposure to hundreds of synthetic food dyes, artificial flavors, flavor enhancers (such as monosodium glutamate), and preservatives. After a period of total abstinence from foods with additives, you may begin reintroducing foods—one at a time—while looking for behavioral reactions to specific additives. Foods showing no strong reaction can usually be reintroduced into the diet.

Naturally, an intervention of this magnitude requires the cooperation of the entire family. It's especially important that you consult with your child to make sure that he is willing to go along with the sacrifices that might be necessary to make the effort a success. Otherwise this diet becomes an externally controlling force that he might well attempt to sabotage. Depending upon his age, he can be involved in learning about the different additives, discovering how to read the ingredients section of different packaged foods, and exploring creative cooking ideas that are additive-free. Also, make sure to get support from other families participating in the Feingold diet. The Feingold Association of the United States can put you in contact with participating families, and also supply you with shopping guides, creative recipes, and information regarding what to watch out for in popular restaurants and fast-food establishments. The Feingold diet isn't for everyone, but for those who can benefit, it represents a healthy, drug-free way to improve your child's attention span and behavior.

RESOURCES

Ben Feingold, *Why Your Child Is Hyperactive* (New York: Random House, 1974).

Ben Feingold and Helene Feingold, *The Feingold Cookbook for Hyperactive Children* (New York: Random House, 1979).

The Feingold Association of the United States, Box 6550, Alexandria, VA 22306; 800–321–FAUS.

Michael Jacobson, *Eater's Digest: The Consumer Factbook of Additives* (New York: Doubleday, 1972).

John F. Taylor and R. S. Latta, *Special Diets and Kids: How to Keep Your Child on Any Prescribed Diet* (New York: Dodd, Mead, 1987).

Limit Television and Video Games

Parenting expert John Rosemond wrote a column recently that suggested there might be a link between the amount of time American children spend watching television and the epidemic of learning disabilities and attention deficit disorder in our country. His article provoked a storm of controversy, as pediatric neurologists, psychiatrists, and psychologists wrote in stating that A.D.D. is "a medical-neurological problem which is biologically based and probably in large part . . . genetically inherited." Rosemond nevertheless stuck to his guns and suggested that there is a growing body of evidence supporting his viewpoint. I would tend to agree with him. I'd also add video games, such as those available from Nintendo, to the equation.

Earlier in the book, I pointed out how our media-driven "short-attention span society" may form a kind of cultural backdrop to the incidence of kids who have trouble paying attention to parental or teacher directions. Television certainly is one of the prime suspects in this trend. Psychiatrist Matthew Dumont writes, "I would like to suggest that the constant shifting of visual frames in television shows is related to the hyperkinetic syndrome. . . . There are incessant changes of camera and focus, so that the viewer's reference point shifts every few seconds. This technique literally programs a short attention span. . . . I suggest that the hyperactive child is attempting to recapture the dynamic quality of the television screen by rapidly changing his perceptual orientation."

By creating high-impact audio and visual information in short blasts, television (and also video games) may be secretly undermining some natural attentional mechanisms in the human mind. Educator Jane Healy, author of *Endangered Minds: Why Our Children Don't Think*, points out how television advertisers have recognized that one of the best ways to capture a viewer's attention is by capitalizing on the brain's instinctive responses to danger. Through the use of sudden close-ups, pans, zooms, bright colors, sudden noises, and other attention-getting mechanisms, television programmers (and video game designers) may be reducing the child's natural vigilance, or ability to remain actively focused on events taking place in the real world. And since children who are having their "thrill and danger" centers constantly provoked by TV and video games are given no immediate context for responding (since TV viewing is a passive activity and video game responses are limited to slight hand movements on a joystick or other manual device), this pent-up need for physical response can manifest as overactivity, frustration, or irritability.

There is substantial evidence to support the view that television-watching can also promote aggressiveness in children. In a famous experiment, one set of children was exposed to a short film in which a man acted aggressively against a large inflatable toy clown (a Bobo doll). Another set of kids was shown a film in which the same man behaved in a quiet and non-aggressive manner. Close observation of the children in play situations after viewing revealed that those who had observed the film of the man acting violently tended to act more violently themselves, while those who saw the man acting non-violently tended to be more peaceful. In another study, two groups of boys were exposed to different kinds of films. One group saw five violent movies, one each day, while the other group saw five non-violent films. The boys' behavior was then observed as they went about the course of their lives. Results conclusively showed that subjects exposed to the violent films showed an increase in several kinds of aggression against others, while those who saw non-violent films failed to show these kinds of changes. And when one considers the fact that, according to the American Psychological Association, children who watch two to four hours of TV a day have witnessed 8,000 murders and 100,000 other acts of brutality by the time they leave elementary school, there can be little doubt that excessive television viewing of violent programming can have a damaging impact on children's behavior.

Television and video games also negatively affect children's behavior by taking them away from activities that are more active, multisensory, and intellectually, socially, and emotionally nourishing. Social critic Jerry Mander, author of *Four Arguments for the Elimination of Television*, writes, "It is bizarre and frightening ... that many parents use television as a means of calming hyperactive children. It would be far better to calm them with physical exercise, sports, wrestling, hugging, bathing, and a lot of direct attention that gives them wide-ranging sensory and intellectual stimulation.... The worst thing one can do for a hyperactive child is to put him or her in front of a television set. Television activates the child at the same time that it cuts the child ... off from real sensory stimulation and the opportunity for resolution."

Even after this long litany of negatives, however, I'm not sure I'd go along with parents who would completely prohibit television viewing and video games for their hyperactive children. First of all, I wouldn't be honest in saying so, since I am a child of the Television Revolution and continue to find television viewing a satisfying activity when taken in measured doses. Second, television and video games connect children to society, and to deprive your child of access to what other children are engaged in puts him at a disadvantage when he goes to school or plays with friends and hears them discussing television shows or video games he has never seen. Third, research suggests that children labeled hyperactive seem to have the ability to divide their attention between television viewing and other activities going on around them without having their comprehension of either stimulus negatively affected. Finally, television watching and some video games, properly mediated through adult participation, can lead to increased abilities in a number of visual-spatial and critical thinking skills, including understanding of plot, characterization, and how individual scenes relate to the whole (and as we'll see in strategy #18, the use of video games to facilitate biofeedback training can help children learn valuable focusing skills).

Consequently, I'm suggesting here that you *limit* rather than eliminate your children's television watching and video game play. Harvard pediatrician T. Berry Brazelton suggests one hour a day during the school week and not more than two hours on weekends as a reasonable goal for TV watching. Guidelines are less available for video game play but surely should not exceed these limits, and more probably should be combined with TV viewing (e.g., one hour of TV and/or video games per day). In addition, you should *eliminate* violent programming from your child's TV & video game schedule as much as possible. If your child's favorite program happens to be violent (and it's very likely it will be!), then sit down with him and watch it together. When violent activities happen, talk with your child about them, share your own feelings, and listen to your child's reasons for preferring this type of programming. If the violent program or game seems clearly related to violent behavior in your child, then explain to your child your reasons for not allowing it and be consistent in restricting access. Meet with your child on the weekend and plan a schedule of television watching or video play for the coming week. Encourage him to explore new types of TV programs or video games that may be equally stimulating but in a non-violent way. Use the VCR to record excellent children's programming for later viewing, and go to video stores together to rent movies or video games that both of you can enjoy. Most importantly, make the times that your child *is* watching TV or playing video games opportunities for growth rather than trivial distraction.

R E S O U R C E S

Action for Children's Television, 20 University Road, Cambridge, MA 02138; 617–876–6620. Advocacy group encouraging quality television programming for children. Publishes booklets including *TV Smart Book for Kids* and *How to Treat TV with TLC*.

KIDSNET, 6856 Eastern Avenue, NW, Suite 208, Washington, DC 20012; 202–291–1400. Clearinghouse for information on children's programming.

Frances Moore Lappe, *What to Do After You Turn Off the TV* (New York: Ballantine, 1985).

Jerry Mander, *Four Arguments for the Elimination of Television* (New York: Morrow Quill, 1978).

National Coalition on Television Violence, P.O. Box 2157, Champaign, IL 61824; 217–384–1920.

Harold Schechter, *Kidvid: A Parent's Guide to Children's Videos* (New York: Pocket Books, 1986.

Dorothy Singer and Helen Kelly, *Parents, Children, and TV: A Guide to Using TV Wisely* (Chicago: National PTA, 1984). This is a pamphlet available from the National PTA, 700 North Rush Street, Chicago, IL 60611.

Dorothy G. Singer, Jerome L. Singer, and Diana M. Zuckerman, *Use TV to Your Child's Advantage: The Parent's Guide* (Washington, DC: Acropolis, 1990).

Marie Winn, *The Plug-In Drug: Television, Children, and the Family* (New York: Penguin, 1985).

#4

Teach Self-Talk Skills

Most people remember from their childhood the spelling rhyme "*i* before *e*, except after *c*," and the steadfast chant of "The Little Engine That Could" ("I think I can, I think I can . . ."). But few people realize that these memorable phrases and others like them represent useful thinking strategies that can help children cope with the world around them. Over the past few years, cognitive psychologists have encouraged children and adults to engage in "self-talk" as an important personal-growth tool. Self-talk represents a process whereby an individual develops key phrases that can guide him through a complex task or difficult situation. He then learns to repeat these phrases to himself at appropriate times of need.

Self-talk is proving to be quite useful in assisting children with attention and behavior problems to develop self-control and reflection skills. It can be employed as a means of controlling anger. If your child gets into fights, for example, you might teach him to say one or more of the following phrases silently to himself when someone provokes him: "Easy does it," "Keep cool," "Chill out," "Relax," or the well-known self-talk phrase: "Sticks and stones may break my bones but words will never hurt me." Self-talk can also be used to help children organize themselves. If you want your child to clean up his room, for example, you might suggest he use a self-talk phrase in the form of a question: "Now let's see, where do I begin?" This question serves as a prompt to help him initiate a coordinated set of actions and might be followed by "Okay, that's done. What do I do next?"

At school, self-talk can be used to remember problem-solving strategies. If your child has to solve a math word problem that uses large numbers, for example, you might suggest he say the following self-talk strategy to himself: "Read the problem. Substitute smaller numbers. Solve the simpler problem. Solve the original problem." In helping your child prepare for a test, you could recommend the following self-talk procedure for items that have him stumped: "Find out what I'm supposed to do. Consider all the answers. Stop and think. Mark my answer. Check the answer."

Finally, self-talk can be used to help a child form a more positive image of herself as a learner. Many children already use self-talk, but in a negative way. They'll get problems wrong in school or receive criticism from a teacher or peer and then, often unconsciously, say something like "I'll never get it right," or "I'm so stupid," or "You dimwit." (Often these phrases are learned from classmates, parents, and other behavioral models.) Self-talk training can help these kids turn their negative self-talk ("You'll never be able to do it") into positive self-talk ("I can do it if I try").

A number of research studies support the use of self-talk in helping children with attention and behavior problems focus, organize, and cope with life. Two Canadian researchers found that children who learn to engage in self-talk become less impulsive. At the University of Montana, psychologists discovered that when children were given self-talk strategies, they were more likely to focus on copying tasks. More recently, children labeled A.D.D. were seen as more likely to use task-relevant private speech than so-called normal students.

My own feeling is that this approach probably works best with kids who are highly verbal rather than those who process information more through visual or haptic (kinesthetic) modes. Sydney Zentall's work at Purdue University suggests that kids who are labeled A.D.D. are less likely to be verbal when they are asked to be so. But when they're not *supposed* to be talking, they talk quite a bit. This suggests that training programs attempting to spoonfeed set phrases to these kids might not work. Once introduced to this approach and given examples of how it works, however, students might take the method and use it in their own way.

The usual procedure in training kids to use self-talk involves four stages. In the first stage, ask your child to say the key phrase out loud.

In the second stage, tell her to whisper the phrase. In the third stage, suggest that only her lips move. In the fourth stage, ask her to say the phrase silently (or covertly). This process of internalizing language is seen as a key to helping children develop self-control strategies. Let your child develop her own phrases (after being given some examples) rather than using the ones you give her. These unique expressions of her own personality are more likely to be remembered than externally imposed phrases. Finally, have fun with this activity! You might play a game called "What Am I Silently Saying?" in which each person has to guess what self-talk phrase the other is covertly repeating in his mind. Ultimately, self-talk should be regarded as a regular part of life rather than an "add-on" to life's responsibilities. And for your child, it could make quite a difference in how she thinks about herself.

Resources

Douglas Bloch and Jon Merritt, *Positive Self-Talk for Children* (New York: Bantam, 1993).

Center for Cognitive Therapy, University of Pennsylvania, 133 S. 36th Street, Room 602, Philadelphia, PA 19104. This organization maintains a referral list of cognitive therapists who can help children develop self-talk skills.

Susan Isaacs and Wendy Richey, *I Think I Can, I Know I Can: Using Self-Talk to Help Raise Confident, Secure Kids* (New York: St. Martin's, 1991).

#5

Find Out What Interests
Your Child

One of the latest theories to hit the A.D.D. movement is that these kids don't really have an attention deficit—they have a *motivational deficit*. According to this view, A.D.D. children have a neurological disorder that creates an insensitivity to consequences (rewards, punishment, or both). This theory attempts to explain why children labeled A.D.D. are so inconsistent in their attention and behavior levels—at times seeming to be very absorbed, and at other times tuning out or misbehaving. Proponents of this view suggest that there are possibly genetic flaws that cause decreased activation in the "reward centers" of the brain and that "A.D.D. children" require more frequent and more intense rewards (as well as medication) to make up for this deficit.

I think it makes much more sense to view this motivation issue from a non-medical perspective. Kids labeled A.D.D. don't have a motivational deficit. They have motivations toward *other* goals—ones that are considered unimportant by A.D.D. proponents. And, conversely, they're not always motivated by the things that authorities *want* them to be motivated by. The manipulative rewards that drive so-called normal people—praise, a letter grade on a report card, a weekly allowance—aren't always effective with kids labeled A.D.D. These kids are more likely to go their own way and be driven by inner motivations and interests. It has been said of the so-called A.D.D. child that when he gets absorbed in something, he *really* gets absorbed—sometimes for hours at a time.

What then are these interests? You won't find out from the A.D.D. community. For as I mentioned above, A.D.D. kids are interested in doing things that A.D.D. professionals generally consider unimportant. Why, otherwise, would there be essentially no literature in the A.D.D. field that explores the range of interests among children who receive that label? Why don't we know if kids labeled A.D.D. love lizards, astronomy, rocks, music, field trips, carpentry, or thousands of other things? It's because A.D.D. proponents are much more focused on what A.D.D. kids *aren't* interested in: lectures, textbooks, worksheets, boring routines, rote skills, and so forth. Apparently these are the things A.D.D. professionals consider most important in life—why otherwise would they claim that non-interest in them qualifies children for a neurologically based motivational disorder?

Since, as I've pointed out in earlier chapters, so-called A.D.D. children make up a heterogeneous group of kids, it's possible to speculate that their interests are similarly diverse and broad-ranging. An important first step in helping children with attention and behavior problems to achieve success in life requires that parents and professionals discover what really interests them. After that has been established, the next step involves feeding the flames of enthusiasm by helping to develop their interests.

The following list of 105 activities represents only a small number of the full range of possibilities, but it nevertheless can help you to begin to focus in on the interests of your child:

action figures	boats	computers
airplanes	the body	cooking
aquariums	bubbles	dancing
art	cards	digging
astronomy	carpentry	dinosaurs
balloons	cars and trucks	dolls
balls	cartoons	drama
baseball	cheerleading	drawing
baseball cards	chemistry set	eating
bicycling	clay	ecology
biographies	clocks	electricity
birds	clothes	electronics
blocks	coin collecting	finger paints
board games	coloring	fishing

football	miniature soldiers	secret codes
gardening	money	sewing
geography	movies	singing
hiking	music	skateboarding
history	musical instruments	skating
hockey	other cultures	sky watching
insects	pets	soccer
jungle gym	photography	stamp collecting
kites	pictures	storytelling
Lego blocks	playhouse	stuffed animals
lizards	playing	swimming
machines	poetry	talking
magic	puppets	telephoning
magnets	puzzles	television
make-believe	radios	telling jokes
makeup	reading books	traveling
map reading	rubber stamp sets	tree climbing
marbles	running	video games
martial arts	science fiction	water
math	Scouts	weather
microscopes	seashells	writing

The best way to discover your child's interests is to observe him during times when no one is telling him what to do. How does he spend his free time? What are the things he does that fill him with enthusiasm, excitement, interest, and passion? What are the activities that most absorb his energies and attention? Once you've discovered what they are, work delicately to help fan the flames of interest by providing resources that can help draw out or extend the activity. One teacher working with a "hyperactive" boy named David, for example, noticed that he was fascinated with birdsongs, insects, animals, trees, and anything else having to do with the outdoors. She provided David with a typewriter, a tape recorder, a camera, and a pair of binoculars and gave him opportunities to go outdoors to observe nature, record its sounds and sights, and write about what he saw when he was back in class. Likewise, a mother of a twelve-year-old son labeled A.D.D. helped to fuel his interest in animals by bringing into the house a turtle and some hermit crabs that he could care for and study.

It's important not to overwhelm a child's interests with too much adult "help." Many times, children prefer to engage in hobbies and activities by themselves and might resist adult intrusions, however well-intentioned. Regard your child's interests—no matter how trivial they may seem or how far removed from the "practical" world—with a sense of honor and respect. It may be your child's personal interests rather than any standard set of A.D.D. treatments that will lead him to a successful future. One parent related to me how her distractible and fidgety daughter, from age nine to age eleven, created an imaginary world of "weepals." There were 164 of these fanciful creatures in all—and for each one she gave a special name, personality, and set of unique characteristics. She even created houses and furniture for them. Now, at the age of twenty-three, she's translated this interest into a successful career coordinating several departments of a law firm! What interests your child?

RESOURCES

Steveanne Auerbach, *The Toy Chest: A Sourcebook of Toys for Children* (Secaucus, NJ: Lyle Stuart, 1986).

Jerry Dunn (ed.), *Tricks of the Trade for Kids* (Boston: Houghton Mifflin, 1994). Kids learn from experts how to throw a frisbee, do a magic trick, juggle, make a video, tie a knot, twirl a baton, draw an animated cartoon, and much more.

Edmund Scientific, 101 East Gloucester Pike, Barrington, NJ 08007. Send for this company's free catalog, which offers several different science kits and other accessories.

Johnson Smith, 4514 19th Street, Court E, P.O. Box 25500, Bradenton, FL 34206-5500; 813-947-2356. This company offers inexpensive toys, gizmos, and novelty items that children aged eight to twelve will find especially interesting. Free catalog.

#6

Promote a Strong Physical Education Program in Your Child's School

When I was a teacher of children with learning and behavior problems, I found that my students were almost invariably quieter, more focused, and more socially appropriate just after they had come in from a physical education or recreational period. (The only exception was if they had gotten into fights during competitive games.) Teachers I've talked with about this back me up. In fact, it's well-known among experienced teachers that if a class gets too jumpy, one effective "trick" is to let them run around the school one or more times (or engage in a similar physical activity) to "blow off steam."

Few schools in the United States, however, actually provide the kind of physical catharsis that even so-called normal children require every day—let alone those kids labeled A.D.D. who may have even greater need for physical release. One survey of PE programs in Texas revealed that students were moderately to vigorously active during less than 9 percent of the PE class time—adding up to about 10 minutes per week. Much of the time students were watching others work out or waiting for their turn to get involved. On a national level, only four states require physical education classes in all grades, while thirty-six states allow classroom teachers who lack credentials in fitness and sport to teach physical education to elementary school students. Finally, a report sponsored by the Kellogg Foundation revealed that only 1 percent of class time in PE classes was spent on aerobic activity.

Fortunately, there are some excellent PE programs throughout the country that serve as models for what high-quality physical education might look like in your child's own school. At Galindo Elementary School in Austin, Texas, children take daily walks and even keep "walking journals" in which they record the things they see, how they feel, and conversations they have with peers. In the Bogalusa, Louisiana, public schools children engage in a "Superkids-Superfit" program that involves dance, rope-skipping, parachute play, walking, jogging, and aerobics. In addition to their regular PE class, students in Bogalusa also engage in "afternoon perk-up" sessions consisting of physical exercises students do next to their desks. At the Bettendorf Middle School in Bettendorf, Iowa, students regularly bicycle along a thirteen-mile bike path before lunch, canoe in a city park lagoon with canoes provided by the park board, and also play golf to improve their fitness levels.

A recent study suggests that kids with hyperactive or aggressive traits may improve their behaviors if they engage in regular vigorous physical education. Hugh Stevenson, track and cross country coach at U.S. International University in San Diego, reported on efforts to improve physical education programs for children: "We're already seeing effects, especially on hyperactive, aggressive kids.... Students who ran and participated in jumping or field exercises, for forty minutes a day, at least three times a week showed less aggression on the days they ran than on the days they did not."

If you're interested in getting your child's school to institute a strong physical education program, here are some guidelines. The National Association for Sport and Physical Education (NASPE) recommends that elementary school pupils receive at least thirty minutes of PE every day, and that secondary school students have at least forty-five minutes of the subject daily. At least 50 percent of the time should be "active" time in which students are engaged in physical activity. In addition, some experts recommend that PE programs for kids with behavior problems should emphasize individual sports over team sports. Pediatrician Jeffrey L. Alexander points out that "many children with ADHD excel in activities that focus more on individual skills than on teamwork. Examples: wrestling, karate, swimming, fencing, track and field, and tennis."

You can help establish a strong PE program in your child's school in several ways: by serving on a school site council or PTA committee dedicated to improving PE in the school; by offering to serve as an aide in PE classes or as a volunteer monitor during playground time; by helping to build or repair physical education equipment; or by holding fund-raisers to buy needed resources (including having a schoolwide "fitness fair"). When you support a strong PE program at your local school, you'll help to provide your child with yet another avenue for channeling his energies and enhancing his self-esteem.

RESOURCES

Amateur Athletic Union (AAU), 160 HPER Building, Bloomington, IN 47405. Write for the AAU's free physical fitness program guide. Teachers with disabled students can call the AAU at 812-335-2059 for ideas on how to modify exercises.

American Sports Institute, P.O. Box 1837, Mill Valley, CA 94942; 415-383-5750. Advances sports as a positive force for keeping kids in school and promoting academic achievement.

Creative Walking, P.O. Box 50296, Clayton, MO 63105; 800-762-9255. Write or call for information on setting up a school walking program.

National Association for Sport and Physical Education. To order this organization's report, "The Shape of the Nation," which surveys physical education requirements in all fifty states, call 800-321-0789.

President's Council on Physical Fitness and Sports, 450 5th Street, NW, Suite 7103, Washington, DC 20001. Write for the council's booklet, "Get Fit!" which includes information on the President's Challenge, a series of exercises to build flexibility, strength, and endurance.

#7

Enroll Your Child in
a Martial Arts Class

A common sight on many playgrounds around the country these days is children practicing their karate, judo, and tae kwon do moves. Inspired by the Teenage Mutant Ninja Turtles, Mighty Morphin Power Rangers, and a flurry of movies featuring superheroes such as Bruce Lee, Chuck Norris, and Jean-Claude Van Damme, today's kids from five to fifteen seem intent on practicing martial art techniques that have their origins in Eastern traditions dating back several hundred years or more. The students in my special education classes were no exception. Many of them would creep through the classroom day only to spring to life during recess time, practicing flying kicks against backboards, handchops through the air, and feinting moves against any and all who might care to join in.

Now it appears that these martial art skills could prove to be a wonderful vehicle for the training of self-control, concentration, and respect for others among children who've been labeled as hyperactive or A.D.D. According to developmental pediatrician Jeffrey Alexander, "Karate may be one of the best examples of a sport that is therapeutic for the ADHD child." Karate and other martial art disciplines help children with attention and behavior problems in several ways. First, they train children to control their boundless supplies of energy. For kids who seem to be at the mercy of their own chaotic energy systems, these sports offer a chance to begin directing physical and mental energy in a focused way. Second, they empower kids to feel good about themselves by enhancing their capacity to defend themselves, improving their physical coordination, and developing a skill that is highly valued in their peer group. Third, they promote respect for others through the ritual courtesies (e.g., bowing) and ethical values each art employs. Finally, they give kids an acceptable way of handling aggressive feelings without hurting themselves or anyone else.

Although most people think of martial arts as a highly aggressive sport that can prove fatal if used with enough intensity, the basis for most of these disciplines is purely defensive. In fact, a theme running through most of the martial arts is that defensiveness is the best way of outsmarting one's enemy. Rather than confronting a perceived threat with an all-out frontal assault, many martial art teachers counsel students to use their opponent's own energy to bring them down. Some aikido masters, for example, are known for their ability to disable individuals without even touching them!

There are many differences, however, among the wide range of martial arts taught currently in this country. Perhaps the most widely known of them, *karate* (a Japanese word meaning "empty hand"), stresses defensive blocks and the use of kicking and striking techniques. In karate, students place intense mental and physical concentration on the intended point of impact—usually a block of wood or a point a few inches in front of an opponent. In *judo*, also a Japanese art (but derived from the Chinese word meaning "gentle way"), emphasis is placed on throwing one's opponent and using pressure on different points of the body to disable an individual. *Aikido* (Japanese for "mind-meeting way") teaches defensive-like techniques similar to those of judo, but with less emphasis on making physical contact with one's opponent. *Tai chi* is a non-contact Chinese system of physical actions performed in slow motion as a meditative exercise. There is also *tae kwon do*, a Korean form of karate that concentrates on kicking; *kenpo*, an Americanized version of Eastern martial arts that combines traditional skills with modern boxing techniques; and *karobics*, a combination of karate, tai chi, and aerobics, among many more systems from cultures around the world.

To find a suitable martial arts class for your child, look first for low-cost children's classes taught through community and fitness centers, after-school programs, or recreational centers. There are also many excellent programs available through private businesses that often operate as storefront enterprises. You can find out about these by flipping through the yellow pages under "martial arts instruction." Make sure that the instructors are certified by a reputable national or international organization. Take some time with your child to observe a lesson or two so that you both feel comfortable with the place. Don't hesitate to ask the instructors questions or share any concerns you might have. Some courses for children include lessons on defending against bullies or potential child molesters as well as methods for respecting the rights of others. Once your child has enrolled, help keep his interest level high by regularly giving him a chance to show you what he's learned, by going together to observe adult demonstrations of martial arts, and by encouraging him to stick it out when he feels bored or discouraged. Once he begins to see how martial arts is positively transforming his whole attitude toward himself and others, he may never want to quit!

RESOURCES

Terrence Webster-Doyle, *Facing the Double-Edged Sword: The Art of Karate for Young People* (Middlebury, VT: Atrium Society Publications, 1988). The book includes directions for focusing energy, handling bullies, avoiding conflict, and choosing a karate school. Atrium Society Publications can be contacted at P.O. Box 816, Middlebury, VT 05753.

8

Discover Your Child's Personal Learning Style

I taught a remarkable group of kids during my five years in special education classrooms. They included a boy who held the national swimming record for breaststroke in his age group; a girl who was a model for a national department store chain; a boy whose science fiction sagas had us all wondering what he would think of next; a girl who was being investigated by parapsychologists for psychic abilities; several students with superior artistic skills; kids who were natural leaders, mechanical wizards, musicians, mathematicians, and more. What they all had in common was difficulty with the traditional classroom model of workbooks, lectures, and standardized tests—a difficulty that sometimes showed itself in learning problems and sometimes in behavioral or attentional problems.

What I discovered in my years of working with these kids was that each one of them was a learner—and that each one learned in a different way. Later on I was able to explain what kinds of "learning styles" each of these students had when I discovered the theory of multiple intelligences. About fifteen years ago, Harvard researcher Howard Gardner wrote a book called *Frames of Mind* that challenged the common belief that people are born with a fixed intelligence that can only be discovered through IQ tests. Instead, Gardner said, there are at least seven distinct ways of being smart, and one can discover these ways by examining how people solve real problems and create meaningful products. These intelligences are as follows:

1. *Linguistic*—the intelligence of words. A highly linguistically intelligent child likes to read, writes easily, tells great stories, and can memorize facts. This child needs such things as books, audio tapes, writing implements, writing paper, diaries, dialogue, discussion, debate, and stories.

2. *Logical-Mathematical*—the intelligence of reasoning. A child that shows high levels of logical-mathematical intelligence enjoys math and/or science, handles number problems easily, does well with brainteasers and logic games, and is attracted to logical patterns. This child needs such things as logical problems to explore and think about, science kits, math manipulatives, trips to science museums, and brainteasers.

3. *Spatial*—the intelligence of pictures and images. The highly spatially intelligent child draws well, remembers visual details, thinks visually, and may be attracted to video games. This child needs such things as art activities, Lego materials, videotapes, movies, slides, imagination games, mazes, puzzles, illustrated books, and trips to art museums.

4. *Bodily-Kinesthetic*—the intelligence of physical skill. The child that has high levels of bodily-kinesthetic intelligence likes to work with his hands, may be a good athlete, needs to move in order to learn, and often gets "gut feelings" about things. This child needs such things as role play, drama, movement, building materials, sports and physical games, tactile experiences, and hands-on learning.

5. *Musical*—the intelligence of melody, tone, and rhythm. The highly musically intelligent child enjoys listening to music, has a good sense of rhythm, often has a pleasant singing voice, and may play an instrument. This child needs such things as sing-along time, trips to concerts, musical instruments, music lessons, records and tapes, and opportunities to be in choir or band.

6. *Interpersonal*—the intelligence of getting along with other people: the strongly interpersonally intelligent child usually has many friends, enjoys socializing, shows empathy for others, and is gener-

ally quite cooperative. This child needs such things as friends, group games, social gatherings, community events, volunteer opportunities, cooperative learning, mentors, apprenticeships, and clubs.

7. *Intrapersonal*—the intelligence of self-knowledge. The highly intrapersonally intelligent child has a good sense of his personal strengths and weaknesses, possesses self-confidence, often sets goals for the future, and is usually able to reflect upon past experience and learn from it. This child needs such things as secret places, time alone, self-paced activities, private hobbies, opportunities to make choices, and independent study.

It's important to understand that every child has ability in all seven of these areas. However, each child differs in the ways in which she expresses each ability. Gardner points out that starting in early childhood, children show "proclivities" for, or inclinations toward, one or more of the intelligences. For example, one child will spend a great deal of time rhythmically banging on pots and pans (showing early evidence of musical intelligence), while another will enjoy drawing (spatial intelligence), and still another prefers to engage in hands-on activities (bodily-kinesthetic and spatial intelligences).

Once a child enters school, however, there tends to be an emphasis upon two of the intelligences: linguistic and logical-mathematical. Schools focus most of their attention on reading, writing, math, and science. If a child has natural strengths in these areas, then he will probably do quite well in school. However, if he has difficulties with linguistic and logical areas, then he may well end up with the A.D.D. or LD (learning disabled) label (or both), even if he possesses high levels of ability in the other five intelligences. In my own research, I discovered that children with school problems most often showed particular strengths in those intelligences *least* honored in the classroom, particularly bodily-kinesthetic and spatial intelligence.

A person with high levels of bodily-kinesthetic intelligence seems to be at particularly high risk for the A.D.D. label. This child needs to learn about things by touching them, by moving around, by building with his hands, and in other ways getting physical with the learning process. If this student has to spend several hours sitting quietly in a classroom listening to lots of linguistic (verbal) information from the teacher, filling out linguistic worksheets, and reading linguistic materials (such as textbooks), then he doesn't have an opportunity to shine in his area of

strength. He's likely to respond to this confining scenario with restlessness, fidgeting, inattentiveness—in short, many of the symptoms of
A.D.D.

Students with strengths in some of the other intelligences may also
be candidates for the A.D.D. label. Highly interpersonal students who
don't have an opportunity to learn by teaching others, working in cooperative groups, or engaging in social learning games may respond by
talking with neighbors out of turn, passing notes, or engaging in other
disruptive behaviors. Musically inclined students who can't learn new
material by singing it, rapping, or learning with background music may
begin tapping rhythmically on the desk, singing under their breath, or
moving their bodies around to some imagined tune. Highly spatial students who don't have the opportunity to learn through visual thinking,
art-related activities, or other spatial approaches may be the daydreamers, doodlers, or space cadets of the class. Each of these students is
sending a message to the teacher through their misbehaviors or behavioral "symptoms": "Teacher, this is how I learn. And if you don't teach
me in the way that I learn, I'm going to do it anyway—and it's going to
drive you crazy!"

The solution to this problem is to create classrooms that teach to all
seven of the intelligences in Gardner's model. That might mean on
Monday, a teacher would introduce a lesson on the skeletal system
by having the class play Simon Says (e.g., "touch your clavicle") for a
bodily-kinesthetic approach. On Tuesday, the teacher might assign each
person a bone in the body and have the class members form a gigantic
"people skeleton" while singing "Them Bones" for an interpersonal-
musical approach. On Wednesday, students might share stories of having broken bones in the past (intrapersonal intelligence). Thursday
might see the class drawing pictures of bones or visualizing the skeletal
system in their mind's eye (spatial intelligence). Friday could involve
counting the number of bones in the class (206 times the number of students in class) and reading some textbook material on the skeletal system (logical-mathematical and linguistic intelligences). By the end of the
week, every student in class would have had his or her strongest intelligence addressed.

I'd like to suggest that if our nation's classrooms taught more often
in this multiple-intelligences way, we'd have fewer students identified as
A.D.D. Students would have frequent experiences of being taught in the
way they most easily learn. The strongly bodily-kinesthetic child would
be able to channel much of his distractible, hyperactive, impulsive be-

havior into physical experiences that are academically rewarding. Similarly, highly musical, social, spatial, or intrapersonal students would be able to show their strengths frequently in the classroom and would have less need to "act out" the intelligences inappropriately.

This new approach to teaching has received growing levels of support from the education community and from the broader society as well. If you'd like to see your child learning in a classroom that honors and celebrates all seven of the intelligences, then get involved with a school curriculum committee, volunteer in the classroom to teach academic skills through some of the neglected intelligences, share curriculum resources with your child's teacher, and gently persist in your quest to provide your child with an opportunity to learn by doing what he does best.

Resources

Thomas Armstrong, *In Their Own Way: Discovering and Encouraging Your Child's Personal Learning Style* (New York: Tarcher/Putnam, 1987).

———, *Multiple Intelligences in the Classroom* (Alexandria, VA: Association for Supervision and Curriculum Development, 1994).

———, *Seven Kinds of Smart: Identifying and Developing Your Many Intelligences* (New York: Plume/Penguin, 1993).

Linda Campbell, Bruce Campbell, and Dee Dickinson, *Teaching and Learning Through Multiple Intelligences* (Tucson, AZ: Zephyr, 1993). Contact the publisher at Zephyr Press, P.O. Box 66006, Tucson, AZ 85728-6006.

Howard Gardner, *Frames of Mind* (New York: Basic Books, 1983).

———, *Multiple Intelligences* (New York: Basic Books, 1993).

David Lazear, *Seven Ways of Knowing: Teaching for Multiple Intelligences* (Palatine, IL: Skylight, 1991). Contact the publisher at Skylight Publishing, 200 E. Wood Street, Suite 250, Palatine, IL 60067.

———, *Seven Pathways of Learning: Teaching Students and Parents about Multiple Intelligences* (Tucson, AZ: Zephyr, 1994).

#9

Use Background Music
to Focus and Calm

"Music has charms to soothe the savage breast," goes the old saying. But does this apply to the hyperactive breast as well? I think it does. Many parents of kids who've been labeled A.D.D. or hyperactive have told me that their children may have trouble attending to words (teachers' instructions, parents' directives) but not to music. In fact, they even suggest that for some of these kids, music serves as a real asset in helping to calm and focus them during study periods.

Even more surprising, it appears that for certain kids, highly stimulating music—such as rock music—may exercise a calming effect (in the same way perhaps that psychostimulants like Ritalin help settle down the hyperactive child). In one study conducted at the Oregon Health Sciences University in Portland, kids who'd been labeled attention deficit disordered showed a significant reduction in motor activities (in other words, less hyperactivity) when they listened to rock music through individual headsets. Researchers speculated that the rock music stimulated the cerebrum; that the prominent beat overrode surrounding environmental distractions providing a focus for the kids; and finally, that the repetitive beat tended to produce a reduction in skeletal muscle tension, which translated into reduced motor activity. An earlier study at a children's residential facility in New York similarly showed that "hyperactive children" who listened to popular music (in this case the Beatles' *Magical Mystery Tour* and *Sgt. Pepper's Lonely Hearts*

Club Band) while working on arithmetic problems were more accurate than when they worked in silence. These two exploratory studies, while not conclusive (they both involved small subject populations), offer some support for the use of music in helping kids labeled A.D.D. calm down and focus.

Rather than leap to the conclusion, however, that all kids labeled A.D.D. need to listen to rock music to settle down, I would recommend talking with your child about whether music has been helpful in the past in calming or focusing him, and if so, what kinds of music. If your child responds positively, I would suggest an experiment in which he's allowed to study or engage in other home tasks with his preferred music for a few days, and then without the music for the same amount of time. Then you can sit down with your child and compare the results, including a look at productivity and accuracy of work completed, as well as attitudes and feelings that came up, and things you might have noticed about the beneficial or detrimental aspects of the music. For school settings, you could approach a teacher and suggest a similar experiment. I let students in my special education classes listen to their favorite music on headsets as long as they were making progress. Music was not allowed if it seemed to be distracting or disturbing individual students in any way.

If highly stimulating music (like heavy metal, rap, or hip-hop) doesn't help, then you might suggest other forms of music to provide a gentle auditory background to a child's home or school environment. I know teachers who have used certain classical and contemporary pieces—as well as environmental recordings or "white sound"—as background while students were engaged in study sessions. This may be particularly important if students are attempting to study in settings that are filled with noisy distractions including chatter of other students, machinery noises, or even overhead aircraft. One study conducted at Eastern Kentucky University revealed that high levels of linguistic noise (students talking) proved quite distracting to "hyperactive children," thus white noise or other sound mufflers may help mask class chatter. In another study, students at an elementary school situated near Los Angeles International Airport had more difficulty solving math problems and tended to give up sooner on learning tasks than control groups because of the airplane noises. In his book *The Healing Energies of Music*, counselor and teacher Hal Lingerman suggests some of the following classical pieces for dealing with different conditions:

For Hyperactivity:

Bach, "Air on the G String"
Grieg, *Holberg Suite*
Beethoven, Symphony no. 6 (first and second movements)
Pachelbel, Canon in D
Hovhaness, *Mysterious Mountain*
Mozart, Concerto for Flute and Harp
Vivaldi, *The Four Seasons*

To Control Anger:

Bach, two Concertos for Two Pianos
Handel, Harp Concerto
Dexter, *Golden Voyage I*
Schubert, Prelude to *Rosamunde*
Dowland, lute music
Gluck, "Dance of the Blessed Spirits" (From *Orfeo ed Euridice*)

For Relaxation and Reverie:

Debussy, *Clair de Lune*
Halpern-Kelly, *Ancient Echoes*
Lee, *Celestial Spaces* for Koto
Copland, *Appalachian Spring*
Stivell, *Renaissance of the Celtic Harp*

In addition to selecting music on the basis of mood, try using different types of music at selected times of the day. It may be that certain kinds of music, for example, are more effective at the beginning of the day (stimulating and awakening music) while other pieces might be selected for bedtime (lullabies or other forms of soothing and calming music). In earlier historical times and still today in some cultures, music is prescribed to treat emotional and physical illness much as today's physicians prescribe medicine. For your child's attentional and behavioral difficulties, music may well turn out to be the "good medicine" you've both been searching for.

Resources

Helen Bonny and Louis Savary, *Music and Your Mind* (Barrytown, NY: Station
Hill, 1990). (The publisher can be contacted at Station Hill Press, Station
Hill Road, Barrytown, NY 12507.) The book includes a comprehensive "dis-
cography" of musical recordings with indicators of the types of emotions
each is likely to arouse.

Steven Halpern and Louis Savary, *Sound Health: The Music and Sounds that
Make Us Whole* (San Francisco: Harper & Row, 1985).

Institute for Music, Health, and Education, 250 Arapahoe Avenue, Boulder, CO
80302. This organization explores the use of music and sound stimulation to
treat learning difficulties.

Hal A. Lingerman, *The Healing Energies of Music* (Wheaton, IL: Quest, 1983).

Music for Little People, Box 1460, Redway, CA 95560. This mail-order company
provides recorded music appropriate for kids. Its free catalog includes a
section on "lullabies and quiet times" as well as more stimulating music
(classical, children's classics, and sing-along).

Laurie Sale, *Growing Up with Music: A Guide to the Best Recorded Music for
Children* (New York: Avon, 1992).

#10

Use Color to Highlight Information

Very young children live in a world of color. Their toys are brightly colored. Lavish colors fill their illustrated books. "Favorite" colors inspire strong feelings. But then children go off to school. And as they proceed through the grades, they confront quite a different world, one ruled not by color but by black and white. They write their compositions in black pencil on white paper. They read textbooks full of black words against a white background. They copy words written in white chalk on a "blackboard." They may even forget what their favorite color was. However, recent research suggests that some kids who are labeled A.D.D. or hyperactive may hold on to this attraction to color as they progress in school. For these kids, a black-and-white world might be a real detriment to learning, and the deliberate use of color in highlighting material could well be an important key to their academic success.

At the forefront of this new research into the impact of color on children labeled A.D.D. is Sydney Zentall, professor of special education at Purdue University. Zentall and her associates studied child and adolescent responses to the use of color in copying written material. They discovered that when color is used to help highlight specific features of letters (i.e., on the most common areas of letter error for cursive writing), children labeled A.D.D. made fewer errors in copying than when the material consisted solely of black letters. Color appears to draw their attention to the most important features of specific letters and helps to guide their work in copying the letters. Zentall also discovered that when children labeled A.D.D. are presented with letters on a screen, they are more likely to be attentive to them if they're in color. She does caution, however, that color can also serve as a distraction if it is not integrated in a meaningful way into the material being learned (e.g., colorful designs and pictures included around the borders of educational materials simply to jazz them up may distract some of these kids away from the material to be learned).

What this research suggests is that parents and teachers should incorporate the meaningful use of color into schoolday activities and homework sessions as much as possible, including the use of some of the following materials: colored pencils, colored chalk, colored markers, colored paper, and colored transparencies (for overhead projectors). Color should be used to highlight specific words, numbers, or text. For example, if the child is studying spelling words beginning in *th*, the *th* might be highlighted in one color and the rest of the word in another color. In arithmetic, odd numbers might be colored blue and even numbers red, or in learning the times tables for the threes, every third number might be colored green. Children should also be taught how to use a colored highlighter pen to underline relevant material as they study (for example, with a history assignment, highlighting in red all the significant names, in green the important dates, in yellow the relevant places, and in blue the central ideas).

Some educators even suggest using a child's favorite colors to enhance their overall learning environment. Barbara Meister Vitale, author of *Unicorns Are Real: A Right-Brained Approach to Learning*, provides children with an assortment of colors (e.g., paper, fabric) and lets them choose the color that makes them feel calmer, more attentive, or more productive (they do this at the beginning of each day, since a child's favorite or preferred color may vary from day to day). Then they cover their work area with the color. Vitale writes, "Often the children demonstrated positive changes in behavior and concentration. One child in particular never seemed to stop moving. He seemed everywhere at once, always at the wrong time. His favorite color was red. When I asked him why the color red made him sit still and think better, he said, 'It makes me feel warm and heavy. The others make me want to fly.' " By tuning in to your child's unique hue preferences, you may be helping him move through school, and life, with flying colors.

R E S O U R C E S

Barbara Meister Vitale, *Unicorns Are Real: A Right-Brained Approach to Learning* (Rolling Hills Estates, CA: Jalmar, 1982). This book includes several "color-friendly" activities, including "Eating Color," "Rolling in Color," "Color Writing," and "Rainbow Letters."

#11

Teach Your Child to Visualize

A few years back, I was demonstrating some new techniques for teaching spelling in an upstate New York elementary school classroom and was stymied by an eight-year-old boy named Billy in the front row who refused to stay in his seat during most of the lesson. When I got to the part of the lesson where I have students visualize their spelling words, however, I was amazed to see Billy return to his seat and remain perfectly still while he covered his eyes and "looked" intently at his imaginary words. Not surprisingly, the letters in his mind's eye would not remain stable, and I spent a few minutes working with him individually on strategies for making the words stand still. Later on, I realized that something more important than a spelling lesson went on that afternoon: Billy was able to transform his external physical hyperactivity into internal mental motion. And by internalizing his outer activity level, he was able to gain some degree of control over it.

The imagination represents an important potential resource that kids labeled A.D.D. can draw upon to help them learn, attend, and behave. Albert Einstein (himself a behavior problem in school) once said in reference to his own thinking processes, "The imagination is everything." He conducted "thought experiments" (e.g., visualizing what it would be like to ride on a beam of light) that were instrumental in helping him to formulate the theory of relativity. Many others in history have used their vivid imaginations to better society, including naturalist

Louis Agassiz, Elias Howe (inventor of the sewing machine), Robert Louis Stevenson, and nuclear physicist Niels Bohr. These thinkers, like many kids labeled A.D.D., were "daydreamers." The only difference was that these eminent individuals used their daydreams productively. With the proper guidance, so-called A.D.D. kids can also thrive through their imaginary gifts.

Even A.D.D. experts admit that "A.D.D. children" have good imaginations. Unfortunately, the experts all too often regard good imaginations as problems. Describing one child's "free flight of ideas" during a school lesson about upcoming presidential elections, pediatrician Robert A. Moss, author of *Why Johnny Can't Concentrate*, writes, "Six-year-old Amanda starts to think about George Washington and the cherry tree. The child is then reminded of the cherry tree in her own front yard. Amanda raises her hand and, when called upon, remarks: 'The tree in our front yard has pretty yellow leaves on it.' Amanda has not been listening to the teacher at all and has no idea who the two presidential candidates are." Yet Amanda clearly *has* been listening, and is applying her own vivid imagination to the lesson. A teacher who recognizes the value of imagination would ask questions to draw out Amanda's connections of trees to presidents, and perhaps even suggest that she imagine special trees in front of the yards of the current presidential candidates.

There are many ways of using visualization as a tool for learning, attention, and behavior. As in the spelling example cited in the beginning of this section, visualization can be used to teach traditional academic subjects. Students can be helped to look at their "inner blackboard" (for some kids labeled A.D.D. it may be more of a mental movie screen or other highly dynamic image). They can place onto their mental screen spelling lists, times tables, math formulas, or other material to be learned. Students can also visualize what they've read after reviewing a textbook, or picture what they've heard after hearing instructions from the teacher. For students who are better visualizers than verbalizers, this strategy may be particularly effective.

Psychologists and educators have also helped impulsive and hyperactive children use imagery as a means of self-control. In one study, children were taught "the Turtle Technique," a procedure for responding to the aggressive or provocative behaviors of peers. This self-help strategy involved the child's imagining that he was a turtle withdrawing into its shell. The child was to pull his arms close to his body, put his head down, and close his eyes while relaxing his muscles. Results revealed significant decreases in aggressive behavior when used in conjunction with problem solving and group support. In another example, a psychologist working with a "hyperactive girl" used fantasy to help her deal with her behavior. Asked to imagine her favorite animal, the girl fantasized a pony who always wanted to go too fast. Initially, when the girl tried to "pull on the reins," the pony only wanted to go faster. However, she discovered as she worked through this imaginary scene that if she said "whoa" very softly and persisted in a gentle way, the pony was able to respond and go more slowly. This spontaneously occurring imagery suggested that the girl did in fact possess the necessary self-control skills for slowing down in her own life.

In a similar way, children labeled A.D.D. can be assisted in forming their own personalized mental images to help them cope with their behavior or with the actions of others. Some images that you can suggest to your child could include the following:

For Calming Down:

♦ a special place in nature (e.g., lake, woods, mountains)
♦ a favorite trip (e.g., amusement park)
♦ an imaginary journey (e.g., to a magical land)
♦ a secret place (e.g., tree house, fort)

For Focusing:

♦ a favorite color
♦ a favorite toy
♦ a special hero
♦ a favorite movie

For Responding to Criticism:

♦ ducking arrows (of criticism)
♦ letting the breeze (of criticisms) pass around
♦ allowing the criticism to fall off like water from a duck's back
♦ fending off the bad words with an imaginary light-saber
♦ putting an imaginary protective white light around him

For some kids labeled A.D.D., the best imagery scenarios will be unlike any of those suggested above. As discussed above, some kids may require high levels of action in their mental imagery and may actually "calm down" when they create highly dynamic images such as monster trucks crashing against each other or dinosaurs locked in mortal combat. For these kids (and for other kids as well), it may be better to ask them to create their own personal "calming down" or "focusing" imagery. Take care not to judge your child's images simply because they don't fit your own idea of what she should be seeing. Then, you can instruct your child when she feels out of control to summon up the appropriate image to help her cope. Additionally, it may be helpful to suggest to your child that she form a mental picture of herself acting calmly, or responding appropriately to criticism, or focusing on schoolwork. These mental pictures of success may well become self-fulfilling prophecies if engaged in on a regular basis. You may even want to suggest to your child that she draw or paint her images and keep them as reminders. Not every child will be able to create imagery, and for some kids imagery may be too disturbing or agitating to create the desired effect. But for those who have vivid imaginations and a willingness to use their visual minds to better their lives, success may be just a picture away.

Resources

Richard DeMille, *Put Your Mother on the Ceiling: Children's Imagination Games* (New York: Viking/Penguin, 1976).

Robert H. McKim, *Experiences in Visual Thinking* (Boston: PWS Engineering, 1980).

Maureen Murdock, *Spinning Inward: Using Guided Imagery with Children* (Boston: Shambhala, 1987).

Mike Samuels and Nancy Samuels, *Seeing with the Mind's Eye: The History, Techniques, and Uses of Visualization* (New York: Random House/Bookworks, 1975).

Joseph E. Shorr, *Go See the Movies in Your Head* (New York: Popular Library, 1977).

#12

Remove Allergens from the Diet

My introduction to the relationship between food and behavior came in 1976 at an educational conference in Montreal, Canada, that featured as its theme nutrition and learning. At that conference a wide range of speakers—including Ben Feingold, William Crook, Alan Cott, Marcel Kinsbourne, and other nutrition pioneers—spoke about how ordinary foods that we eat everyday (wheat, chocolate, and milk for example) can sometimes play havoc on a sensitive child's brain chemistry. As a special education teacher, I could see in some of my most unruly students physical symptoms—puffy red eyes, stuffy nose, stomachaches, and headaches—that seemed to go along with their difficult behavior. I also observed how the behavior of some students could go sky high a short time after lunch.

Since that time, scientists have discovered much more about the relationship between diet and the symptoms of hyperactivity and "attention deficits." In a 1982 double-blind placebo-controlled study conducted by Bonnie Kaplan and her associates at the University of Calgary in Canada, twenty-four preschool boys who had been identified as hyperactive took part in a ten-week program that removed from their diets foods containing artificial flavors, colors, and preservatives, as well as any substance the family reported might affect the child (including such things as chocolate and milk). Results suggested that more than half of the subjects showed a significant improvement in behavior.

And in a 1985 study reported in the prestigious British journal *Lancet*, seventy-six overactive children were provided with an "oligoantigenic diet" for four weeks. (An oligoantigenic diet is a diet that contains few varieties of food—basically meats, potatoes, rice, fruits, and vegetables—and thus one that is likely to be free of food allergens.) Those children who improved on the diet went on to the next phase of the study and had selected foods from their prestudy diet reintroduced. If a food appeared to provoke a negative behavior reaction, it was withdrawn from the diet. These suspected food allergens were then administered under placebo-controlled double-blind conditions (neither the family nor the researchers knew whether a substance was a suspected allergen or a neutral food). Sixty-two of the seventy-six kids improved overall as a result of the diet change. The most common allergens reported were food colorings and preservatives. But specific foods were also implicated, including (in order of prevalence) soya, cow's milk, chocolate, grapes, wheat, oranges, cow's milk cheese, chicken eggs, peanuts, maize, fish, oats, melons, tomatoes, and ham.

These scientifically controlled studies provide strong evidence that, at least for some children with behavior problems, removal of allergens from the diet may be an important component in any treatment plan. Although research on the link between A.D.D. and overt allergies such as asthma, atopic eczema, or hay fever is controversial, some physicians have suggested that certain children with A.D.D. may suffer from "hidden food allergies." Author and physician William Crook compares allergies with an iceberg: common allergies like hay fever and eczema lie on the surface and are easy to spot, but a broad range of subtler allergies lurking beyond detection and caused by common foods can likewise play havoc with people's lives. The symptoms of such allergies may include: irritability, hyperactivity, fatigue, inability to concentrate, stuffy nose, dark circles under the eyes, puffiness around the eyes, abdominal pain, and headaches.

Crook suggests that parents who suspect their kids may have a hidden food allergy start them on an "elimination diet": a diet that includes most meats, vegetables, fruits and nuts, rice and water, but eliminates dairy products, sugars, wheat, eggs, corn, chocolate, cola, and certain fruits and vegetables. To implement the diet, Crook advises following a multistep procedure. First, prepare menus that contain the approved foods. Second, keep a diary of your child's behavior symptoms starting three days before the diet. Third, eliminate suspected foods for five to ten days or until your child's symptoms show significant improvement lasting forty-eight hours. Fourth, begin to add suspected foods—one each day. Finally, if a specific food seems to provoke a behavior reaction, don't give it to your child anymore and wait until symptoms subside before adding any new foods. It's very important to the success of this diet that you enlist the support of your child. Involve him in the decision to begin the diet, in the selection and preparation of foods and menus, in shopping for foods, and in recording in his own personal diary some of the potential "dietary culprits" as well as the observed benefits of this new way of eating. (You might even make a game of it: "Catch the Culprit.") And remember: what may be eating your child could be what your child is eating!

RESOURCES

William Crook, *Help for the Hyperactive Child* (Jackson, TN: Professional Books, 1991).

———, *Solving the Puzzle of Your Hard-to-Raise Child* (New York: Random House, 1987).

Marjorie H. Jones, *The Allergy Self-Help Cookbook* (Emmaus, PA: Rodale, 1983).

Vicki Lansky, *The Taming of the C.A.N.D.Y. Monster* (Wayzayta, MN: The Bookpeddler, 1988).

Nutrition Action Healthletter, published by the Center for Science in the Public Interest, 1875 Connecticut Avenue, NW, #300, Washington, DC 20009.

Doris Rapp, *Is This Your Child? Discovering and Treating Unrecognized Allergies in Children and Adults* (New York: Quill, 1992).

Lendon H. Smith, *Improving Your Child's Behavior Chemistry* (New York: Pocket Books, 1976).

#13

Provide Opportunities for Physical Movement

During one of my education workshops on learning styles, a teacher shared the story of a boy in her fourth grade classroom who was quite hyperactive and couldn't seem to focus on the material she was trying to teach him. One day, she asked him to water the plants while she went on with her teaching, and was surprised to learn afterward that he managed to absorb a great deal of her lecture material while doing the chore. Later on, I ran into a similar account in Maureen Murdock's book *Spinning Inward:*

> A former third grade student . . . could never sit still while I demonstrated a lesson on the chalkboard. He had to poke the child sitting next to him or rock back and forth in his chair, distracting both me and the rest of the class. . . . I asked Tony if he would sponge off the art/clay table while I presented a phonics lesson to the class. . . . After the lesson I quizzed the class about the rules I had presented for vowel blends and Tony got a perfect score of 10. He had never received a score higher than 3 before.

In both of these cases, it seems as if the students involved needed to *move* in order to learn. It may be that many students who are labeled A.D.D. share this need. Unfortunately, most of these kids are expected to learn under classroom conditions where students must sit quietly at their desks for long periods of time. It's understandable, then, why many of them squirm, wiggle, and show other "warning signs" of A.D.D.-type behavior.

Such students should be provided with opportunities at home and school to channel their physical energy in ways that are not disruptive to other class members. Sadly, many in the A.D.D. field seem woefully unprepared to comprehend this important learning need in children. In the book *Otto Learns About His Medicine: A Story About Medication for Hyperactive Children*, the narrator comments, "The medicine would help Otto keep still long enough and pay attention long enough to learn what he needed to know." Implied here is the belief that children need to *keep still* in order to learn. Similarly, one of the key slogans used in the A.D.D. community is "STOP, LOOK, AND LISTEN." It may be much more appropriate for some of these kids to *"GO*, LOOK, AND LISTEN."

In guidelines written by the Education Committee of the parent advocacy group CH.A.D.D., teachers are advised to "seat A.D.D. students near teacher's desk," and "place A.D.D. student up front with his back to the rest of the class." This particular advice, however, risks having the child twist, turn, jump, and spin in plain view of every member of the class, much to the class's amusement and possibly the child's as well. In questionnaires I've given to teachers in my own workshops, I've received much more sensible advice about seating arrangements that take into consideration the child's need to move. One teacher suggested, "Sit the child near a wall so s/he can be standing or wiggling without getting in someone else's way." Another teacher shared the following story:

> I had a tall, hyperactive 6th grade girl whose "attitude" was terrible. I noticed she got up a lot (disturbing others). I offered to let her have a seat in the back. She stood up almost *all* the time after that but got much more out of what was going on in class. Attitude/behavior changed, and academics improved.

Several teachers shared the strategy of providing a wiggly child with *two* desks at opposite sides of the room. That way, if the child gets out of his seat, he'll always have somewhere to go! Still other teachers recommended frequent changes in activities so that kids are regularly on the move. Some of the suggested variations in activities include standing, sitting at a desk, kneeling or lying on the floor while studying, working at a study carrel, meeting with small groups on a rug, moving from one activity center to another, and doing work outside of the classroom in other parts of the school or as fieldwork in the wider community.

One teacher reported building a special desk for a boy named David who was always on the move. This desk was more like a lectern in that it allowed David to stand up while doing his work, but it also included sturdy armrests and a padded back so he could sit when he wanted to. An old sewing machine foot lever was attached to one of the legs so that David could keep his feet busy while he worked. The teacher reported that David's calling out and neck-craning stopped, as did his constant fidgeting and touching of others. David commented that "now I can get some work done without getting tickles inside me." David has since grown up and become an innovative teacher himself, teaching kids with behavior and learning problems.

In China, children start their schoolday with a warmup of tai chi, an Oriental system of graceful and stylized movements. Similarly in the United States, teachers can provide students with special physical energizers throughout the day to help discharge or channel restless energy. An exercise break helps *all* kids, but especially those who are at risk of being labeled A.D.D. Examples of activities to use throughout the day include Simon Says, simple aerobic exercises set to music, a run around the school, folkdancing, calisthenics, and indoor ball games using balloons.

Movement activities can and should be a regular part of the academic program as well. Students can role-play history lessons or act out reading passages. They can learn spelling words by standing up on the vowels and sitting down on the consonants, or acquire knowledge of the times tables for the threes by counting while moving in a circle and skipping on every third number. They can "walk" their letter shapes, and create an algebra equation by having class members form a group equation where each child represents a different mathematical symbol (e.g., $2x + 1 = 5$). There are thousands of learning activities teachers can provide students at all grade levels that engage children in physical movement.

At home, there are also many opportunities to provide channels for appropriate physical movement. During homework sessions, allow your child to lie on the floor if that feels more comfortable, or to find some other posture (even standing up) that helps get the job done. Permit him to get up frequently and move around if that seems to be his style—he may get more done in short bursts than in long, drawn-out attempts to get him to sit still and finish his work. If you have a rocking chair, a hammock, or porch swing, these may be places where your child can read and/or study while moving at the same time. If you have a stationary bike, it can often be fitted with a special rack to allow for reading. Even an old swivel chair may help your child work out the wiggles while he studies. Above all, keep in mind that your child's hyperenergy only becomes a problem when the environment around him fails to find a constructive use for it. Once you've begun to accept your child's need for motion, you can set out to provide him with some truly "moving" learning experiences.

Resources

Anne G. Gilbert, *Teaching the Three R's Through Movement Experiences* (New York: Macmillan, 1977).

Gail Neary Herman and Patricia Hollingsworth, *Kinetic Kaleidoscope: Activities for Exploring Movement and Energy in the Visual Arts* (Tucson, AZ: Zephyr, 1993).

#14

Enhance Your Child's Self-Esteem

During the 1992 CH.A.D.D. annual conference, Harvard Medical School professor Robert B. Brooks read a creative writing sample from one of the A.D.D.-identified children he works with in his practice as a clinical psychologist. The child wrote, "Going to school has been like climbing up a steep mountain. Each step is a battle against icy winds. Sometimes I get knocked down. My body is numb. I'm clawing up a steep cliff. I look up and my struggle has hardly begun." This painful description may be representative of many kids who are labeled A.D.D. Perceiving the world in a different way, having a different kind of behavioral rhythm, and struggling with inner conflicts, many of these children end up being ostracized or taunted by peers, harshly evaluated by teachers, and severely punished by parents for misbehavior. Then, as if to add insult to injury, these kids are labeled as "deficit disordered." It's no wonder that their sense of self isn't too rosy.

Although research on the self-esteem of children labeled A.D.D. is still in the early stages, a preliminary study lends support to the idea that A.D.D.-identified kids may have significantly lower self-esteem than their so-called normal peers. A.D.D.-diagnosed boys aged eight to twelve years were compared, by means of the Self-Perception Profile for Children, with non-A.D.D. boys of the same age range. Researchers concluded that "A.D.D. boys" tended to view themselves as significantly less competent than the control group in areas of scholastic competence and global self-worth. An earlier study by Jan Loney in the Department of Psychiatry at the University of Iowa similarly showed that "hyperactive" fifth and sixth graders scored significantly lower on a self-esteem inventory than so-called normal students at the same age. Younger "hyperactive students" in the same study did not show lower self-esteem levels, suggesting that children develop lower self-esteem as a result of the kinds of negative experiences they accumulate from home and school as they grow up.

Given this state of affairs, it is extremely important—probably more important than anything else discussed in this book—to develop the self-esteem of your child. Unless your child has a positive core of self from which he can move strongly into the world, he won't have the strength to withstand the kinds of challenges that life inevitably delivers. The development of a strong and positive sense of self occurs as a result of your child having life experiences acknowledged and validated by significant people around him, including support from parents, teachers, and peers. One of the greatest enemies to self-esteem is the put-down: "Why can't you act like your sister?" or "You're the sloppiest student I've ever had in my class!" or "Oh look, here comes Hyper Henry!" On the other hand, one of the best self-esteem builders is the use of affirmations or validating statements: "I really love the way you smile!" or "You've got such a great sense of rhythm!" or "Hey, you were great in yesterday's ballgame!" Validation is different from praise, which is often used in a manipulative way to reinforce positive behavior. Validation should emerge out of a genuine and spontaneous feeling of appreciation for your child's existence as a unique and special person. By having his most positive features mirrored by those he cares about, your child learns to internalize this positive sense of self and grows up with a healthy sense of his own personal worth. Here are some specific strategies for developing your child's self-esteem:

 ♦ Have a "success-sharing" time during dinner or in the evening where everyone in the family has a chance to talk about at least one great thing he did during the day.

 ♦ Encourage your child to keep a "success-scrapbook" containing awards, memorabilia, photos and pictures of himself doing things he feels proud of, and anything else that contributes to his sense of self-esteem.

◆ Suggest that your child create a tape recording where he shares things he likes about himself and/or things he does really well. He can then replay it whenever he feels down and needs some moral support.

◆ Ask your child, "If you could be any animal, which one would you be?" Then suggest that he learn more about his animal and the positive traits that go along with it.

◆ Draw pictures together as a family depicting favorite activities and scenes of family members "doing what they do best"; share the pictures and keep them up around the house as reminders of everybody's positive qualities.

Most of the above activities can also be incorporated into a classroom curriculum. The teacher might have a "student of the week" program in which the strengths, talents, and gifts of each child are highlighted. Self-esteem educator Jack Canfield suggests that classes have "strength bombardments" in which each child sits in the middle of a circle while classmates "bombard" her with positive statements (e.g., "You're a good drawer," "I like it when you share your paper with me," "You can run really fast"). Have interviews or puppet shows in which students highlight each other's positive qualities. Gear writing assignments to an exploration of personal attributes ("Write a poem about all the neatest things about you").

Self-esteem development ultimately needs to go beyond a collection of activities. At its heart, self-esteem education should touch every part of a child's life, and show itself in all the ways that you help your child handle conflict, overcome obstacles, and meet challenges. However, it all begins with a deep-seated belief in the ultimate goodness of your child. As Spanish cellist Pablo Casals put it: "We should say to each child, do you know who you are? You are a marvel! You are unique!" If this was the message we gave to our kids, and children took that message into their hearts, believed it, and lived their lives on the basis of it, what a wonderful world this would be.

RESOURCES

Dorothy Corkille Briggs, *Your Child's Self-Esteem* (Garden City, NY: Doubleday, 1975).

Jack Canfield and Harold C. Wells, *100 Ways to Enhance Self-Concept in the Classroom* (Boston: Allyn & Bacon, 1976).

Jean Illsley Clarke, *Self-Esteem: A Family Affair* (San Francisco: Harper, 1984).

Stephanie Marston, *The Magic of Encouragement* (New York: Pocket Books, 1992).

Betty B. Youngs, *How to Develop Self-Esteem in Your Child: 6 Vital Ingredients* (New York: Ballantine, 1991).

15

Find Your Child's
Best Times of Alertness

Spring fever. The afternoon siesta. The Monday blahs. Most people are familiar with each of the above terms. But few know that there is now an entire field of study dedicated to charting human responses to changes over time. The field of *chronopsychology* studies the effects of biological rhythms on physical, cognitive, and emotional dimensions of human behavior. And because these built-in rhythms affect the human *attention span*, what we learn from chronopsychology may be quite helpful in assisting youngsters who've been identified as having attention deficits. It may, in fact, be possible to identify when your child's best times of day are in terms of focused attention, problem-solving ability, and memory skills.

The most prominent temporal rhythms that all humans experience are the *circadian rhythms*, which occur in twenty-four-hour solar and twenty-five-hour lunar cycles. During these cycles, there is a fluctuation in the efficiency of neurotransmitter molecules that chemically regulate normal rest and activity cycles. According to Timothy Monk, director of the Human Chronobiology Program at the University of Pittsburgh School of Medicine, overall alertness tends to rise through the morning in most people to a noonday high and then declines steadily throughout the afternoon. Short-term memory seems to peak at about nine in the morning, while long-term memory appears to function best at about three in the afternoon. Problem-solving skills peak in the morning and then fall during the afternoon and evening. Monk suggests that the differences between a person's performance during "best" and "worst" times of day can be significant (for example, as much as 10 percent on a memory quiz).

Research suggests that the above findings hold up when applied to kids labeled hyperactive or A.D.D. In one study, conducted at Northwestern University, "hyperkinetic students" performed better on a number of problem-solving tasks in the morning and exhibited more interference, off-task behavior, non-compliance, and minor motor movements in the afternoon. In another study, funded by the National Institute of Mental Health, "hyperactives" were most restless during the afternoon.

The implications of these findings for helping kids with attention problems are compelling. Given the importance of circadian rhythms on attention, teachers should probably schedule activities requiring short-term memory (e.g., pop quizzes, drill, lecture, fact-based responses) and problem-solving (e.g., math tests, science experiments) in the morning hours. Afternoon seems generally to be a much better time for more open-ended experiences (e.g., reading for pleasure, art, music) and activities involving motor activity (e.g., PE). Robert Sylwester, professor of education at the University of Oregon and a specialist in the role of the brain in learning, agrees: "It makes sense to schedule curricular priorities that require rapt attention and precise response during the morning, when it's easier to maintain attention. It is also logical to schedule interesting activities that demand less precision and sustained attention in the afternoon, when students' inherent interest in the activity will elevate their attention level."

You may want to keep a diary over a period of a week or longer (and have your child do the same if possible) to see whether his activity rhythms match those described above. If he seems to be most alert in the morning, then evening may be the *worst* time of the day for doing homework, and you may want to suggest that he work on it in the morning *before* going off to school. On the other hand, if you discover that your child is more of an "owl," or night person, then he may be hitting his stride in attention and learning only after school gets out! In that case, carrying over school tasks not completed into the evening time may be entirely appropriate. In addition, if you discover that your child's teacher is scheduling the afternoon period with tests, lecture, drill, and "seat work," and your child is having difficulty paying attention, then it may be wise to confer with the teacher and/or a school administrator about loosening up that time period to allow for more open-ended activities. In any case, it may be very important to your child's success in school, and in life, if you and he can discover those special "islands of alertness" during the day and year where he really shines.

#16

Give Instructions in Attention-Grabbing Ways

One of the most common problems that troubles parents and teachers, and one that can particularly vex parents and teachers of kids who've been labeled A.D.D., is that of giving a child instructions ("Take out the garbage," "Put your name in the upper-right-hand corner of the page) and not having them followed. Whether the erring child "didn't hear" (as kids often claim), "forgot" (another good excuse), or, as A.D.D. experts assert, failed to comply because of some central processing deficit is a moot point. What really matters is finding a way to get kids to follow instructions. Having this happen would make just about everybody's life a little bit easier.

Some A.D.D. experts suggest that one important solution to this problem involves cutting down on excess verbiage in those instructions. "State specific, one-step, ten-words-or-less commands to the child (e.g., pick up the pencils or go to the back of the line, etc.)" says one A.D.D. educator's guide. Another A.D.D. point of view counsels parents that *repetition* is the key. A.D.D. authority Ellen Gellerstedt, assistant professor of pediatrics at the University of Rochester School of Medicine and Dentistry, advises parents to be "parrots." "Since these kids act on impulse," says Gellerstedt, "you have to be prepared to remind them five thousand times about what they're supposed to be doing." Unfortunately, these suggestions, while probably true, are not fail-safe. They also show a certain lack of creativity—a lack that *pervades* the

A.D.D. movement. There are in fact many other ways of grabbing a child's attention that can be enjoyable for both parent and child even as they deliver the message home.

A key principle in developing "attention-grabbers" is to make them vivid and compelling. According to Tony Buzan, author of *Use Both Sides of Your Brain*, people are more likely to attend to and remember something if it moves (kinetic), is colorful, imaginative, exaggerated, and/or absurd. University of Oregon educators Robert Sylwester and Joo-Yun Cho point out that our complex attentional system evolved from primitive conditions in which we needed to "quickly recognize and respond to sudden, dramatic changes that signal physical predatory danger, and to ignore or merely monitor the steady states, subtle differences, and gradual changes that don't carry a sense of immediate alarm." Some kids labeled A.D.D. may easily pick up on the system's built-in bias for high contrast, novelty, and emotional overtones, but they may have greater difficulty shifting into an attention style in which things are monitored in a more predictable and even monotonous way. In fact, Purdue University researcher Sydney Zentall makes the point in her research of stating that "A.D.D. kids" have a definite preference for *novelty* in acquiring new information.

What then are some novel or "attention-grabbing" ways of giving instructions? Music is one way. Zentall shared the story, in an address to the CH.A.D.D. national conference, of parents who were at their wit's end in coming up with a good way to remind their child of certain tasks that needed to be done. "So what they did," reports Zentall, "is they put the child's favorite song on the beginning part of [a] tape, and then they left a list of the kinds of things the child was to do after school when she came home and then the end of the tape was the rest of her song. That child would race home to get her personalized tape every day." Similarly, I had a mother write to me about how she had the most success gaining the attention of her four-year-old son when she *sang* her instructions to him. This reminds me of the world-famous pianist Arthur Rubinstein, and how as a child he refused to talk or respond to the words of others. So his family started to sing to him, and it got so that he could recognize others by their particular tunes!

Visual metaphor is another great way of delivering an important message to kids in a compelling way. On one episode of the popular TV sitcom *Home Improvement*, Tim Allen wanted his kids to clean the house but wasn't having much luck with traditional approaches. So he used a Western metaphor: "It's high noon in Dodge City. Quick, cover the windows! Wyatt Dirt's come to town to clean up that Dust Bunny Gang!" In another case, a creative mother who was tired of telling her kids to turn off the lights when they left the room said to them, "When you leave a room, remember to turn on the dark." Kids love looking at the world in unfamiliar ways. By portraying the task to be done in a novel manner, you are more likely to get kids to pay attention and follow through.

You can take any message you wish to convey to your child and connect it to words, pictures, music, physical actions, or sensory cues and have one or more of these ways make an impact on your child. For example, if you wish to remind your child of his job to take out the garbage, here are some strategies you could use:

♦ Work out a prearranged signal with your child that will alert him to what he needs to do. For example, hold your nose while standing next to the garbage can and say, "Pee-yew! That garbage sure stinks!"

♦ Draw on a miniature chalkboard a picture of a garbage can. Point to the can, then to your child, and then to the outside.

♦ Pantomime the act of taking out the garbage.

♦ Get a photo of some garbagemen at work and tack it onto your child's bulletin board on the morning of the day he's to take out the garbage.

This business of giving and receiving instructions can be especially motivating to your child if he has a role in the creation of specific "cues." He might want to create a series of "cue cards" with either key words in large colorful print ("GARBAGE," "PICK UP ROOM," "SET TABLE"), or pictures that he's drawn himself (a garbage can, a messy room with an arrow pointing to a clean room, a properly set table, etc.) which anyone in the family can then pick up and show him if he's forgotten to do something around the house.

At school, the same approach can be used by the teacher to focus the attention of the whole class or of specific individuals. Teachers have already been using many of these techniques as part of their attention-getting "tricks of the trade." For example, playing a piano chord or flicking the lights on and off signals silence in many classrooms. Some teachers indicate a need for silence by having students hold up one arm while making the "shhhh" sign with the index finger of the other hand. Other teachers recognize the importance of *touching* a child when giving specific instructions, or writing the instructions down in addition to giving them orally. To grab a child's attention, teachers sometimes have been known to throw a beanbag to them to jolt them into alertness before telling them what they needed to do. Other teachers have worked out specific bodily cues to remind individual kids to return to their work: a nod, a glance, a wink, or even a secret handshake. So you see, parents or teachers needn't become parrots endlessly squawking the same refrain over and over again. If anything, parents and teachers should be more like peacocks, proudly displaying an elaborate and colorful plummage of strategies for catching a child's attention and then awakening the desire to respond.

#17

Provide a Variety of
Stimulating Learning Activities

Some parents might look at this strategy and think: "My kid is already stimulated. Too much so. If anything, he needs *less* stimulation!" This sort of thinking used to govern the way professionals viewed and treated "hyperactive kids." In the 1940s, many in the field believed that certain children were extra sensitive to environmental input and reacted to this overstimulation by becoming hyperactive. According to this view, "hyperactive children" (or "minimally brain damaged" kids, as they were called then) needed to be placed in school environments where stimulation was drastically reduced. These settings became known as "Cruickshank classrooms," named after William Cruickshank, one of the major proponents of this treatment method and an early pioneer in the field of special education. Cruickshank classrooms were veritable exercises in educational minimalism. Teachers removed bulletin boards and pictures, covered over windows, disconnected intercom devices, removed all furniture except what was absolutely essential to the program, separated students from each other, and placed each child in a cubicle three feet square. Female instructors were even advised not to wear red lipstick, as it was feared that this would overstimulate the child!

Current thinking on this matter, however, has it exactly the reverse. It's now believed that many kids who are labeled A.D.D. may in fact be *underaroused.* This belief is based upon a concept employed by Purdue University special education researcher Sydney Zentall. According to

Zentall, every living organism has a biologically determined level of optimal stimulation and a homeostatic means of regulating that level. In other words, if stimulation from the outside world is too strong, the organism will respond by restricting activity and avoiding stimulation. On the other hand, if stimulation from the world is not strong enough, then the organism will respond by initiating stimulation-seeking activity. It is believed that many so-called A.D.D. kids function in this latter condition. They appear to require a larger dose of stimulation from the environment than the average person, and if they don't get it, then they attempt to create it by making their *own* stimulation (i.e., through hyperactive behavior). This helps explain why psychostimulants such as Ritalin are effective with many of these kids. It was once thought that psychostimulants produced a paradoxical effect on children by calming them down instead of revving them up. But in this perspective, psychostimulants seem to add the extra zip that the "hyperactive child" needs in order to achieve an optimal level of arousal.

The most exciting implication of Zentall's research is that proper stimulation from the learning environment can also help to optimize the arousal state of these children. In fact, Zentall has conducted research showing that appropriate types of stimulation in a classroom setting actually function to calm many of these children down. In one experiment, Zentall compared the performance of "hyperactive children" in high-stimulation and low-stimulation rooms. The high-stimulation environment contained brightly colored pictures and posters on the walls, colorful carpets, Christmas lights strung across the room, a cage of mice hung from one wall, and popular rock music playing in the background. The low-stimulation environment was just a bare room with white walls and gray floors—a Cruickshank-type setting. Children went into each room and completed an academic task involving locating and circling letters of the alphabet in sequential order from a large array of letters. The behavior of the child was observed by an examiner and recorded electronically through an activity meter (a motion indicator strapped both to the child's wrist and ankle). Results indicated that "hyperactive kids" were significantly less active in the high-stimulation room and performed an academically related task no worse than when placed in a low-stimulation environment. Not all stimulation is necessarily beneficial, however. In other research, Zentall reported that high levels of talking in a classroom setting can be distracting to some of these kids and can result in higher activity levels.

Zentall's research suggests that home and school environments for "hyperactive kids" should be exciting, novel, and stimulating places of learning—not boring, repetitive, worksheet wastelands. Quoting from one of her "hyperactive heroes," Friedrich Nietzsche, Zentall points out that "habit is a great deadener," and that kids identified as A.D.D. hate restrictions on activities, repeating things over and over again, and waiting their turn for an activity. "Because of their preference for novelty," says Zentall, "youths with ADHD are more likely to change their focus of attention. This need for change is also called failure to sustain attention but really what it is is a need for change."

The type of school environment this sort of learning style cries out for is one with lots of stimulating learning activities that are continually changing (a feature which, of course, is beneficial to *all* students). Fortunately, there are plenty of model schools around the country that feature a dazzling array of learning possibilities. For example, at the Underwood Elementary School, in Raleigh, North Carolina, students can choose from a hundred electives, including "Coastal Ecology," "Creative Drama," "Magical Math," "Architecture Around Us," and "Crystal Ball" (the study of the future). At South Medford High School, in Medford, Oregon, students have staged benefit rock concerts for the hungry, written novels, built riverboats, choreographed dance performances, produced TV commercials, and constructed laser beams.

In these activity-based programs, students may study one subject in a number of different ways. For example, instead of reading a dull history textbook and answering the questions at the back of the book, students might build replica artifacts used during that time, interview people in the community who are experts in that period, keep journals of what it might have been like to live at that time, listen to music of the era, draw murals, create dioramas, or put on a play that reenacts the period. As one mother of a child labeled A.D.D. put it to me once, "Justin, a hyperactive child who has problems with ideas on paper, can quite easily become Mariano Vallejo, a nineteenth-century Californian. He can also get fellow actors to produce a creditable performance." Here is a list of some novel learning activities your child might benefit from in school:

watching films
creating art
listening to musical recordings

keeping journals
developing projects
drawing
map-making
interviewing
peer teaching
model building
doing puzzles
taking field trips
producing videos
conducting laboratory experiments
creating animated cartoons
reading illustrated books and magazines
listening to books on tape
using computers
studying animals and plants
using math blocks
measuring things
surveying opinions
holding discussion groups
taking part in simulations
brainstorming
storytelling
photography
visualizing
taking part in activity centers that change frequently

The philosopher George Santayana once said, "A child educated only at school is an uneducated child." This suggests that the home environment should also be regarded as a place where stimulating learning activities can abound. Engage your child in highly stimulating multisensory activities, including some of the following:

♦ Put natural food coloring in bread dough and make sculptures that can be eaten after they're baked.

♦ Purchase a rubber stamp set and let your child create her own messages, signs, and compositions.

♦ Buy a stopwatch and time different activities (e.g., walking around the house, standing on one foot, threading a needle).

♦ Place some diluted dishwashing liquid in a sink or a bowl and use various implements (e.g., straws, hollow cans, plastic tubing, wire loops), to dip into the solution and blow bubbles with.

♦ Put a variety of timely objects into a "time capsule" (e.g., a Tupperware container), and then bury it ceremoniously in the back yard.

♦ Obtain an empty appliance box and using art materials turn it into a house, car, mountain, post office, store, or anything else.

♦ Take a walk and look for only round things, or dogs, or red things, or things that look broken, or tall things, or any other category you care to dream up.

Using the theory of optimal stimulation as a framework, it stands to reason that the closer to optimally stimulated the child is, the less need there will be to create stimulation artificially through psychostimulants such as Ritalin. That such drugs may be used primarily to help kids adjust to boring, routine-ridden, repetition-plagued classrooms says more about the sad state of many schools than it does about the so-called deficits of these kids. The theory of optimal stimulation challenges us to create vital educational environments where *all* kids can reach their true potential.

Resources

Thomas Armstrong, *Awakening Your Child's Natural Genius: Enhancing Curiosity, Creativity, and Learning Ability* (Los Angeles: Tarcher/Perigee, 1991).

Steven Caney, *Steven Caney's Playbook* (New York: Workman, 1975).

Vicki Cobb, *Science Experiments You Can Eat* (Philadelphia: Lippincott, 1972).

Susan Kovalik, *ITI: The Model-Integrated Thematic Instruction* (Village of Oak Creek, AZ: Books for Educators, 1993).

Randy Moberg, *TNT Teaching: Over 200 Dynamite Ways to Make Your Classroom Come Alive* (Minneapolis: Free Spirit, 1994).

Joanne Oppenheim and Stephanie Oppenheim, *The Best Toys, Books, and Videos for Kids* (New York: HarperCollins, 1993).

Susan K. Perry, *Playing Smart: A Parent's Guide to Enriching, Offbeat Learning Activities for Ages 4–14* (Minneapolis: Free Spirit, 1990).

18

Consider Biofeedback Training

I sat down in front of a computer screen at an exhibit during a recent A.D.D. convention and had a trained practitioner attach electrodes to my head. "Frankenstein returns!" I thought as I sat there all wired up. On the screen was a white box with a small green box inside of it and two small green boxes on either side of the larger white box. I noticed that as I sat there, the green square inside the white box fluctuated in size. Sometimes it even burst the boundaries of the white box. Also, the two side green boxes kept fluctuating in size, and sometimes they touched the sides of the large white box. "Make the center green square fill up the white box," said the technician. "And try to keep the two side boxes from touching the white box," she added. "How?" I wondered aloud. "Just do whatever it takes," came the reply. So I set to work. It was kind of like a mental video game. No joy sticks or mouse to operate. Just my pinball-wizard mind. "Hey! This is fun!" I thought as I started to rack up some points.

What I was experiencing was a taste of biofeedback, one of the promising new non-drug treatments for kids labeled A.D.D. Biofeedback essentially refers to any kind of instrumentation used to measure internal physiological states. Biofeedback has been around for about twenty-five years and has become a standard part of the treatment program for many individuals with migraines and other kinds of pain. However, its use with kids identified as A.D.D. is relatively new. Different forms of biofeedback exist that measure, among other things, heart rate, blood flow, the electrical resistance of skin, muscle tension, and brain waves.

Changing brain waves seems to be the primary task involved in using biofeedback with an "A.D.D. population." The human brain generates very small amounts of electrical current that can be measured on an electroencephalogram (EEG). These currents vary in amplitude according to the state of mind of the individual. For an adult in a quiet resting state, most of the EEG record will consist of alpha waves from the back of the head that repeat themselves at about ten hertz (a hertz is an international unit of frequency equal to one cycle per second). A more rapid rhythm associated with a state of focused and alert attention in the central and frontal portions of the brain occurs at eighteen to twenty-five hertz and is referred to as beta waves. Rhythmic slow waves at frequencies between four and seven hertz—called theta waves—are normal in infants and young children but tend to decrease during the elementary school years. These waves are associated with daydreaming, hypnogogic imagery, and a wide focus of attention.

It's believed that some children labeled A.D.D. produce more theta (wide focus) and less beta (narrow focus) activity. Biofeedback with these kids attempts to help them produce less theta and more beta, thus improving their ability to focus and concentrate. One of the key researchers in the field, Joel Lubar, professor of psychology at the University of Tennessee, cautions, "I don't want you to get the impression that theta is bad and beta is good necessarily. Theta has been identified for many years with creativity and with visual imagery. . . . Beta on the other hand is involved with a closed focus, a fixed focus, detailed concentration to the exclusion of a lot of extraneous stimuli."

Children attempt to increase their beta and decrease their theta by engaging in biofeedback sessions much like the one I had: facing video screens that pose different kinds of challenges. The format of the visual feedback presented varies from program to program. In one version, as long as a child is producing beta, bright colors advance around a wheel accompanied by tones going up the musical scale. In another, the trainee has to keep an airplane above a certain line (while producing beta) to keep the red lights off. Typically an individual will go through a series of from thirty to fifty sessions, one or two sessions per week, each lasting approximately an hour.

It's clear to see that such a treatment method has many attractive features for a child. It works like a video game, has bright colors and sounds, provides immediate feedback, and offers rewards for a job well done. But does it work? Although well-controlled studies are just now being done, there is preliminary evidence to suggest that this approach is worth a second look from parents seeking non-drug alternatives for their A.D.D.-labeled kids. In the best overall review of the literature, conducted by Steven W. Lee of the University of Kansas, it was concluded that while methodological problems exist with current studies, biofeedback in conjunction with other approaches appears to have promise for reducing some of the symptoms associated with hyperactivity.

There are certain guidelines that parents should follow when considering a biofeedback program for their children. First, consider this as an *adjunctive* treatment to be used with other approaches and not as a foolproof method of eradicating A.D.D. symptoms. Steer clear of any practitioner who claims 100 percent cures or makes other excessive claims about the effectiveness of biofeedback. Second, biofeedback training may not be appropriate for your child if he is clinically depressed, suffers from seizure disorders, is under seven years of age, or has psychotic episodes. Third, work with a practitioner who is clinically certified and has plenty of experience working with kids with attention problems. Ask about prior experience—some biofeedback technicians go to work after only three days of training. Finally, remember that the machine doesn't create the results, the child does. Different children do different things to create the changes in brain waves. Some children visualize, others get physical feelings or think specific kinds of thoughts. It's what kids do with their mind that helps create the new behaviors—the machine merely serves as a medium for change.

RESOURCES

Association for Applied Psychophysiology and Biofeedback, 10200 West Fortyfourth Avenue, #304, Wheat Ridge, CO 80033-2840; 303-422-8436. This organization is a professional association of researchers and clinicians using biofeedback in a variety of applications. The AAPB will provide parents with the names of certified practitioners in their local area. Send a selfaddressed stamped envelope with your request.

#19

Activate Positive
Career Aspirations

While traveling to Europe a few years ago, I happened to sit next to a man who told me in the course of our conversation that he had been recently identified by his physician as A.D.D. As we talked, I learned more about the man and in particular about his livelihood. It seems that he worked as a media consultant for a large church association and flew all over the world shooting documentaries. Later on, I thought more about his work, and it soon began to dawn on me that this was a man whose occupation matched his behavioral tempo. In a nine-to-five job that required lots of sitting, I could only imagine that he would have been miserable. As it turned out, situated in a job that involved frequent changes, moving at high speeds in transit, and encountering new scenarios at every turn, I could well appreciate what he told me during our time together: he loved his work.

It seems critical to me that we help children who've been labeled hyperactive or A.D.D. to see that there are positive futures up ahead for them. Many of these kids suffer through years of frustration in classrooms only expecting to find more of the same once they leave school. Yet it may be that for many of them, the real world could offer the chance to display strengths and abilities that a narrow classroom curriculum never could. I'm reminded of the short-attention-span radio announcer in Phoenix who interviewed me while I was on a book tour. He shared with me the story of his verbal clashes with teachers while in high school and of his low self-esteem as a student. It was only after he left school that he was able to use his gift of gab in a positive way.

Unfortunately, it seems as if the A.D.D. world is sending out the wrong message to its children when it broadcasts the results of follow-up studies with children labeled hyperactive who grow into adulthood. According to these studies, somewhere between 30 to 70 percent of A.D.D. children will grow into A.D.D. adults. These adults will have more car accidents, less education, and more job instability than the average person. In addition, they will show more of a tendency to abuse drugs and to have trouble with the law. These statistics are disturbing: they convey an underlying generalization that if you're an "A.D.D. child" then the chances are better than even that you've got a rocky road ahead of you.

This needn't be the case. Most of the individuals in those studies didn't have the benefit of the kinds of broad-based interventions shared in this book. Moreover, it's possible to turn the above statistics around and note that up to 70 percent of all kids labeled A.D.D. will grow up *normal*. Furthermore, if one digs a little deeper into these outcome studies, some interesting findings emerge. In one longitudinal study conducted at McGill University, for example, schoolteachers rated the "hyperactive" group as inferior on all items of a behavioral questionnaire. However, when these individuals grew up and entered the workforce, their employers rated them as no different from their "normal" colleagues. The researchers commented, "Possibly the many choices of types of work vs. the lack of choice of schools or activity within a school are factors resulting in competence in one situation and failure in the other. In addition, if a hyperactive subject does not like a particular job or an employer, he is free to try and find another; hence, he can eventually find a work environment in which he can function satisfactorily." Another study revealed that far more individuals identified as A.D.D. became self-employed than so-called normal adults. They're more likely to take their life in their own hands and make something of it.

What this means is that your child may find his true place in life only when he can get out into the real world and discover a vocation that allows him to do what he does best. In order to ensure that he *finds* his true vocation, however, you need to begin stimulating his career aspirations from an early age. That doesn't mean pushing him into a job description that matches *your* idea of what he should do, but rather in letting him know that the kinds of traits he possesses are valuable out there in the workplace. In terms of the characteristics associated with A.D.D.-like behavior—need for novelty, change, imagination, movement, and spontaneous expression—there are many work roles that fit the bill, including

- self-employed businessperson
- free-lance writer, artist, or editor
- airline pilot or train engineer
- disc jockey or radio announcer
- traveling salesperson
- music or dance therapist
- forest ranger
- recreational worker
- itinerant teacher (moves between classrooms or schools)
- radio, television, or newspaper reporter
- police officer or firefighter
- nature photographer
- building contractor
- craftsperson
- artist or sculptor
- inventor or designer
- private detective
- community ombudsman
- truck, bus, or taxicab driver
- family-practice physician
- free-lance researcher
- farmer or ranch worker
- choreographer or dancer
- athlete or coach
- lecturer or workshop leader
- aerobic or fitness instructor
- surveyor, cartographer, or architect
- Peace Corps worker
- fashion model
- public relations consultant

You can help stimulate career aspirations in your child by exposing him to a wide range of these and other high-variety, high-action, high-movement vocations through trips to the library and exposure to vocation-oriented movies and television programs. (I remember formulating my first career goal while watching a Disney special about people who flew airplanes into the eye of a hurricane. I wanted to be a hurricane hunter: perhaps one of the ultimate jobs for a high-action person!) Also, introduce your child to successful people who themselves were considered hyperactive in childhood. These individuals serve as living examples of positive futures and can point the way to specific career goals.

Ask your child from time to time what she'd like to be when she grows up. You might even suggest that she draw a picture of what she sees herself doing twenty-five years from now. Talk with her about her aspirations and take her comments seriously. Don't try to discourage her if she seems to want to take up a vocation you feel is unsuitable or unrealistic. If a child is motivated enough to want to follow even a seemingly low-action, low-change, low-novelty career like tax accountant, for example, then she may be willing to adjust her behavioral tempo to the demands of the job. She may surprise you. Help feed her dreams while still showing her the wide range of options that are open to her in other areas. Mythology expert Joseph Campbell counseled his students to "follow your bliss." By helping to stoke the flames of your child's personal career ambitions, you're making a significant contribution toward her success in life. You're also helping society by ensuring that your child's energies work *for* the culture rather than against it.

Resources

Thomas Armstrong, *7 Kinds of Smart* (New York: Plume, 1993). Includes a chapter matching careers to different intelligences.

Richard Nelson Bolles, *What Color Is Your Parachute?* (Berkeley, CA: Ten Speed Press, 1994). This job search book is designed for adults but contains such a marvelous collection of skills, talents, and abilities matched to job descriptions that it can serve as a good reference work in looking over career possibilities with your child.

Thomas Hartmann, *Focus Your Energy* (New York: Pocket Books, 1994). This is a book for those "A.D.D. adults" who are looking for ways to match their energies to their careers.

20

Teach Your Child
Physical-Relaxation Techniques

As a teacher of "hyperactive children," I frequently noticed how *tense* many of these kids were as they wrestled with math problems, struggled to learn the rules of a new game, or grappled with any new learning task. It was almost as if these kids were bursting at the seams with energy; it took all their effort and resolve—expressed in muscular tension—to control themselves. Add to this the frustrations they experienced from not fitting in, the problems they encountered with peers out on the playground, and the criticisms they received from siblings, parents, and other teachers, and what we were looking at in many cases were students under a great deal of *stress.*

While there are many possible ways of relieving this stress, certainly one important tool involves the use of physical-relaxation exercises that a student can learn quickly and use frequently whenever he feels under pressure at home or at school. These exercises provide an immediate relief from muscular tension, offer a channel for discharging excess energy, supply a means of allaying anxiety, and give the child a way to focus attention on something solid and specific—the physical body—to help ground awareness in the here and now.

There are several different kinds of relaxation training systems. Possibly the oldest is hatha yoga, an ancient Hindu system of physical postures, or *asanas*, designed to rejuvenate physical, mental, and spiritual health. More recently, in the 1930s, Edmund Jacobsen developed progressive relaxation, a method of alternately tensing and relaxing the various muscle groups of the body, and around the same time J. H. Schultz created autogenic training, a process of imagining warmth, heaviness, or other physical sensations in different parts of the body. Still other methods of relaxation include visualization, aerobic exercise (such as jogging, swimming, or calisthenics), biofeedback, and various forms of meditation. These methods have been used for years to treat a wide range of conditions, from anxiety and depression to asthma and hypertension.

A comprehensive review of the literature, conducted by Neil C. Richter, professor of psychology at the University of South Carolina, suggests that physical relaxation is an effective treatment for hyperactivity when used in conjunction with other supportive measures. In one study, fifteen children diagnosed by physicians as hyperactive listened to progressive relaxation tapes twice a week over a six-week period and, with assistance, practiced relaxation techniques. Children significantly improved on a number of behavioral and physiological measures. Studies suggest that progressive relaxation training is particularly effective when the subject controls the pacing and when the training is extended out over several sessions.

When teaching your child relaxation methods, it may be helpful to use picture metaphors in describing the specific physical activities he should engage in when doing the exercises. Some of the following scenarios may be helpful. Your child can do most of these exercises seated in a comfortable position or while lying down on a carpeted floor.

♦ *Balloon*: Take a deep breath as if you were a balloon blowing yourself up large; then slowly let the air out of the balloon. Repeat two or more times.

♦ *Robot/Rag Doll:* Make your body as stiff as a robot's for several seconds, then make it as limp as a rag doll's for several seconds. Repeat two or more times.

♦ *The Cat:* Lying facedown on the floor, begin to stretch like a cat; stretch arms, legs, arch the back, yawn, just like a cat. Repeat two or more times.

♦ *The Elevator:* Imagine that you're in a cozy elevator. You feel it slowly descending, and as it does, you feel more and more relaxed.

♦ *The Honey Jar:* Try this one standing up. Imagine that you're moving in a jar of honey: you need to move very slowly.

Make sure to do these exercises with your child at first (or have a sibling or friend there as a support), and then gradually withdraw as he becomes competent in using them. You may find that your child wants to modify them or develop his own unique exercises. That's great! The more these exercises become a part of your child's life, the more he is likely to use them.

Physical relaxation needn't always consist of formal techniques. According to author and pediatrician T. Berry Brazelton, your child can develop his own self-comforting methods to deal with stressful events. "When ADHD children start building toward a crisis," says Brazelton, "they need a way to withdraw from the stimulation and regain control. If he already has such a pattern—thumb sucking or rocking, hugging a lovey or turning away—point this out to him and help him use the pattern *before* the crisis occurs. If he doesn't have a way to comfort himself, you'll need to teach one." Other ways to relax include

- ♦ throwing a ball against a wall
- ♦ listening to music
- ♦ playing with pets
- ♦ spending time with favorite relatives or friends
- ♦ gazing at clouds or other natural events
- ♦ taking a walk
- ♦ spending time in a "secret place" (e.g., a fort or a treehouse)
- ♦ taking a nap
- ♦ playing with a favorite toy
- ♦ daydreaming

Life has never been as stressful as it is now, in this complex society. By teaching your child to use physical-relaxation strategies, you're empowering him with techniques that he can use for the rest of his life.

RESOURCES

Rachel Carr, *Be a Frog, a Bird, or a Tree* (Garden City, NY: Doubleday, 1973).

C. Gaylord Hendricks and Russell Wills, *The Centering Book: Awareness Activities for Children, Parents, and Teachers* (Englewood Cliffs, NJ: Prentice-Hall, 1975). This book includes several relaxation exercises.

Mary Stewart and Kathy Phillips, *Yoga for Children* (New York: Fireside, 1990).

#21

Use Incidental Learning to Teach

While conducting a workshop for the Orton Dyslexia Society, I reserved a portion of the day for teachers to present their own innovative teaching strategies. A group of teachers came to the front of the room and began teaching a somewhat dry lesson on the California Gold Rush. It was late in the afternoon and the attention of most of the audience (myself included) was sagging. Suddenly, there burst through the door at the back of the room a person dressed up in Wild West clothes, shouting that he was John Sutter and that he'd just discovered gold. As he moved through the audience talking about his great discovery, he threw chocolate kisses wrapped in golden tinfoil to the crowd. Wow, did *that* get our attention! That day we learned about California history in a vivid and memorable way.

This story is important because it highlights something that tends to get lost in all the talk about "attention deficit disordered" children. And that is that *all of us* are attention deficit disordered when the material is boring enough, and often it's something incidental or peripheral to the teaching (in this case, the person bursting into the room) that best captures our attention.

The fact of the matter is that many children labeled A.D.D. are actually very good at paying attention. They're good at paying attention to what they're *not supposed to be paying attention to*. In the classroom, they hear Joey telling Suzy about what happened to Billy during recess. They see the funny drawings that Ed made on the chalkboard before class started (drawings the teacher hasn't even noticed yet). They pay attention to their own inner thoughts: daydreams about being somewhere else besides school—perhaps at an amusement park or camping in the forest. They pay attention to everything except the teacher—who drones on and on much like the science teacher in the television sit-com *Wonder Years* or the adults in the *Peanuts* television specials (they all sound like this: *"wock-wock-wock-wock"*). These students pay attention to everything except for the worksheet pages that lie in front of them dead on their desk.

In other words, their real "difficulty" often has to do with paying attention to things that do not interest them. Most of us learn the ability to attend to tedious things early in life. We develop the capacity to prop our hands under our chins and put a look of interest on our faces even when the subject matter is boring us to death. Children who are at risk of being labeled A.D.D. often are not able or willing to put on appearances in this way. In many ways, some of them are like infants or toddlers—actively exploring whatever comes their way, moving quickly from one thing to another, like bees seeking nectar in flowers.

We should not be too quick to consider this sort of attentional style a disorder. After all, during early childhood human beings engaged in some of the most powerful learning they will ever experience in their lives. Young children master complex tasks like walking and talking by letting their attention be drawn to what interests them and by absorbing knowledge in *incidental* ways. It seems as if millions of years of evolution have endowed a human infant with this inborn drive toward spontaneous exploration, curiosity, and the need for variety and novelty so that there would always be in the human species the capacity to search for new possibilities—a decided asset when outer conditions change and adaptation is required.

It may be that some children who are labeled A.D.D. possess this special adaptive capacity for incidental learning even as they grow older. Unfortunately, most classroom learning is based upon "central-task" learning. That task may involve attending to the teacher's lecture and ignoring all the other sounds going on in the room and beyond. Or it may require circling the right multiple choice item, filling in the blank with the right word, finding the main idea in a reading passage, or identifying the governing hypothesis in a science experiment. And yet perhaps 98 percent of everything we have ever learned in our lives came from incidental learning. Parents and educators need to capitalize upon the "A.D.D. child's" capacity for incidental learning in developing strategies that reach out and teach them.

An entire field of teaching has emerged over the past twenty years that is based upon the capacities of individuals to learn quickly and easily through incidental learning. Variously called superlearning, suggestopedia, or accelerative learning, this innovative approach to learning attempts to replicate the learning conditions of the human infant by creating an environment in which knowledge is absorbed in pleasantly incidental ways. Students are asked, for example, to listen to rhythmic classical or baroque music while in the background the teacher repeats the information to be learned (e.g., spelling words, foreign language vocabulary, history facts, math formulas). Students are told that they don't have to listen to the teacher's voice or concentrate on the words. They just need to relax and enjoy the music. The academic material is incidental to the act of listening to the music. In addition, the teacher may introduce new information by embedding it in colorful posters and then hanging the posters on the wall a week or two before the actual lesson. No attention is called to the material. Students absorb it as part of their incidental or peripheral learning.

There are several other ways that teachers can use incidental learning to help students achieve. Most teachers are familiar with interruptions to their lessons (e.g., bells ringing or the lawn mower going on outside). These are events that affect the attentional mechanisms of *all* students. Most teachers try to oppose the interruption by speaking more loudly, admonishing the students, or perhaps using a special behavior modification program to reward "good listeners." In the context of incidental learning, however, teachers attempt to bring the interrupting stimulus *into the lesson*. So if the teacher is giving a lesson on the Civil War and the bell rings, she can announce: "That bell signals the end of an era in U.S. history." Or, if students are reading a story about the attempts of a child named Paul to win new friends, and suddenly a class begins to pass through the halls outside, the teacher might say: "And now you can hear some of Paul's friends going by."

The essential rule here is, If children aren't paying attention, find out what they *are* paying attention to and then put the material they need to learn smack dab in the middle of their field of attention. So if a student is busy talking with a buddy while the teacher is trying to teach, the teacher should take the friend aside, teach him the lesson, and then the next time the student whispers to his friend, the friend can whisper to him the mini-lesson! Or if the child is talking out impulsively in class about irrelevant things, the teacher should find a way to tie his comments to the lesson. For example, in a lesson on solids, liquids, and gases in science, if the student blurts out, "I have a new Ninja Turtle," the teacher can ask, "Is your Ninja Turtle a solid, a liquid, or a gas?" This can "lasso" the child back into the fold. Finally, teachers can try the "John Sutter" approach: teach the most important instructional material of the day to a student, a classroom aide, or a parent volunteer, and then have him burst into the classroom vividly shouting it out or presenting it in some other vivid way.

At home parents can apply many of the same rules about incidental learning in getting their kids to attend to and follow through on everyday tasks. Here's one scenario of what this might look like:

> Mom is telling Mike to take out the garbage. Mike doesn't seem to hear her and goes on playing with his miniature cars and trucks in his bedroom. Rather than wear out her vocal cords, Mom goes into Mike's bedroom, gets down on the floor with him and starts playing with the cars. "This one is a garbage truck, Mike. See, the garbage man is getting out in front of our house. He's saying to his buddy, 'We can't collect the garbage here, Ed, because Mike hasn't brought it out yet.' " Mike looks up at Mom and zooms out of the room in the direction of the kitchen, where the garbage is waiting for him.

In the above example, Mom went right into Mike's "attentional field"—his play world of miniature toys—and wove her instructions into the images of his private world. She used incidental attention to deliver the message. Too often, parents or teachers dismiss the child's "failure to comply" as a threat, a nuisance, or a warning sign of A.D.D. If the content of the child's incidental attention is first given some respect, then it may be much easier to move his attention to where you'd like it to be.

Resources

International Alliance for Learning, 1725 South Hill Street, Oceanside, CA 92054-5319. This organization is a professional association of educators concerned with applying principles of superlearning to the classroom.
Sheila Ostrander and Lynn Schroeder, *Superlearning* (New York: Delta, 1979).
Colin Rose, *Accelerated Learning* (New York: Dell, 1985).

#22

Support Full Inclusion of Your Child in a Regular Classroom

At a conference I attended recently in Colorado, sixteen hundred parents, educators, and administrators gathered together to argue persuasively for the inclusion of children with special needs—including those with Down's syndrome, cerebral palsy, and other severe disabilities—in a regular classroom environment. I left the conference feeling inspired by the attitude toward diversity that seemed to run like a thread through each of the workshops. I learned about school programs across the nation that are breaking down the traditional divisions that have divided regular and special education. I learned about classrooms that have "de-labeled" children and taught them according to their unique gifts. I learned about programs in which kids with emotional, learning, and physical difficulties shared their interests, ideas, and feelings with kids considered "normal" or even "gifted." The underlying philosophy seemed to be that *every* child—labeled or not—has special needs that regular classrooms should be designed to meet.

Unfortunately, this spirit of celebration and diversity does not appear to extend to the world of A.D.D. The parent advocacy group for attention deficit disorder, CH.A.D.D., has come out officially as being *against* the concept of full inclusion. According to its executive director, Wade F. Horn, "While many children with special needs can and should be served in the regular education classroom, many other children must have access to a full continuum of services and placement settings."

These other services that Horn refers to include some of the following settings:

◆ Resource room programs in which children leave their regular classrooms for one or more hours per day to work with specialists in areas of need

◆ Special classes in which children leave regular classrooms all day to receive small-group instruction designed to meet their special needs

◆ Special public school buildings geared toward children with particular problems or disabilities

◆ Private residential schools (paid for at public expense) that are geared toward handling a child's difficulties twenty-four hours a day

To many parents of children who've been labeled A.D.D., these "exclusive" special education options sound all too tempting. It simply makes intuitive sense that if a child is having trouble in a regular classroom environment, he ought to be removed from that environment and placed in another setting where he can succeed. Then, when he's "better," he can be placed back in the regular program. That's the theory, anyway.

The truth of special education, however, is something altogether different. Special education is its own self-contained universe, with its own special tests, special texts, special materials, special jargon, and special *problems.* Your child has every chance of entering a world where he will be defined according to his *disability.* Like a prison, the special ed classroom could be the place where your child will learn special misbehaviors from the school's real troublemakers. Kids in regular classrooms can begin looking at your child as a freak, a " 'tard," or worse. Teachers in regular programs begin to see your child as a "disabled" learner. Instead of being surrounded by teachers and curricula that seek to draw out the best from your child, the special education classroom is likely to spend a great deal of time concentrating on your child's weak points. How many adults would like to have their own personal limitations highlighted six hours a day, five days a week?

Not all special education classrooms are like this. Many special-class programs exist that are taught by highly committed teachers who seek to bring out the best in every child, who use state-of-the-art learning strategies, and who work intensively to get the child back into a regular classroom environment as soon as possible. However, these programs are probably the exception, not the rule. Besides, there's something larger going on here than just a teacher and a classroom. It's the Special Education System, with its own ethos of deficit, disorder, and dysfunction that does the most damage to children. At its best, it's like a maze filled with red tape, testing, time lines, and eligibility criteria that parents need to patiently endure in order to get special services for their children. At its worst, it's like a mechanical monster that eats up children, judges them according to tests far removed from reality, sorts them according to their problems, feeds them boring special education workbooks and behavior modification programs, and keeps them locked in a cycle of failure for the rest of their school days.

For these reasons, parents of children already labeled A.D.D. are well advised to think in terms of full inclusion in the regular classroom for their kids. If need be, you can still have your child go through the special education maze to receive special services. Federal law provides parents with important rights to push for special services if your child needs them. But you can specify that these services be delivered in the regular classroom environment. That means that a certified special education teacher can go into the regular classroom and work with your child on specific goals at certain times during the day. In some programs, this special teacher can team up with the regular classroom teacher to work with so-called normal kids as well as "disabled" so that your child won't be stigmatized by being singled out for special treatment. The downside of this approach is that you need to subject your child to the often negative impact of diagnostic testing, screening, and labeling.

A better way is to seek to have your child's unique needs met in a regular classroom without having to be labeled as "other health impaired," "learning disabled" or some other qualifying label. Meet with your child's teacher to discuss your child's special learning interests, abilities, limitations, and needs. Many schools have School Study Teams that meet to discuss how a child's needs can be met in a regular classroom before having to consider special education options. If necessary, get involved in that process and work cooperatively with teachers to see that your child's needs can truly be served in a normal environment. Identify helpful strategies from this book or others that can be transplanted into the classroom and discuss these ideas with your child's teacher. If the teacher or school resists change, and insists on a "one-size-fits-all" philosophy in the regular classroom, then you need to consider the following options:

♦ Look for another teacher in the school who may be more flexible.

♦ Look for another school in the district that may be more accommodating to your child's needs.

♦ Use the special education laws to get special services for your child in the regular classroom.

♦ Consider non-public-school alternatives (see strategy #24, "Consider Alternative Schooling Options").

When discussing possible options with school personnel, be on guard if they suggest either retaining your child at his grade level another year or placing your child in a regular classroom environment that is "tracked" for a slower group of students. Research suggests that kids who are retained a year or more are at increased risk for dropping out of school in the future, and children who are placed in slower academic tracks or ability groups receive a substandard education compared with those in higher tracks.

The advantages of your child being fully included in a non-labeling, non-tracked classroom are many. First, your child will be exposed to positive role models for behavior from many of the students. Such contact may be instrumental in helping your child to develop important social skills if this area has been a problem in the past. Second, your child won't be singled out as a special ed kid (a child in one classroom commented that the *ed* in *special ed* referred to "extra dumb"). Instead, your child will function as a "normal" person—a non-label most kids desperately cling to during their growing-up years. Third, your child will be exposed to the same subject matter as everyone else instead of taking a separate curriculum in a special ed class. This means he will be less likely to fall significantly behind his peers and will be exposed to the same content as everyone else. Finally, he will encounter a rich diversity of learning styles and backgrounds among his peers instead of being in a group where everyone shares the same label. In a society like ours that is becoming increasingly diverse, it's especially important to provide kids with the message that differences are good! In a truly inclusive classroom, your child's differences can be celebrated along with everyone else's.

RESOURCES

Winifred Anderson, Stephen Chitwood, Deidre Hayden, *Negotiating the Special Education Maze* (Englewood Cliffs, NJ: Prentice-Hall, 1982). This book is a nuts-and-bolts guide to getting services for your child using the special education laws.

Lori Granger and Bill Granger, *The Magic Feather: The Truth About "Special Education"* (New York: Dutton, 1986). This book chronicles one family's odyssey to secure special help for their child, and the problems that arose once they entered the special education system.

Winners All: A Call for Inclusive Schools. This 1992 report is available from the National Association of State Boards of Education, 1012 Cameron Street, Alexandria, VA 22314. The report features descriptions of successful inclusive education programs.

#23

Provide Positive Role Models

What do Winston Churchill, Peppermint Patty, Thomas Edison, and Curious George all have in common? They represent examples of A.D.D.-like behaviors seen in a positive light. And for kids labeled A.D.D. who tend to look at themselves in a negative way, it's particularly important to learn about characters—both fictional and real—who are admired by others for the healthy traits they embody. Study of these characters can lead to children identifying with them and beginning to see themselves more positively.

A look back through history reveals a stunning array of individuals who, were they transplanted into contemporary public schools, might well have been candidates for the A.D.D. label. Thomas Edison's biographer, for example, had this to say about Edison's schoolteacher: "The minister, of course, taught by rote, a method from which Alva [Thomas Edison] was inclined to disassociate himself. He alternated between letting his mind travel to distant places and putting his body in perpetual motion in his seat. The Reverend Eagle, finding him inattentive and unruly, swished his cane. Alva, afraid and out of place, held up a few weeks, then ran away from the school."

In their fascinating study of four hundred eminent individuals throughout history, Victor and Mildred Goertzel described Winston Churchill as "hyperactive . . . [with] poor peer relationships." His experiences in school were frequently disastrous. In his first school, Winston kicked the headmaster's hat to pieces. He was taken out of this school and placed in a school run by two kindly ladies. "In this benign atmosphere," say the Goertzels, "Winston was called the naughtiest small boy in England by his dancing teacher." He was frequently permitted to leave the classroom and run about in the schoolyard to release his exuberant energies. His later school experiences at Harrow were similarly difficult. He refused to study mathematics, Greek, or Latin and was placed with the lowest group of students.

Similarly dramatic accounts can be given for countless other individuals whose restless, impulsive, or distractible energies in childhood were later channeled into their important life's work. Some of the more well-known examples are the following:

♦ Sarah Bernhardt was expelled from school three times: once for imitating a bishop, once for throwing stones at the Royal Dragoons, and once for climbing a wall to visit a young soldier.

♦ Will Rogers was incorrigible at school and ran away from home.

♦ Orville Wright was suspended from school because of his mischievous behavior.

♦ Pope John XXIII was sent home with a note saying he continually came to class unprepared; he did not deliver the note.

♦ Ludwig van Beethoven was rude and ill-mannered toward his friends and was subject to wild fits of rage.

♦ Arturo Toscanini was an obstinate and disobedient boy; once he made up his mind not to do something, nothing could make him change his mind.

♦ Louis Armstrong spent time in an institution for delinquent boys.

♦ Paul Cézanne had a bad temper and would stamp his feet in hysterical rage whenever he felt thwarted.

♦ William Wordsworth was described before his eighth year as a "stubborn, wayward, and intractable boy."

♦ Arthur Conan Doyle was aggressive and continually involved in fights; he would break rules deliberately so he could show others how well he could take the punishment.

Other examples of distinguished adults who were difficult or restless children include Nikola Tesla, William Randolph Hearst, Enrico Fermi, Huey Long, Ignacy Jan Paderewski, François Truffaut, Vincent van Gogh, John Keats, Charles Darwin, Mary Baker Eddy, Florence Nightingale, and Friedrich Nietzsche. As Victor and Mildred Goertzel explained it, "These burgeoning, exploding, often highly verbal boys and girls were undoubtedly problems in their classrooms. They were too eager to get at the truth of things to be satisfied with lip wisdom."

One needn't only look at history, however, to find excellent examples of positive role models for kids labeled A.D.D. Relatives, friends of the family, and teachers who were hyperactive in childhood provide more immediate sources of inspiration. In one case, a boy labeled hyperactive was being introduced to the head of a recreational program and related this story: "Dad started telling the Rec Leader about me and he just laughed and says, 'No problem, Mr. J. I was, too [hyperactive], and so was Tom Edison and two of my buddies who are in think tanks now.' . . . And when he told who were the new ones that day all he said was, 'Glad to have you, Dave, I know your brother' . . . just like I'm like the other kids."

Sometimes these positive connections occur within the family. Author James Evans, in his autobiographical work An Uncommon Gift, writes about how his hyperactivity was dealt with inside of the family matrix. "My hyperkinesia . . . was a novelty to most people, and was accepted by my parents as healthy. . . . My parents assumed that I would grow out of my energetic stage, just as my father had done." It's this notion of okayness and the feeling of connectedness to successful adults that makes such a huge difference in a young person's developing sense of competence and self-esteem.

You can help your child discover positive role models by going to the library to find biographies or autobiographies of eminent individuals who struggled with behavior or attention problems in childhood, by researching the family tree for relatives who were particularly restless yet successful, by reading children's books that include characters modeling some of these traits (for example, Curious George, Ramona Quimby, and Laura Ingalls Wilder), and by posting cartoon strips that feature energetic and unpredictable characters (for example, Dennis the Menace, Peppermint Patty, Calvin and Hobbes, and even Garfield!). Your child may even want to do a school project featuring one or more of his favorite "hyperactive heroes." By focusing attention on successful individuals who were also hyperactive, distractible, or impulsive as children, your child may soon begin to believe a very important truth: "If *they* can be successful, then so can I!"

R ESOURCES

Victor Goertzel and Mildred G. Goertzel, *Cradles of Eminence* (Boston: Little, Brown, 1962).

Westridge Young Writers Workshop, *Kids Explore the Gifts of Children with Special Needs* (Santa Fe, NM: John Muir Publications, 1994). Peers are the positive role models in this student-written book.

#24

Consider Alternative
Schooling Options

Countless parents have written to me over the past several years sharing their stories of children with behavior or learning difficulties floundering in public school programs. Many of these parents have an almost identical three-act story:

Act 1: They were contacted by school administrators and told that their child had "a problem."

Act 2: The child was tested, identified as A.D.D., LD, ED, BD, or some other alphabet-soup term, and referred to a special education program.

Act 3: The child continued to have difficulties in special education, and in some cases became even worse, prompting new meetings and tests, and sometimes new labels, to chart the child's educational future.

Most of these parents remained stuck in this humorless pedagogical play for the rest of their child's school career. However, a few did not. These parents essentially wrote an Act 4 that involved taking their children out of the public school system and either putting them in a private alternative school or schooling them at home.

One of the first parents I knew about that explored a non-public-school option was an old friend who related to me the difficulties her son had in first grade. She went in for a conference with her son's regular classroom teacher and a specialist. "They handed me a report which had all these activities checked 'unsatisfactory' and 'needs improvement.' I was really surprised. I thought to myself, 'This is very strange. I mean, first grade? How can a kid be doing so poorly in first grade? He's only been here six weeks!'" After testing, her son was placed in a special education program. "Suddenly Jimmy didn't want to go to school anymore, hated school, was miserable at school. It was during that year that one morning he ran away." After more behavior problems, Jimmy's mom decided to take him out of school and place him in a private alternative school that emphasized individual learning styles. "The attitude at New Horizons," she related, "was, Let's not make any prejudgments. Let's start with the idea that different kids learn at different rates. Let's not put pressure on kids to be at a certain level at a certain time. Above all, let's not interfere with their natural love of learning." The effect of the school on Jimmy's growth was phenomenal. "They took all the pressure off. He was like a different child. He couldn't wait to get to school."

Not all private schools can create this sort of miracle turnaround. In fact, many private schools—especially those that describe themselves as "academic" or "back to basics"—are actually more confining and inflexible than the average public school classroom. However, thousands of private alternative schools exist around the country that share New Horizon's philosophy of honoring individual differences in learning. Some of them are Montessori programs in which students can work at their own pace on learning materials. Some are Waldorf schools, a philosophy of education that emphasizes the arts in teaching skills and content. Many others are uniquely designed schools established independently by parents and educators working together to create real alternatives for children in their community. While not all of these programs cater to or even welcome kids who've been labeled A.D.D. or LD in the public schools, many schools don't even ask about previous school labels and prefer not to know. One director of a Vermont private school told me that she throws away the cumulative folders students bring in from public school programs because she doesn't want to let the biases of previous teachers influence her own image of the student.

Another private school director wrote in a letter to me that kids with the A.D.D. label do come into their school but the label ceases to have much meaning. He writes, "We often find out through informal conversation, often after months of attendance at the school, that this or that student was diagnosed as hyperactive (or A.D.D., or ADHD, or whatever the current fashion is). Yet we never have a problem with these students, since our program is entirely and exclusively based on student-initiated activity, and students control their time and their actions without interference from adults. In fact, the only students who have ever posed serious problems are the few that have been subject to prolonged administration of drugs such as Ritalin, who are sadly often at sea in an environment where they are not subject to strict controls."

Many parents have gone even further and decided to homeschool their previously school-labeled children. Currently homeschooling appears to be on the rise as a national trend, with an estimated 200,000 families across the country teaching their children at home. Although such an approach demands a great deal of time and patience from parents, who must spend hours a day teaching and planning instruction for their kids, many parents of kids labeled A.D.D. apparently feel it's worth it.

One mother, writing in the national homeschooling journal *Growing Without Schooling*, shared the story of her son Matt, who was diagnosed as A.D.D. in the first grade, medicated, and referred to a special education program in the second grade. "Matt's teachers gave stickers for each week's completed assignments," she writes. "These were openly displayed in the classroom. The children who didn't have many stickers were called 'dumb,' 'flunker,' or 'stupid,' by their classmates. . . . Children with behavior problems were threatened with not being allowed to go on the yearly overnight camping trip. Instead of helping, this threat made the kids, including Matt, more anxious, resulting in more behavior problems." After more difficulties in third grade, the family decided to homeschool him. "We saw an immediate improvement in all areas. . . . He is currently studying oceanography and American history, especially Civil War battles and modern military machinery. He can tell you more about aircraft, tanks, and ships than most adults we know. . . . He enjoys learning again and our whole family is a lot happier."

The stories related above suggest that non-public-school alternatives may be warranted in cases where kids are not thriving despite repeated attempts in both regular and special education to make things work. If you decide on either of these two options (alternative school or homeschooling), make sure that you're ready to make the commitment. Some private schools are expensive and may require a certain amount of hours per week in parent volunteer time. Make sure that you are comfortable with the school's philosophy, that you visit a classroom with your child if allowed, and that you see to it that teachers are certified by the state or a recognized educational association.

Homeschooling requires a major time commitment from at least one parent to plan a child's curriculum and then more time to follow through on instruction and evaluation of work. In some states, parents must be supervised by state-appointed educators. To make things easier, commercially available homeschooling programs exist to guide the process (write to Growing Without Schooling for more information). But to be effective, homeschooling needs to be designed around the needs, abilities, and interests of your child. It's also recommended that you network with other homeschooling parents to schedule social events so that your child has contact with kids his own age. Whether you decide on an alternative school or a homeschool for your child, you could very well be providing him with a label-free environment in which he can learn in his own way.

Resources

American Montessori Society (AMS), 150 Fifth Avenue, New York, NY 10011.

Association of Waldorf Schools of North America, 17 Hemlock Hill Road, Great Barrington, MA 01230.

David and Micki Colfax, *Homeschooling for Excellence* (New York: Warner, 1988). This book gives one family's story of how the parents sent three of their sons to Harvard after years of homeschooling.

Daniel Greenberg, *Free at Last: The Sudbury Valley School* (Framingham, MA: Sudbury Valley School Press, 1987). This book tells the story of one independent alternative school that honors and celebrates learning differences.

Growing Without Schooling, 2269 Massachusetts Avenue, Cambridge, MA 02140. This is a national organization of homeschoolers originally founded by progressive educator John Holt. It publishes a bimonthly newsletter, helps homeschoolers connect with each other, assists families in learning about legal procedures in each state for setting up a homeschool, and runs a mail-order service for relevant books and learning materials.

25

Channel Creative Energy
into the Arts

As part of my practicum experience for a master's degree in special education, I helped direct an arts resource room in a residential summer
program for children with a variety of special needs. We worked with
small groups regularly throughout the day using a broad range of ex-
pressive media including paints, collage, mask-making, drawing, finger-
painting, and woodwork. Many of the kids in the summer program were
hyperactive, distractible, aggressive, and sometimes completely out of
control when in the more academically oriented classrooms. But when
they came into our arts resource room, they seemed like different people. Somehow their chaotic or random energies flowed naturally into the
art materials that we had available for them.

  Many children who are labeled as hyperactive or A.D.D. appear to
possess huge reserves of creative energy that simply aren't being
tapped and appropriately channeled. When I attended one of
CH.A.D.D.'s national conferences, I noticed a poster on the wall that
read: "America Needs: Energy, Creativity, Ingenuity! A.D.D. Kids Have
It! Give Them a Chance." I agree wholeheartedly with this statement.
However, when I phoned one of the most respected A.D.D. researchers
in the field and asked her about research that had actually been done on
the creativity of kids labeled A.D.D., I was told that there was none. She
did offer a study she'd done indicating that kids labeled A.D.D. tell more
novel stories than so-called normals. Later on, I discovered one general

article and three citations in hard-to-get journals suggesting that kids who had been diagnosed as A.D.D. and were also identified through intelligence tests as "gifted," tended to have higher levels of picture-based creativity than "gifted" kids who weren't labeled A.D.D. Other than these studies, however, there was nothing. Yet there are thousands of studies telling us what A.D.D. kids *can't* do. This is a tragedy, since it suggests researchers are more interested in the deficits of these children than in their potentials.

If children labeled A.D.D. *do* in fact possess hidden reserves of creative energy, then the use of the arts, including music, dance, theater, and painting, could represent an important ingredient in helping them become successful people. While research is sorely lacking in this area, I've come across several anecdotal reports pointing to the value of the arts with kids labeled A.D.D. A mother recently wrote me telling me about her young daughter, who was quite unfocused in the classroom yet at home could dance for hours on end. Similarly, Cynthia Swope, a second-grade teacher at a Tennessee elementary school using a program known as Discipline-Based Art Education, has noticed that several of her "A.D.D. students" seem to excel in art while displaying "impressive critical thinking abilities." And a recent *Ladies' Home Journal* article featured an "A.D.D. child" who essentially saved the school's orchestra from being cut out of the budget when he wrote an impassioned plea to the district superintendent, saying, "Making music is one of the only things I can do better than my friends. . . . I don't think it's fair to cut the music program."

I don't think it's fair that kids labeled A.D.D. aren't being given more of an opportunity to display and express their creativity. Fortunately there are several things you can do at home to help your child channel his energy through the arts. First, locate an area of the house where you can set up a "make-a-mess corner." Some supplies to provide would be paint and brushes (with easel), drawing paper and colored pencils, collage materials such as old magazines, wallpaper samples, colored cloth, paper, and glue, fingerpaints, and modeling clay. Make sure the corner is in a part of the house where your child can get messy without it being a big problem, perhaps by covering the floor with newspaper or putting the center in the basement or garage. Here are some other ideas:

♦ Get an empty appliance box and create a puppet theater with your child. Purchase some simple puppets at a toy store, or make your own out of old socks, and let your child put on puppet shows with her friends.

♦ Save hand-me-down clothes and put them in a sturdy container for use as a "costume box." Let your child dress up and put on special skits, plays, or dances dressed up as she wishes.

♦ Create a "musician's corner" stocked with simple percussion instruments and a tape recorder. Here your child can tape her own performances or play her favorite music.

Finally, for kids with special abilities and strong motivation, consider music lessons, dance classes, or art programs in which they can develop their talents in a more structured way. Above all, don't push your child into these activities, and try to keep a respectful distance from her creative work unless she invites you to become involved.

At school, push for a strong arts program that includes classes in music, dance, theater, and the visual arts. Unfortunately, these programs are all too often the first to be cut when there is a budgetary problem. Yet for your child, they may represent the places in school where she achieves her greatest successes. Encourage your child's teacher to incorporate the arts into regular classroom activities. When I taught in the public schools, I had a regular "choice time" during the day when my students could draw, make art projects, listen to music, or be creative in other ways. Teachers can also bring the arts into the curriculum by having students role-play history lessons, draw pictures illustrating math problems, and create raps and songs about characters in the literature they're reading. Think of your child's hyperactive, distractible, or unfocused behaviors as creative energy simply looking for a place to flow. By providing your child with art materials and an appropriate setting for using them at home and at school, you can serve essentially as a human resources engineer and help your child's creative waters find their right level.

Resources

Teresa Benzwie, *A Moving Experience: Dance for Lovers of Children and the Child Within* (Tucson, AZ: Zephyr, 1988).
Mona Brookes, *Drawing with Children* (Los Angeles: Tarcher/Perigee, 1986).

Don G. Campbell and Chris Boyd Brewer, *Rhythms of Learning* (Tucson, AZ: Zephyr, 1990).

Avery Hart and Paul Mantell, *Kids Make Music: Clapping and Tapping from Bach to Rock* (Charlotte, VT: Williamson, 1993).

Viola Spolin, *Theater Games for the Classroom* (Evanston, IL: Northwestern University Press, 1986).

Sally Warner, *Encouraging the Artist in Your Child* (New York: St. Martin's, 1989).

26

Provide Hands-on Activities

"Put that toy away!" "Stop fiddling with the pencil sharpener!" "Can't you learn to keep your hands to *yourself*?"

Do these comments sound familiar? If you have a child, or have ever taught a child, then you're probably all too familiar with these or similar phrases. And if that child has been labeled A.D.D., then you've possibly experienced more than your share of stories along this line. Yet for all the trouble such behaviors seem to cause, I want to suggest that behind these annoyances lies an important need for your child: to have direct hands-on experience with the world.

When humans learned to use their hands to create tools they made a quantum leap in evolution. During the first eighteen months of life, according to Swiss child researcher Jean Piaget, all thinking takes place through physical experiences. The infant grasps, claws, squeezes, pinches, pats, pushes, and otherwise manipulates the environment to learn more about it. As the child matures, he begins to internalize the world. However, even during the elementary school years, Piaget says that the child still requires the use of the external world as a reference point for all thinking activities. To learn, says Piaget, the child must manipulate the world. To learn about fractions, for example, he needs to cut apples into segments or pies into slices and not simply read a textbook or do pencil-and-paper math problems. To learn about maps, he needs to create a three-dimensional map out of papier-mâché or clay and not simply look at a map.

Some children have a greater need for this kind of activity than others. Art educator Viktor Lowenfeld spoke of the *haptic* learner. Haptic individuals (from the Greek word *haptos,* meaning "laying hold of") need to have direct physical contact with something in order to learn more about it. According to Lowenfeld, "An extremely haptic individual ... relies upon his sense of touch and body self as his main means of becoming acquainted with and reacting to his environment." Often this hands-on preference becomes a part of the adulthood of these individuals and proves to be instrumental in the realization of their life's work. Former Stanford creativity professor Robert McKim writes, "Consider the sculptor who thinks in clay, the chemist who thinks by manipulating three-dimensional molecular models, or the designer who thinks by assembling and rearranging cardboard mockups. Each is thinking by seeing, touching, and moving materials, by externalizing his mental processes in a physical object. Many contemporary thinkers, in science and engineering as well as art and design, respect the fertility of this venerable form of ... thought."

From my contacts over the years with parents and teachers who have worked with children identified as A.D.D. or hyperactive, it's apparent to me that many of these children appear to be haptic or "hands-on" learners. One mother of an A.D.D.-labeled son wrote, "My son has a great gift for working and creating projects with his hands. ... He loves to build with cardboard, tape, has made his own laser gun, etc." A teacher commented in one of my questionnaires about a student described as hyperactive that "Tommy has become one of my greatest helpers in the class. He is very good with 'fixing' things, be it to glue a face to a magnet, [to repair] the pencil sharpener, or find missing items." Violet Oaklander, a child psychotherapist, talked about her practice of doing woodworking with some children identified as hyperactive: "They will make wonderful things, experiment with new ways of making books, boxes, airplanes, etc.... Once a faculty member ... walked into the room unexpectedly to observe a student teacher ... and remarked, 'These look just like ordinary normal children!' Indeed, they were just like the rest of us!"

Since it is clearly the case that many kids labeled A.D.D. do have a high need for hands-on activities, here are some socially appropriate ways for them to satisfy that need so that they don't end up becoming a hands-on nuisance!

♦ *Give your child something to do with his hands while he's in-volved in stationary activities.* If your child has to sit for long peri-ods in a car on a trip, for example, make sure he has materials to keep his hands busy. Some possibilities would be: hand-held video games (e.g., Gameboy), small puzzles (e.g., Rubik's Cube), miniature action figures, yarn for making cat's cradles or other string forms, and an Etch-a-Sketch or other simple drawing device. Some teachers have told me that they give their "handy" kids a rubber squeeze ball, some beeswax to mold, or even a balloon filled with "ooblick" (a mixture of corn starch and water) to manipulate and that this keeps them quiet and calm at their desks.

♦ *Provide opportunities for tactile stimulation.* Some teachers have created a "tactile tub" consisting of a small plastic wading pool filled with any of a number of substances, including water, oatmeal, sand, cornmeal, shredded paper, Styrofoam packing beads, or flour, among other ingredients. This environment provides plenty of tactile stimulation as kids scoop up the material, rub their hands in it, and use it to form islands, castles, or other fantasy creations. You can also keep a "feely box" filled with fun things to touch, such as felt, silk, sandpaper, duct tape, bubble packing sheets, or a soapholder with lots of little suction cups on the back. You can put a "mystery object" in a box and have your child attempt to identify it only by touch. You might be surprised at how good your child is at this activity.

♦ *Supply 3-D building materials for free play.* Anything that allows your child to create three-dimensional forms using some kind of build-ing unit can feed his hands-on hunger. Examples include Lego blocks, an Erector set, Lincoln Logs, d-stix, Tinkertoys, simple wooden blocks, pattern blocks, plastic connector beads, origami, clay, and, playing cards for building "houses." Provide an open space where your child can work over a period of time at ongoing projects.

♦ *Use manipulative materials to teach academic subjects.* The Montessori and Piagetian revolutions in education spawned a wide range of hands-on materials that teach math concepts in concrete ways, including Cuisenaire rods, Dienes blocks, unifix cubes, geo-boards, tangrams, number-blox, and other math manipulatives. These materials allow children to explore logical patterns in a hands-on way. For example, putting small cubes of wood together to form groups of ten or a hundred provides a way of learning about place value. To learn science concepts, students can do hands-on science experiments. For example, they can use measuring equipment to learn about the metric system or put together a miniature skeleton from chicken bones to learn about anatomy. In literature and history, students might create dioramas, models, and artifacts to illustrate the plot of a novel or a historical period. Even reading can become hands-on if you provide special books: pop-up books, scratch-'n'-sniff books, touch-'n'-feel books, and books kids can take apart and put back together in a different way.

There are many other ways of feeding your child's need for hands-on activity at home or in school. In one school, a teacher throws a bean bag to a student while asking a question about the lesson. This requires the student to think and act at the same time—something many hands-on learners are very good at. In another school, students who are referred to the principal for behavior problems can sit in the office and pet the school cat. Having animals around is very important for many kids with high-touch needs. One parent allows her child to "fingerpaint" the shower walls with shaving cream (it's so easy to wash off). Another lets her child "paint" the sidewalks with water on a hot day (it evaporates in the heat). In these and other ways, you can keep your child from becoming too "touchy," help him "grasp" new material, and provide strategies that allow him to get a "good grip" on his life!

R E S O U R C E S

Cuisenaire Company of America, Inc., 12 Church Street, Box D, New Rochelle, NY 10802. This company is a mail order supplier of many math and science manipulatives, including the original Cuisenaire rods.

The Editors of Klutz Press, *Kids Travel: A Backseat Survival Kit* (Palo Alto, CA: Klutz, 1994). This book of activities for trips includes several accessories to make the time go by faster. Klutz Press also publishes books that come with hands-on materials such as a book on juggling sold with juggling balls.

#27

Spend Positive Times Together

When Albert Einstein was four years old, his father showed him a magnetic compass. Einstein later said that this experience awakened in him a desire to figure out the mysteries of the universe. When Thomas Edison was eight, he ran away from school when the teacher called his mind "addled." His mother didn't believe that her son was stupid and taught him at home. In each of these cases, parents played a key role in the success of individuals who had school difficulties yet went on to become among the greatest thinkers in history. It was the positive time that these parents spent with their kids that helped create turning-point moments for them.

Parents are truly a child's first teachers. Nature maintains the dependence of children on parents for several years after birth so that parents can help mediate a child's adaptation to the environment. If the relationship between parent and child is filled with yelling, arguing, fighting, and other negative interactions, then the child's adaptation to life will be troubled. On the other hand, a positive relationship between parent and child prepares the child for a full and active participation in the world. This positive relationship is forged from all the little moments that parents and children spend together: moments of playfulness, creativity, respect, problem-solving, wonder, silliness, curiosity, and delight that parent and child mutually share. If these moments are absent, the child is left without a beacon to light her way through life.

It's understandable, then, that children instinctively crave positive contact with their parents. Citing a study of 2,500 fifth graders, author Zig Ziglar writes, "The one thing that upset children the most was spending too little time with their parents." Ziglar points out that "for a child, love is spelled T-I-M-E." When a group of "A.D.D. boys" were asked to select their favorite rewards for positive behavior from a list that included games, television, toys, and candy, time spent with parents led the list. Unfortunately in many households where time is stretched thin by working parents and a faster pace of life, positive time spent between parents and children is a scarce commodity. And in families where a child has already been experiencing behavior difficulties, much of this precious time can be wasted in arguing, fighting, and other struggles.

Research is loud and clear on the impact of a positive parent-child relationship upon a child's later success. In one famous longitudinal study of children in Hawaii, positive emotional support in the early years of life was seen as crucial to later emotional well-being and academic achievement. In another study on the impact of "positive contact" in the family, mothers who spent more positive time with their children used fewer communications in the form of directives and "unmodified power" and more communication in the form of praise and social conversation. Research on children who seem to respond exceptionally well to stressful events, the so-called invulnerable child, shows that such kids have in common one thing: "one good, strong secure relationship with a parent or with another adult." There is also significant evidence pointing to the impact of positive parental involvement in a child's school life on later academic success.

These studies all point toward one unifying guideline for parents: *spend regular positive time with your child.* Don't wait for the positive time to happen: *make* it happen by scheduling it into your day. For some busy parents, this may involve having a special time with your child before breakfast or after dinner on weekdays. But make sure that it happens regularly even if for only thirty minutes a day. Here is a list of some of the positive things you can do together with your child:

- read a book
- go for a walk
- play a board game
- listen to music
- tell funny jokes
- look at family scrapbooks
- draw pictures
- play catch
- sing songs
- take a car ride
- go to the zoo
- have a pleasant talk
- go out for dinner
- cook something
- build something
- repair something in the house
- play one-on-one basketball
- go on a picnic
- visit a historical site
- do a puzzle
- do a craft project
- watch TV (and talk about what you see)
- play with the dog or cat
- do card or magic tricks
- write a letter
- visit a museum
- play a sport (e.g., bowling, tennis)
- do a science experiment
- solve a riddle
- look at your child's collections (e.g., cards)
- phone a relative
- put on music and dance
- meditate or pray
- learn something new
- go miniature golfing
- look up information in the encyclopedia
- plan a trip
- play video games
- tell stories
- read magazines
- work with clay
- ride bikes
- make music (with instruments)
- play with toys
- do volunteer or charity work
- solve brainteasers

In addition to the activities listed above, plan on being available for special events in your child's life, including teacher conferences, Little League games, the school play, music recitals, and transition times like birthdays and graduation. Also, consider daily events such as meals and bedtime as regular opportunities for positive contact with your child. At mealtimes talk together about the day's news and good things that happened at school, or share funny jokes or stories. At bedtime, read a favorite book or tell a bedtime story, listen to your child share things he did during the day, and end with I-love-yous and reassuring hugs and kisses. By providing your child with a safe and loving parent relationship, you're helping to install "shock absorbers" in your child's heart and mind that have a lifetime guarantee.

RESOURCES

Steve and Ruth Bennett, *365 TV-Free Activities to Do with Your Child* (Holbrook, MA: Bob Adams, 1991).

————, *365 Outdoors Activities to Do with Your Child* (Holbrook, MA: Bob Adams, 1993).

————, *365 Ways to Reclaim the Family Dinner Hour* (Holbrook, MA: Bob Adams, 1994).

Jane Healy, *Is Your Bed Still There When You Close the Door?: How to Have Intelligent and Creative Conversations with Your Kids* (New York: Doubleday, 1992).

Vito Perrone, *101 Educational Conversations with Your Fourth Grader* (New York: Chelsea House, 1993). Books for kindergarten through twelfth grade by Perrone, a Harvard education professor, are also available from Chelsea House. These books provide ideas for conversation starters to discuss important ideas.

28

Provide Appropriate Spaces for Learning

In the classic television sitcom *WKRP in Cincinnati,* one of the radio station's employees, Les Nessman, puts masking tape on the floor surrounding his desk to mark off the boundaries of his tiny office space. Those brave souls who dare trespass over the line must reckon with Les's indignation at having his personal space violated. Not too unlike Les Nessman, every child needs an appropriate personal space in which to learn. For children identified as A.D.D. who are often "on the move," or who have a "wider" attentional focus, this space may need to be even larger or more flexible than that of the average child.

Unfortunately, many of these kids have to learn in overcrowded classrooms that allow for little flexibility and under conditions that may even worsen hyperactive symptoms. When animals are crowded into cages for long periods of time, symptoms of stress—including aggression and hyperactivity—occur at epidemic levels. Similar results can be observed in human populations. Rutgers University professor Carol S. Weinstein comments, "Nowhere [but in schools] are large groups of individuals packed so closely together for so many hours, yet expected to perform at peak efficiency on difficult learning tasks and to interact harmoniously." Her review of research suggests that crowding in classrooms may be related to symptoms of nervousness, dissatisfaction, less sociability, and more aggression.

Child development expert Alexander Thomas and his colleagues in-

dicate that overcrowding in large urban housing projects may also contribute significantly to the problem of hyperactivity in some children.
They write, "We suspect that some, if not most of the 'hyperactivity'
complained about in the PRWC [Puerto Rican working class] children
was due to the circumstances of their environment. The families usually
had several children and lived in small apartments in which even the
normal fooling around and active play of a youngster greatly impinged
on others and could appear to the family as excessive motility. Furthermore, those children who temperamentally had a high activity level
were even more likely than others to be cooped up at home for fear that
if they ran around in the streets they would be in special danger of
accidents."

Crowding isn't the only problem in providing appropriate spaces for
learning. School and home spaces may trigger or worsen symptoms of
hyperactivity if they are *underarousing*. Classroom design expert Anita
Olds describes some of the problems in many bureaucratically engi-
neered schools: "The barrenness and homogeneity of the physical pa-
rameters of classrooms can deaden arousal and interfere with children's
capacities to stay alert and attentive. Cold, shiny tile floors, multiple
chairs and tables of identical design and hard finish, dull-colored walls
lacking recesses or changes in texture, ceilings of uniform height, which
dwarf the size of the room's occupants, and fluorescent lights, which
spread a constant, high-powered glare over all activities indiscrimi-
nately, all contribute to feelings of boredom, listlessness, and dislike for
the settings in which learning takes place." Previously in this book,
we've examined research suggesting that some kids who are labeled
A.D.D. become hyperactive as a way of stimulating their underaroused
nervous systems. In a bland classroom space such as that described
above, these children probably would find it necessary to create their
own stimulation through fidgeting, daydreaming, socializing, or wander-
ing in order to meet their personal arousal quotas.

The above research suggests that children identified as hyperactive
or A.D.D. require appropriate spaces in which to learn. At school, they
should have their own desk or private learning area. It may even be
helpful to adapt Les Nessman's strategy and mark the space around the
desk with tape on the floor. Make sure all children in the classroom have
their own designated spaces so your child doesn't feel singled out. At
home, your child should have his or her own private study space. It
might be a desk in a corner of the bedroom or a special nook in a base-

ment or study. Make sure, though, that it's comfortable and relatively free of major distractions, such as other people talking.

Classrooms should have a variety of study spaces to accommodate the needs of kids' different energy states. Learning styles consultant Rita Dunn has students studying in a number of innovative spaces including a math tub (a free-standing bathtub that one can lie in only while doing math work), a reading "tee-pee," a couch, a tent, and a rocking chair. In some schools I've worked in, parents have volunteered their time to create special multileveled "lofts," where kids can snuggle into private spaces to study. To provide more variety in classroom spaces, Anita Olds suggests some of the following additions: pillows, plants, soft furniture, kid-sized furniture, mobiles, murals, carpets, canopies, and wall dividers. The same kind of variety should exist in a child's home study areas. Make sure that your child has a role in designing these areas. The space in which your child does his learning should be considered almost sacred—in the sense that he is giving birth to new ideas. Let's treat these areas with respect, then, and give our children the space they need in which to find themselves.

RESOURCES

Anne Levine, Don Kaplan, and Craig A. Berquist, *How to Design and Remodel Children's Rooms* (San Francisco: Ortho, 1988).

29

Consider Individual Psychotherapy

My wife is a child psychotherapist. If you were to walk into her office, you'd see thousands of miniature figures (houses, people, animals, trees, cars, and much more) on shelves and a free-standing tray of sand in the middle of the room. She specializes in sandplay psychotherapy, in which clients create miniature worlds in the sand from some of the innumerable figures available. Over the course of several years, Barbara has worked with many hyperactive children. She tells me that when many of these children enter the sandplay room, their energies are transformed from chaos into purpose by the images they choose for their trays.

There are over 230 different types of child psychotherapy, from talk therapy and play therapy to behavioral and cognitive therapies. What each of these therapies have in common is a process for helping children change for the better. Whether the child comes into the consulting room because of low self-worth, depression, anxiety, hyperactivity, or other problems, the psychotherapist is responsible for creating conditions under which the child can move into a place of greater mastery over his own life.

Regrettably, psychotherapy has been accorded a very low place on the A.D.D. ladder of treatment options. Dorothea M. Ross and Sheila A. Ross, in their comprehensive book *Hyperactivity: Current Issues, Research, and Theory*, wrote in 1982, "Traditional psychotherapy was firmly rejected as a part of the treatment armamentarium for hyperactivity, the major basis for this drastic stance being one methodologically inadequate study." More recently, Barbara Ingersoll, in her best-selling book *Your Hyperactive Child*, voiced the orthodox viewpoint: "Since ... current evidence indicates that the hyperactive child's difficulties are caused by physical malfunctions in the brain, it makes little sense to look to psychological methods for relief. And in fact, there is simply no convincing evidence that psychotherapy helps to alleviate the hyperactive child's inattentiveness, poor impulse control, or motor hyperactivity."

In keeping with Dorothea Ross's and Sheila Ross's statements, I'd like to suggest that psychotherapy may hold great promise for some children labeled A.D.D. Since research suggests that up to 25 percent of "A.D.D. kids" suffer from anxiety disorders and that as many as 75 percent of kids identified as A.D.D. may be depressed, then psychotherapy designed to treat these deeper emotional issues may be extremely important to their future well-being. Moreover, because many of these kids end up being criticized by teachers, ridiculed by peers, and/or punished by parents because of their behaviors, they can end up in a cycle of failure in which punishment leads to anger which leads to more inappropriate behavior leading to more punishment, and so on. Furthermore, some of these kids face specific stresses, such as the loss of a parent through death or divorce, domestic or neighborhood violence, illness, or other troubling experiences. For these stressed-out children, psychotherapy can provide a means of healing emotional wounds.

And while many A.D.D. experts have discounted the potential effectiveness of psychotherapy on the basis of past studies, more current and better designed research suggests that psychotherapy can be quite helpful in the lives of hyperactive kids. For the past twenty years, James Satterfield, executive director of the National Center for Hyperactive Children, in Encino, California, has used long-term (two to three years) talk therapy as an adjunctive treatment with medication, family support, and other approaches. His research suggests that the use of psychotherapy has cut down on future delinquency (including arrest and hospitalization rates) by more than 50 percent.

Depending upon the type of therapy and the specific needs of your child, psychotherapy can provide several different kinds of benefits. In psychodynamic therapy, children can be helped to look at the emotional conflicts that negatively affect them. They can be given a vocabulary for their feelings and may be helped to recognize and appropriately express feelings as a way of coping with the many stresses of their lives. These feelings may be expressed through words, puppets, drawing, music, drama, storytelling, sandplay, or other concrete means, depending upon the particular training of the therapist. World-renowned psychoanalyst Erik Erikson writes about the use of simple block play with a young "hyperactive child." The boy constructed a tower that looked like a body with outstretched hands. Erikson commented that "the whole construction may well echo the teacher's formula for the solution of what worried the boy at the time, namely, how to keep body and brain together, and to make them work in concert." Through an ongoing process of work on the inner life, children can be helped to develop mastery over impulses, better ways of coping with conflict, and higher self-esteem.

Other forms of psychotherapy sidestep the world of feelings and instead concentrate on specific behaviors or habitual ways of thinking. In behavioral therapy (the most widely used form of therapy for A.D.D.-type issues), the therapist helps the parents set up a system of reinforcements to reward specific positive behaviors. They also assist the child in learning how to identify his own negative and positive behaviors and show him ways of shaping new behaviors. In cognitive therapy (sometimes used in conjunction with behavior therapy), children are helped to *think* about their actions in new ways. Children may be helped, for example, to attribute their successes in school to personal effort. They may also be assisted in developing specific self-talk skills as a way of boosting morale and organizing new information. Children can also participate in group therapy with other children to learn how to develop important social skills or take part in family therapy.

Regardless of the particular type of therapy you decide on for your child, make sure that you choose a therapist with solid credentials and specific licensing in her field (see the list of organizations below for referral sources). Psychiatrists are medical doctors with several years of specialization in psychiatry and can prescribe medications. Psychologists have Ph.D.s or Psy.D.s in psychology and special clinical training, and may also be trained in administering diagnostic tests. Other examples of professionals who can be specially trained and licensed to do psychotherapy include social workers, psychiatric nurses, and marriage and family therapists. Make sure to ask about state licenses held and affiliation with local and national professional associations. Once you do choose a therapist, plan on taking an active role in your child's therapy. This may involve meeting periodically with the therapist to discuss your child's progress and learning what you can do at home to support his growth. It may also involve going into personal psychotherapy yourself. Psychotherapy is not a "cure" for attention or behavioral difficulties. But when used in conjunction with other treatment methods, it can provide your child with an important source of support on his way to achieving success in life.

RESOURCES

Jack Engler and Daniel Goleman, *The Consumer's Guide to Psychotherapy* (New York: Simon & Schuster, 1992). This excellent guide includes a section on A.D.D. and instructions on how to find a therapist.

The following organizations can provide referrals for psychotherapists certified within their association (in some cases, the national office will tell you to call a local branch which can then provide the referral):

American Psychiatric Association, 1400 K Street NW, Washington, DC 20005; 202-682-6142.

American Psychological Association, 1200 17th Street, NW, Washington, DC 20036; 202-336-5500.

Association for the Advancement of Behavioral Therapy, 15 W. 36th Street, New York, NY 10018; 212-279-7970. This organization will send guidelines for choosing a behavioral therapist and a membership directory.

National Association of Social Workers, 7981 Eastern Avenue, Silver Spring, MD 20910; 202-408-8600.

National Mental Health Association, 1021 Prince Street, Alexandria, VA 22314; 703-684-7722.

#30

Use Touch to Soothe and Calm

As a teacher of children with learning and behavior problems, I often found myself in situations where a child was out of control: throwing a tantrum, fighting with another student, or simply driven to distraction. At such times, I almost instinctively found it necessary to reach out and touch the child, often just lightly on the shoulder, as a way of making contact and sending a message of reassurance. Anthropologist Ashley Montagu tells us that touch is a strong human need. Touch appears to stimulate the release of endorphins in the brain that have a pain-relieving effect similar to that of morphine. For thousands of years, the "laying on of hands" has been regarded as a potent method of physical and emotional healing. We can learn to use its powerful influence in sensitive ways to help lessen the effects of some of the more disturbing behaviors experienced by children who've been identified as hyperactive or A.D.D.

Kids diagnosed as A.D.D. can benefit from touch in many ways. First, as we've seen earlier in this book, many A.D.D.-labeled children have high needs for stimulation—and that includes tactile and bodily-kinesthetic stimulation as well. You can see this in the way some of these kids interact with their environment: touching the walls and furniture of a room as they pass through it, knocking roughly up against their friends and enemies, fidgeting restlessly while seated at their desks. These kids appear to be trying to provide themselves with adequate physical stimulation.

Sensitive and safe forms of non-sexual touch from parents and teachers can help meet some of these needs.

Second, many of these kids have experienced chronic stress, whether from school problems, peer conflicts, or parent-child tensions, and may have developed muscular tensions that are themselves uncomfortable and that impair learning and attention. Touch can serve as a way of helping to dissolve those tensions and free up constricted muscular energy that can then flow in the child's body in a more natural way.

Finally, with the wide attentional focus that some of these kids have (one colleague referred to them as the "earth as second planet children"), touch can serve to "ground" children to the here-and-now and provide a means of bringing them back to their senses. Author and pediatrician T. Berry Brazelton recommends that parents use "holding" as a way of helping an out-of-control preschooler: "When the child is hysterical, a parent can gently take him into a rocking chair, hold him securely and rock him until he subsides. Then the parent can slowly begin to croon to the child, gradually to talk, and when he is able to listen, to explain to him what he has been through and how he has learned something from it." Brazelton suggests that this approach helps children learn techniques for eventually calming themselves. Several years ago, a group of pediatricians conducted an informal study with twenty-four "hyperactive children" using a similar method of therapeutic holding and achieved dramatic results: "All responded favorably to nondrug therapy; 15 have had almost total remission of both hyperactivity and other symptoms (short attention span, aggressiveness, antisocial behavior etc.)."

There are many ways of providing nourishing touch experiences for your child, including back rubs, hugs, foot massages, and light backscratching. If you massage your child, make sure that your hands are warm, that when you massage you press gently yet with strength (not tentative), and that both you and your child *want* the experience. Older kids may not feel comfortable with formal massage yet may welcome opportunities for tickling, wrestling, or other indirect ways of making body contact.

At school, where physical contact with children is complicated by teachers' fears of sexual-molestation charges, a simple touch on the shoulder or a light hug may be enough to reassure a distraught child or to focus a distracted student back on task. Light physical contact can also be worked into academic experiences. For example, students might spell words on each others' backs. And students can even be taught to give themselves self-massage in areas of tension (for example, "palming," or massaging the muscles surrounding the eyes by placing the hands gently over the eyes and gently rubbing, to relieve eye strain) or to press special energy points (associated with the ancient tradition of acupressure) to help focus and ground awareness. Touch, after all, is simply human energy, and when we learn to apply it in nourishing ways with kids whose energies are off-track, we help them find a place of calm within themselves and assist them in moving with confidence into the world.

R ESOURCES

Ashley Montagu, *Touching: The Human Significance of the Skin* (New York: Harper & Row, 1986).

Marybetts Sinclair, *Massage for Healthier Children* (Berkeley, CA: Wingbow, 1992).

Jeanne St. John, *High Tech Touch: Acupressure in the Schools* (Novato, CA: Academic Therapy Publications, 1987).

#31

Help Your Child with Organizational Skills

Periodically in my classroom we had an SCO (schoolwork cleanout) day, when students went through their desks deciding what to keep, what to throw out, and what to take home. For some students, the job was finished almost before it started, since their desks were so well-organized and maintained on an ongoing basis that virtually no cleanup was necessary. Quite a few students, however, found the task quite challenging. I remember Randy in particular. The inside of his desk usually resembled Mt. Saint Helens shortly after it blew. Randy would peer into the mass of twisted papers, tattered books, and odds and ends collected from home and school, and start to cry. Then, either my teacher's aide or I would go over to him with some reassuring words and begin retrieving items out of the desk, one by one. I'd hold up a paper and Randy would tell me what to do with it (i.e., save it, toss it, or put it aside to take home). This worked quite well, but it was unfortunately about as far as we ever got with Randy's desk organization skills.

Many kids with attentional or behavioral problems have similar difficulties with organizational skills. Among the litany of complaints that parents and teachers have in this area are the following: messy bedrooms, forgotten homework, chaotic study skills, missed chores, and skipped deadlines for school assignments. These outer signs of disarray, however, may simply be reflections of an inner disorganization that can be straightened out with some assistance from a patient and at least somewhat organized parent or teacher. Below are some suggestions for helping your child self-organize in several areas of his school and home life.

Remembering Homework Assignments: Take your child to a stationery or school supply store and let him choose a three-ring notebook that appeals to him. If he chooses a notebook with a blank cover, allow him to color or draw on the cover anything that will help remind him that this is his *homework* notebook. Material to put in the notebook might include

♦ A calendar for recording due dates (your child might want to create his own calendar as an art project)

♦ Special three-hole-punched colored paper for writing down assignments that can then be crossed out or checked off when completed

♦ Lots of regular notebook paper for homework assignments

♦ Several notebook dividers for dividing written assignments by specific school subjects (color coded by subject)

♦ A three-holed "pouch" for carrying pencils, erasers, pens, and even a calculator

For the first few days of school (and periodically thereafter), sit down with your child and review with him his list of assignments, due dates, and the actual homework itself. If your child isn't writing down the assignments or forgets to put them in his notebook at school, phone the teacher and ask her to meet briefly with your child toward the end of the day to make sure homework materials are all ready to go home. If your child is confused about which textbooks to bring home, make a colored book jacket for each text that he can illustrate with pictures relevant to each subject.

Using Study Time Efficiently: Teach your child to read textbook material using a colored highlighter pen, coloring in significant ideas in one color, important dates in another color, and so forth. Help him gain the most information in the quickest period of time by skimming texts for key words, captions under pictures, topic sentences, and any highlighted material. Learning expert Tony Buzan suggests that individuals take short breaks for every twenty to forty minutes of study time; this helps aid recall later on. Your child may want to take breaks even more frequently. Show him how to take notes using "mind-mapping." This note-taking method involves putting a key idea in the center of a blank page, writing down related concepts or ideas spatially distributed around the main idea, and then linking main and related ideas together with straight lines. I like to think of this approach as "hyperactive note-taking"! This method can also be used as a "prewriting" strategy before writing a book report, short story, poem, or other written assignment.

If your child is confused about what to study first, help him learn how to prioritize tasks. Assist him in breaking down each assignment into small tasks and then prioritizing them according to either importance (most important task first, least important task last), or logical sequence ("I have to do this before I can do that"). It may help if he can draw a quick picture to go along with each task as a reminder, or if he puts each task on an index card, spreads them on the floor, and then manually puts them in order.

Organizing Home and School Space: Color-code drawers and shelves to remind your child where clothes and toys go. He might also want to create a graphic symbol for each drawer; for example, a picture of a pair of pants for the pants drawer. Color-code the clothes bar in the closet so that pants are hung up along the blue segment, shirts along the red segment, and so on. Suggest that your child clean up his room using any of the following categories: color (pick up the red things first, then the blue, then the green, etc.), size (pick up the smallest things first, the largest things last), or texture (pick up the smooth things first, the rough things last), or have him create his own organizational category. Store items in clear plastic boxes so that he can see what goes inside.

Guide him in setting the dinner table by using placemats that show the outlines of the silverware, plates, and cups.

At school, help him organize his desk by dividing the inside into sections using colored tape: books go over here, pencils in this section, show and tell items in this square in the corner, and so forth.

Doing Household Chores: Create a family chore chart with pictures and names of family members horizontally across the top of the chart, and then vertically down in columns under each name a series of hooks or pockets. Chores can be put on thick pieces of cardboard and hung from the hooks or placed in the pockets to indicate which individuals are responsible for which chores that day, week, or month. Rotating chores helps keep the experience fresh for your child. Color-code chore tags or paste pictures on them to represent the work involved.

Building Up to Self-Organization: Make sure that your child is involved in the creation of organizational materials. One of the things that bothers me with some of the A.D.D.-related products is that they tend toward bureaucratic overorganization. The poor child can be inundated with mass-produced forms of all kinds: checklists, schedules, calendars, planning sheets, assignment sheets, reward cards, grade sheets, and more. If these materials are simply imposed from without, then they'll probably have little impact. It's probably a better idea to let your child design some of his own forms. Then he's likely to be motivated to use them. Some organizational ideas won't work with your child no matter how long you spend trying to get him to use them. Try out a few of the ideas shared above and see which ones work. In time, and with proper guidance from you and his school, your child will discover those organizational techniques that help him manage his life more effectively.

Resources

Tony Buzan, *Use Both Sides of Your Brain* (New York: Dutton, 1974). This book shows special learning techniques to help your child study, read, problem-solve and think more efficiently and creatively.

Faith Clark and Cecil Clark, *Hasslefree Homework* (New York: Doubleday, 1989). This book provides excellent strategies for creating schedules, planning projects, and keeping a homework journal.

Bobbi DePorter and Mike Hernacki, *Quantum Learning* (New York: Dell, 1992). In this book you'll find specific tips for test taking, note taking, remembering facts, and reading comprehension.

Lawrence J. Greene, *1001 Ways to Improve Your Child's Schoolwork* (New York: Dell, 1991). This book gives helpful advice on dealing with such issues as disorganization, study distractions, following directions, time management, and working independently.

Nancy Margulies, *Mapping Inner Space* (Tucson, AZ: Zephyr, 1991). This well-illustrated, practical manual describes "mind-mapping" in note-taking, studying, or writing.

#32

Help Your Child Appreciate the Value of Personal Effort

"I can't do that, it's too hard!" "Joey made me goof up!" "Teacher doesn't like me, that's why I'm flunking!" These are three of the one million excuses I've heard in my special education classes. Rather than face a challenge head-on, even a challenge they have the capacity to meet successfully, many of these kids instead cop out and look for forces outside of themselves to explain away their difficulties. Of course, this is understandable, given the cycle of failure that many of these kids have been through. After repeated low grades from teachers, rejection from peers, and criticism from parents and siblings, many of these kids just give up. In fact, there's even a term to describe this condition: *learned helplessness*. Scientists first observed this phenomenon in rats who were intentionally given shocks in laboratory cages. At first they were shocked on only one side of the cage, and the rat would escape by fleeing to the other side. However, when the rats were shocked on both sides of the cage, they soon gave up and took the shock wherever it came. They continued to behave this way even when the experiment went back to the original condition of shock on only one side of the cage. They even displayed signs of helplessness when put in water-filled mazes and would have drowned if not rescued by the scientists. They'd given up on life. Kids who experience repeated failure in the classroom and at home undergo another kind of surrender, a surrender of the spirit, when the light of curiosity, initiative, and effort slowly begins to die out.

Research suggests that many kids identified as A.D.D. or hyperactive experience learned helplessness. They often view things that happen to them as being beyond their control. If they do well on a test, for example, they're likely to see it as due to luck, a kind teacher, or easy questions. If they do poorly on a test, they might ascribe their failure to a bad day, a mean teacher, hard questions, or more devastatingly, to their own lack of natural ability. Unfortunately, for many of these kids, labels like "hyperactive" and "attention deficit disorder" provide a further means of attributing difficulties to external causes ("I can't do that 'cause I'm A.D.D."). The use of medications or behavior modification programs also reinforce the child's tendency to look outside of himself for answers to his problems ("I need my pills [or points] to be good").

Successful students are much more likely to look at factors they *do* have control over—especially their own personal effort—as an explanation for both their successes ("I worked really hard on that assignment") or their failures ("I didn't spend enough time reading that question"). We know that one very important reason Asian students seem to perform so much better academically than American students is because they view personal effort as central to their success or failure. And even in the United States, superteachers such as Jaime Escalante, the calculus teacher featured in the movie *Stand and Deliver*, extol the virtues of *ganas*, a Spanish word Escalante used with his students that means "desire" or "will" to achieve something.

One solution, then, seems to be to encourage students labeled A.D.D. to learn how to attribute their performances at home or at school, whether positive or negative, to personal effort. In fact, this is what some cognitive therapists and educators have already been doing in controlled studies as well as in ongoing training sessions. Students are taught to use positive self-attributions while engaged in academic work ("I need to try hard" or "I need to remember what we learned this morning") and then after receiving the results, to connect their performance with a positive attribution ("I did well because I tried hard and used the tips the teacher gave me" or "I didn't do well because I forgot two of the tips"). In one study where a group of "hyperactive" students were taught specific strategies for remembering pairs of unrelated pictures, and then received attribution training, results showed decreased levels of hyperactivity in the classroom and improved self-control.

At home there are several things you can do to help your child have a greater appreciation for the value of personal effort. First, spend time talking with him about the reasons for his successes and failures in school. You might make a list of all the reasons he comes up with for doing well or poorly in his classwork. Then go over the list together, examining each reason and highlighting the ones he has most control over. Encourage him to create a positive attributional statement such as "I do well when I work hard" or "Good things happen when I try." Perhaps he can even make a poster with his positive statement on it to keep near his study area.

Second, share stories with him of individuals who tried hard and succeeded in life; people like Helen Keller, who overcame deafness and blindness to become a world-famous author, and Thomas Edison, who was hyperactive as a child. (It was Edison who said, "Genius is one percent inspiration and ninety-nine percent perspiration.") Read literature together that reinforces the value of persistence, effort, and initiative, including the fable of the ant and the grasshopper, the tale of the tortoise and the hare, and the stories of John Henry and the Little Engine That Could.

Finally, when you see your child showing good effort, let him know it! Author and educator Dorothy Rich, in her book *MegaSkills*, tells of a study in which four groups of children worked on subtraction problems. Group A was told by a teacher's aide to work hard. Group B was told that they *were* working hard. Group C had contact with the teacher's aide but received no comment. Group D had no contact with the aide at all. The group that was told they were working hard did work harder than the others. They completed 63 percent more problems and got three times as many problems right on the next test. Be a cheerleader for your child, then activate his own "inner cheerleader," and watch his grades and motivation rise.

RESOURCES

Dorothy Rich, *MegaSkills*, rev. ed. (Boston: Houghton Mifflin, 1992). This book focuses on ten key qualities to develop in children to help them succeed in life: confidence, motivation, effort, responsibility, initiative, perseverance, caring, teamwork, common sense, and problem solving.

#33

Take Care of Yourself

Over the years, many parents have called, written, or spoken with me in person about the anguish they have suffered as a result of having a child with special needs. Sometimes this pain occurs as a result of frustrating attempts by the parent to get others—especially the schools—to understand and accept their children. As one parent put it to me in an on-line computer message: "You see, I have a dream that I wake up one day and I don't have to explain why my child is the way he is anymore to anyone." At other times, the frustration stems more from direct conflicts with the child. No parent has expressed this sense of heartache better than a Louisiana mother who wrote me and said, "To be honest, I wish I could trade in this child. . . . By ten a.m., this child has worn me down. I am very unhappy. If this were a husband, I would probably divorce him."

In all of the controversy surrounding appropriate ways of helping children labeled A.D.D., the needs of their parents are all too often ignored. Yet research suggests that these parents are themselves victims—victims of the "system" that refuses to understand their children, victims of their children's unpredictable behavior, and victims of other stresses that make effective parenting especially difficult. In one study using the Parenting Stress Index as a measure, researchers found that mothers of "hyperactive" children reported higher levels of stress than parents of "normal" children. The parents in this study expressed feelings of depression, self-blame, social isolation, and incompetence in parenting skills. In another study, parents of children labeled A.D.D. reported elevated levels of depression and anxiety and experienced more stressful events, such as marital difficulties, divorce, and hospitalization, during the previous year than a control group of parents of "normal" children.

These findings suggest that parents of kids diagnosed as A.D.D. may require as much help as their children in coping with stress. Such parents need to discover strategies for taking care of themselves and need to find ways of getting support from their environment if they are to be of much help to their children. A calmer, happier, and more secure parent is in a much better position to respond appropriately to a child's difficult behaviors than one who is angry, anxious, or insecure. In learning effective ways of taking care of themselves, parents also model important self-help skills for their children. Finally, when parents focus attention on their own needs, they liberate themselves from the tendency to dwell exclusively on their child's problems. They begin to see that the world doesn't revolve around their child's "disability," and that simple realization can provide much-needed distance in a stormy parent-child relationship.

There are many ways you can begin to take care of yourself. Perhaps the most immediate way is to learn how to quickly defuse tension when locked in a power struggle with your child. Sometimes all it takes is a few deep breaths to reduce your stress enough to keep from yelling at your child. At other times, you may need to get away from the situation and find a "time-out" space for relaxing. And there will be times, too, that you'll *really* need to take the pressure off and seek a deeper sense of relaxation and contentment. Some possible methods include meditation, yoga, massage, and simple physical exercises. As always, a healthy diet is essential.

It's also important for you to feel as if you have a life away from your child. Most adults need activities that don't involve children and that bring personal satisfaction, activities such as

- watching movies
- reading
- listening to music
- spending time in nature
- going out for romantic dinners with your spouse
- worshiping and praying
- getting together with friends

- ♦ playing sports
- ♦ watching sports
- ♦ going out for nights on the town (plays, musicals, concerts, etc.)
- ♦ taking bubble baths
- ♦ taking trips, cruises, or vacations
- ♦ gardening

Make sure to build in two or three of these or other similar activities each week so that you have a way of recharging your human batteries on a regular basis.

An instrumental part of your self-care program should involve creating effective support systems for yourself. Research suggests that parents who experience a greater sense of social support (from extended family and community sources) see greater behavioral improvements in their children as they go through parent-training programs. Join a parent support group such as CH.A.D.D., which (despite its philosophical shortcomings, which have been detailed throughout this book) provides an extremely helpful system of local chapters around the country that puts parents in touch with others who are going through many of the same problems with their children. You can also create your own support group by advertising in local papers or by putting cards on bulletin boards in community shops.

Tap family resources such as grandparents or friends of the family in getting support. Sometimes just knowing that you can call a relative or friend to get a word of encouragement, sympathy, or advice helps reduce the burden you might feel in a difficult situation with your child. Community resources are also available to support parents. Some towns have a parental stress hotline you can call for immediate advice (check your phonebook). Also, many communities have special parenting centers that offer classes, counseling, and other resources for struggling parents. Finally, consider professional help—including individual or family psychotherapy—in dealing with your parent-child conflicts. By making *you* the focus of attention for a change, you will discover inner resources to enrich not only your experience as a parent, but your experience as a valuable person in your own right.

Resources

Dorothy Corkill Briggs, *Celebrate Your Self: Enhancing Your Own Self-Esteem* (New York: Doubleday, 1986).

Spencer Johnson, *One Minute for Myself: How to Manage Your Most Valuable Asset* (New York: Avon, 1985).

Alix Kirsta, *The Book of Stress Survival: Identifying and Reducing the Stress in Your Life* (New York: Simon & Schuster, 1986). Included in this book are many exercises using yoga, breathing, massage, acupressure, aromatherapy, time management, and more to reduce stress in your life.

Mildred Newman and Bernard Berkowitz, *How to Be Your Own Best Friend* (New York: Ballantine, 1971).

Barbara Sher and Annie Gottlieb, *Teamworks!* (New York: Warner, 1989). This book includes advice on setting up support groups to help you realize your personal dreams.

CH.A.D.D. (Children and Adults with Attention Deficit Disorder), 499 N.W. 70th Avenue, Suite 109, Plantation, FL 33317; 305-587-3700.

#34

Teach Your Child Focusing Techniques

In Aldous Huxley's utopian novel *Island*, there's a mynah bird who repeatedly cries out the same word to all who are within earshot: "Attention! ... Attention! ... Attention! ..." Huxley seems to be using this bird as a reminder of the importance of being alive, awake, and fully aware of our moment-to-moment existence. The ability to attend to the environment is a necessary capacity that has probably existed from the very beginning of evolution of life-forms. After all, an organism that failed to be attentive to its environment was all too often eaten up by a predator and thus could not pass its genes on to the next generation. In today's society, attention demands have become increasingly complex. For the child labeled A.D.D., such demands have more to do with teacher and parent instructions than with avoiding extinction. Nevertheless, the development of attention does represent a kind of survival skill for these kids—at least in terms of their successful adaptation to the society around them. Can this ability be trained? The answer is a solid yes. For thousands of years, human beings have learned to control attention using specially designed meditative techniques. Yogis, shamans, and other practitioners have trained their minds to shut out distracting thoughts, to develop mental tranquillity, and even to control autonomic functions like heart rate and skin temperature.

Current research suggests that focusing exercises or meditative techniques can be successfully used to help children labeled hyperactive or A.D.D. In one study conducted at St. John's University in New York State, twenty-four children meeting the criteria for A.D.D. practiced a type of meditation that involved slow breathing and repeating aloud the Sanskrit word *ahnam* (meaning "nameless"). The actual speaking of the word was phased out gradually until the children were saying it silently. They were instructed to focus their attention on the word, and if their attention wandered, to bring it back to the word. The length of meditation sessions were gradually increased from two to eight minutes. The children were instructed to meditate at least three times per week at home and to record the day and time on a checklist. After four weeks, they were tested on several measures of attention. Meditators experienced significant decreases in their levels of impulsivity and distractibility and increases in their selective attention compared to a control group. Parent ratings of children's behavior also improved during that time.

There are several different kinds of meditation that can be used to help children learn to focus their attention. Perhaps the easiest technique to use with children on the move is a kind of "roving meditation" that involves helping them simply *notice* things in their environment more closely and with greater depth. In her work with children showing hyperactive symptoms, Psychotherapist Violet Oaklander oftentimes follows their rambling explorations and asks questions designed to help them focus on each experience. "Look at that candle," she'll suggest. "What do you see? Feel the wax. Do you notice the orange part?" Then, when the child's attention changes, she'll move to whatever next catches the child's eye.

Once a child shows the ability to settle his focus upon an object for more than a few moments, this experience can be lengthened by suggesting that he spend time looking at an object intently for as long as he can. You might even turn this into a game by seeing how long he can look at an object and then comparing results with other attempts. Make sure the child sees this as enjoyable and not as a grim task to accomplish. Objects to look at might include a candle, a picture, a favorite toy, a tree, a cloud—anything the child chooses to single out for attention. While it's probably best for children to focus on external objects, it may also be helpful for the child to turn the focus inward and concentrate on her breathing, on a visual image in her mind's eye (for example, her favorite place), on a word (like "focus") or an idea (like "I'm a great student"). Then, when distracting ideas come into her mind, she can learn to simply turn the focus of her attention back to the central thought.

Pick a regular time of about ten to twenty minutes each day to work with your child on one of the attention-training or focusing techniques suggested above. It might help if you take part in this activity with your child. Please note, however, that if these activities appear to simply make your child anxious or confused, then stop doing them. However, if your child thinks they're fun and shows increasing levels of capability over time, then it's probably worthwhile to continue.

Training attention has sometimes been compared to housebreaking a puppy. You place the puppy on the newspaper knowing he will wander off. When he does, you pick the puppy up and place him back on the newspaper. He wanders off again, and you continue to place him on the newspaper repeatedly until he finally learns where to go. The mind can wander like a puppy dog. Many professionals and parents of children labeled A.D.D. testify to the fact that these kids' minds often wander as relentlessly as their bodies. Sometimes this is an asset—it makes for wonderful creativity and the formation of new and innovative ideas. But when the time comes for relatively uncreative tasks like taking a spelling test or remembering to take out the garbage, then the ability to focus on the job at hand may turn out to be quite important to your child's successful adjustment to life.

R E S O U R C E S

Deborah Rozman, *Meditation for Children* (Millbrae, CA: Celestial Arts, 1976).

35

Provide Immediate Feedback

When I was a special education teacher, I had a student named Ralph, who was prone to impulsive actions like falling down hysterically on the ground and rolling around on the floor. One day, I brought a camera to school and took a picture of Ralph in one of his "moments." Later on, after he had calmed down, I showed the picture to him and was amazed at the impact it had. He seemed to look at the photo as if the boy in it were someone else. Gradually, though, he began to realize that the person on the floor really was him. I could see little lights go on inside of his head as he started to connect himself to his behavior.

This experience made me realize the importance of providing immediate feedback to kids with behavior and attentional problems. Many of these children go in and out of control without ever becoming aware of the consequences of their actions, without realizing how their actions look to other people, and without really experiencing themselves as the "prime mover" of their behavior. As a result, they find it very difficult to change their behavior. By providing immediate feedback to these kids, we can give them a means of "owning" and taking responsibility for their actions.

Unfortunately, the typical A.D.D. approach to providing feedback is by giving children immediate rewards, such as points or tokens that can be awarded or taken away and eventually traded in for food, toys, and privileges. Such a reward system tends to take the focus off of the child's awareness of his own actions and puts it on a clamor for external reinforcements. This may shape his behavior in a positive direction but doesn't help him confront the reality of his own actions. Fortunately, there are many ways that parents and educators can give kids immediate and frequent experiences of feedback so that they can start to get a real sense of themselves and their impact on the environment.

One of the simplest feedback approaches involves counting. Identify one of your child's problem behaviors (e.g., falling out of his chair) and then count the number of times during the day that this behavior occurs. You might obtain a grocery store counter or some other quick tabulating device to use in keeping track of the behavior. Then, at the end of the day, present the figure to your child in a matter-of-fact way. It's important to give the feedback in a non-judgmental fashion so that your child's defenses aren't aroused. After you've done this for a while, you can have your child keep track of the behavior and tally the results on a graph or chart.

For some children, the feedback will need to be more vivid than a number or even a graph or chart. Purchase an instant camera and take photos of your child when he is demonstrating a behavior you'd like to eliminate. For even more action, use a videocam to record the entire experience. Make sure to show him the photo or play back the videotape as soon after the behavior as possible so that he can more easily connect what he sees on the screen or in the photo to his recent actions. You can also use audiotape (for recording insults or swearing), a behavior diary (to write down specific actions and words used), or a full-length mirror to let your child see for himself what his actions look like the moment he is engaged in them.

You don't need to depend upon technological aids, however, to provide quick behavioral feedback. I've helped students look at their own behaviors by simply imitating what they are doing. If the student falls off their chair, I fall off my chair. If the student whines "I don't wanna do this," I whine too, with the same kinds of inflections and mannerisms. It's important to do this in a way that is non-mocking and non-shaming. A child who feels she is being made fun of will lose the sense of trust that is so important in helping a child develop mastery over her environment. You can also follow the child around and describe verbally what she is doing ("You just pushed a toy off the table, now you've fallen on the ground, now you're running across the room. . . ."). It can also be helpful if you encourage the child to describe exactly what he is doing while he does it. Ultimately, these activities are designed to confront out-of-control kids with a means of observing and then taking charge of their own actions. Although no words may pass between you two (and it's probably wise to avoid long sermons as follow-up to your feedback), when you present your child with accurate, objective, and non-judgmental feedback, essentially you're saying to him: "Is this the way you want to come across to the world?" Many kids, seeing themselves perhaps for the first time, will want to respond, through their responsible actions, with a resounding no!

#36

Provide Your Child with Access to a Computer

I had a mindstorm recently while learning about one of computer technology's most recent innovations: hypermedia. It occurred to me that this leading-edge technology in software design mimics the way that many children who've been labeled ADD actually think. With hypermedia, computer users can move the cursor (a moving light controlled by a mobile "mouse") onto any word or phrase on the screen and by clicking the mouse, they can be shown related information. For example, a person reading Shakespeare's *Romeo and Juliet* might read on a computer screen the line "A rose by any other name would smell as sweet." The person could then click on the word "rose" and be shown other references to roses in Shakespeare's works. Then the person might click on to one of the references and be shown the scene from which that line came, and so on. This process is not unlike the cognitive styles of some individuals labeled A.D.D. One recent book about A.D.D., for example, describes a situation in which "if an adult who has attention deficit [disorder] is mowing the lawn and the bag that catches the grass becomes filled, this individual may make a trip to the garage to empty the bag. He may then note that the car needs to be moved, which may result in his realizing that the oil in the car needs to be changed. The result is that the mowing job gets put on hold." This is hyperthinking! Sure, at times it may take an individual off-track. But it also is a hallmark of a creative and sensitive mind. (Interestingly enough, a number of innovators in computer science, including Apple's maverick wizard Alan Kay, had behavior problems in school.)

Computers seem tailor-made to the needs of many kids who have been labeled A.D.D. Software programs often provide instant feedback (quick answers to questions) and immediate reinforcement (often providing bells and whistles or access to higher levels when the user makes the right choices). They allow the user to control her own pace, thus sidestepping problems that individuals may have complying with external authority. They are often colorful, animated, and graphically interesting to look at. They provide visual, auditory, and tactile stimulation (through use of a mouse, joystick, or keyboard). They are nonjudgmental, take a person from their current level of performance to higher levels in small steps, and can be used alone or with others.

Not surprisingly, then, research suggests that children labeled A.D.D. do very well with computers. In one study, children identified as A.D.D. spent more time and did more problems with computers than with traditional paper-and-pencil tasks. Another study indicated that so-called A.D.D. children attend more closely to software programs that are in the form of games than to straight tutorial programs in which problems are simply put up on the screen to be solved (I like to call these latter programs "electronic worksheets"). Kids labeled A.D.D. also seemed to spend more time on software programs that were relatively unfamiliar to them, and on those that were neither too easy nor too difficult to use.

These findings suggest that parents and teachers should exercise some care in choosing computer software programs for kids who possess "hyperminds." Some software categories that may be particularly inviting include (with specific program titles in parentheses) the following:

- animation programs (Art and Film Director)

- draw and paint programs (Dazzle Draw)

- electronic chess games (Chessmaster)

- spatial problem-solving games (Tetris)

- electronic puzzle kits (Living Jigsaw)

- clip-art programs (The New Print Shop)

- graphic encyclopedias (World GeoGraph)

- singing software (Vocalizer)

- tone-recognition games (Arnold)

- logic games (King's Rule)

- hands-on science experiments (Science Toolkit)

- hands-on Lego models run by computers (Lego Dacta)

- word games (Missing Links)

- interactive storybooks (Just Grandma and Me)

- motion-simulation games (Flight Simulator)

- virtual reality software (Dactyl Nightmare)

- eye-hand coordination games (Shufflepuck Cafe)

- electronic communication bulletin boards (Kidsnet)

- simulation games (Sim City)

- history and geography games (Where in the World Is Carmen Sandiego?)

If you don't have a computer at home, investigate other possibilities, including using a school computer after hours, a computer at the local library, or one at a copy store in your community. Spend time with your child interacting with the software program so that you know that it interests him, is relatively easy to use, and provides an adequate challenge without being too difficult. Do family projects using computers, including playing interactive games, designing greeting cards for holidays using a clip-on art program, and writing family newsletters using a word processing or desktop publishing program. Encourage your child's teacher to use computer software (especially in a game format) to teach reading, math, and other academic skills. And finally, investigate hypertext and hypermedia possibilities. When your child discovers a computer program that "thinks" the same way he does, you might just find that his learning curve suddenly zooms sharply upwards.

RESOURCES

Marion Blank and Laura Berlin, *The Parent's Guide to Educational Software* (Redmond, WA: Microsoft Press, 1991).

Only the Best: The Annual Guide to Highest-Rated Educational Software/ Multimedia for Preschool–Grade 12 (Alexandria, VA: Association for Supervision and Curriculum Development, 1994).

R. Raskin and C. Ellison, *Parents, Kids and Computers: An Activity Guide for Family Fun and Learning* (New York: Random House, 1992).

#37

Consider Family Therapy

If you ever want to raise the hackles of a group of CH.A.D.D. parents, try suggesting to them that A.D.D. may be a result of poor parenting. This, more than anything else you might say (even "A.D.D. does not exist"), will rouse a choir of indignation and anger seldom seen in parent advocacy circles. A defensiveness exists in the A.D.D. community concerning the role of parenting as a potential cause of hyperactive, impulsive, or distractible behaviors in children. When the famous Zametkin study came out in 1991 touting A.D.D. as a biological disorder, the first thing out of the mouths of many A.D.D. experts was a disavowal of the role of parenting in causing A.D.D. "We would hope," Alan Zametkin stated in an interview, "that people would stop blaming parents and bad parenting ... for this problem." Similarly, Sandra F. Thomas, then-president of CH.A.D.D., declared, "Finally, there's going to be recognition that this is not simply bad parenting." A CH.A.D.D. brochure made this position even blunter: "Frustrated, upset, and anxious parents do not cause their children to have A.D.D. On the contrary, A.D.D. children usually cause their parents to be frustrated, upset, and anxious." So now, the tables have been turned. Having troubles with your marriage, job satisfaction, or family life? It could be your A.D.D. child's fault!

Family therapists have a name for this kind of turnaround. They call it *scapegoating*. In family systems theory, each member of a family is seen as an interconnected part of the whole, and each member influences and is influenced by every other member. Problems that arise in individuals within the family are not seen as the unique problem of that person, but rather as a problem in the family system. In this context, hyperactivity in a child may represent a response to some kind of tension existing in the family matrix: between mother and father, between father and *his* father, between siblings, or through other familial combinations.

Regrettably, the identification of one member of the family as A.D.D. or hyperactive makes it all too easy for a family system to continue not to deal with its deeper systemic problems; the problem has effectively been projected onto the child. Professionals then come onto the scene to give official sanction to this scapegoating process. As family therapy pioneer Murray Bowen points out, "Parents can go from one physician to another until the 'feared' defect is finally confirmed by diagnosis. Any defect discovered in physical examination, laboratory tests, and psychological tests can facilitate the projection process. . . . One need listen to such a mother only a few minutes to hear her invoke outside opinions, diagnoses, and tests to validate the projection. . . . Thus, a time-proven principle of good medical practice serves to support the parental projection process in the family." In this perspective, then, an A.D.D. diagnosis may serve to mask deeper family difficulties.

The research is clear that families with A.D.D.-identified kids are not trouble-free. As discussed in earlier sections of this book, there appears to be higher levels of marital distress, parental psychopathology (including depression and anxiety), and other life stresses in such families. A.D.D. experts would argue that most of these problems come about either because of biological factors shared by both parents and child (the genetic "sins" of the father are visited upon the child) or because the biological problems of the child wreak havoc on parental peace of mind ("The kid drove me to it!").

However, when one looks more closely at the inner dynamics of many A.D.D. families, curious things begin to emerge. Why, for example, are A.D.D.-labeled kids more hyperactive, distractible, or impulsive with their mothers than with their fathers, as research suggests? Such findings indicate that A.D.D. symptoms increase or decrease as a function of specific family interconnections. Moreover, a recent study has revealed a strong correlation between marital discord and child behavior problems. The authors of this study commented that "these results are consistent with family theory notions that the child is sometimes the scapegoat of parental distress in the marriage." Although it's true that children's problems certainly affect parental attitudes and behaviors, research indicates (and common sense dictates) a greater influence from parent to child. This, after all, is a biologically directed imperative. Parents, as sustainers and protectors of children's well-being, exercise the critical role in their development, not vice versa. As seen in Chapter 3, even children born with biological predispositions for a more difficult temperament can have these natural traits moderated by parental influence ("parental responses to the child's initial temperament mediated between that temperament and the possibility of the [eventual] development of ... behavioral disturbances"). And even if you believe that A.D.D. *does* cause family problems, researchers suggest that different family structures can significantly affect the outcome of a child's experience with the "disorder."

All of these findings support the use of family therapy as an important potential intervention for many families within an A.D.D.-labeled child. Some family therapists accept the A.D.D. diagnosis and work on helping families cope with the difficulties associated with having a restless or impulsive child in the house. They may provide practical assistance in setting limits, developing effective communication, and enhancing self-esteem. Other family therapists will treat the entire family as the patient and attempt to discover what family patterns, rules, secrets, myths, conflicts, alliances, or other interactions in the family may underlie and even give birth to the A.D.D. symptoms of one family member. Sometimes therapists will look back at cross-generational patterns (including the role of grandparents and other relatives who may have exerted a lasting influence upon current family dynamics) or examine the impact of sibling relationships. Depending upon the therapist and the goals of therapy, family therapy may last a few sessions or go on for several years.

It's especially important to remember that if you decide to consider family therapy as an option, this does not mean that you have to admit responsibility for your child's difficulties. *You are not to blame* for your child's behavioral or attentional problems. What family systems theory suggests is that your child's symptoms do not reside in *him*, but rather are part of a larger structure that includes not only you and your spouse, but your parents and other significant relatives of the present and past. Family therapy, then, offers the possibility not only for the healing of your child, but for your own healing and that of others in your family as well.

RESOURCES

Jane Annunziata and Phyllis Jacobson-Kram, *Solving Your Problems Together: Family Therapy for the Whole Family* (Washington, DC: American Psychological Association, 1994).

Carolyn Foster, *The Family Patterns Workbook* (Los Angeles: Tarcher, 1993).

Both of the following organizations will provide referrals to professional members in your local area:

American Association for Marriage and Family Therapy, 171 K Street, NW, Suite 407, Washington, DC 20006; 202-452-0109.

American Family Therapy Association, 2020 Pennsylvania Avenue, NW, Suite 273, Washington, DC; 202-994-2776.

#38

Teach Problem-Solving Skills

Michael throws a tantrum when he doesn't get to be quarterback in a neighborhood football game. Susan becomes dejected when she receives detention class for constantly coming late to school. Peter complains bitterly that some mean kids punch him during recess.

Each of these children has a problem. Unfortunately, each one also perceives himself as a victim. What each child needs is a proactive way of thinking about his difficulty so that he can come up with solid solutions for dealing with his problem.

Many kids who are labeled A.D.D. have perhaps more than their share of problems: conflicts with parents, squabbles with siblings, school difficulties, peer rejection, and more. Often their response to these problems is to impulsively act out their feelings of anger, disappointment, or rage, rather than deal with the situation directly. At other times, they might respond by shrinking from the challenge and engaging in avoidance behaviors. In fact, many of the classic symptoms of A.D.D. (impulsivity, distractibility, hyperactivity) may at times be nothing more than a child's unthinking reaction to what he perceives as circumstances beyond his control. By teaching children problem-solving skills, we can help them develop alternative ways of confronting life's challenges. When we help kids envision options and develop plans to meet a problem head-on, we're providing them with a way to stop reacting automatically to life through tantrums, fighting, disobeying, forgetting things, lying, being late, and a hundred other ineffective coping strategies. This new-found problem-solving ability can lead to heightened feelings of competence and an enhanced self-image.

Expert problem-solvers are not born—they are made. Problem-solving is a *teachable* skill. In one encouraging study from Toronto's Hospital for Sick Children, twenty-seven boys with attention and behavior problems received individual therapy and had at-home sessions with their families. Half of the boys also received special instruction in problem-solving skills (such as learning how to get along with a sibling or discovering ways of making it to school on time). The parents of those boys who received the additional problem-solving sessions reported the biggest improvement in their children's behaviors. The boys in the problem-solving group also showed the greatest gains on measures of self-esteem.

You can help your child develop problem-solving skills by teaching him a simple four-step plan used by stress-reduction expert Betty B. Youngs in her work with families.

Step 1: *"What's my problem?"*—Help your child define as precisely as possible the nature of his difficulty: not "People are bothering me," but "Johnny slugs me in the arm really hard and it makes me mad!"

Step 2: *"How can I solve it?"*—Assist your child in brainstorming as many solutions as possible. For example: "I could ignore Johnny. I could hit him on the head. I could ask him to stop. I could run and tell the teacher." You may want to have him write these ideas down on a large sheet of paper or individually on index cards that can be arranged and rearranged by order of priority as your child considers his options.

Step 3: *"What's my plan?"*—After your child chooses the *best* option he feels is available to him (and it's important to let *him* choose), you might assist him in thinking about ways to put his plan into action. If he decides, for example, to ask Johnny to stop hitting him, you might help him think about the words he'll use, the timing of his re-quest, and how he might deal with Johnny's possible reactions. If your child feels tentative about putting his plan into action, you could role-play it together first.

Step 4: *"How did I do?"*—After carrying out his action plan, your child needs to learn how to evaluate its results and use what he's learned in solving future problems. If Johnny keeps hitting him, then you might want to help your child examine what went wrong and what he could do differently next time. If the plan succeeded, you can be there to congratulate him on making a wise decision!

You also help your child become an expert problem-solver by modeling it in your own life. The next time you have a problem of your own, whether it's what to do when the TV breaks down (fix it? throw it out? buy a new one?) or handling a rude neighbor who plays music too loud at night (ignore him? talk to him? call the police?), verbalize your thinking processes in the company of your child: "Well, I could call the police, but I tried that last year and he's back doing it. I really should talk to him about it but I'm a little afraid to because he's got such a mean temper. . . ." Consider holding regular family meetings in which each person can bring up problems and get help in solving them. The more experience your child has in confronting and solving the difficulties he encounters in life, the better able he'll be in handling all the little and big frustrations that life brings to his doorstep.

RESOURCES

Linda Schwartz, *What Do You Think? A Kid's Guide to Dealing with Daily Dilemmas* (Santa Barbara, CA: Learning Works, 1993).

39

Offer Your Child Real-Life
Tasks to Do

Psychologist Robert B. Brooks shares the story of working with a troubled boy at McClean's Hospital in Massachusetts. It seems that the kid
was knocking out all the lights on the floor of his residential unit.
Brooks's response was to appoint the boy as a light monitor. His task involved going around the unit and making sure that all the lights were
working, and if they weren't, to replace them. After the boy had assumed his new role, not only did the light breaking cease, but when
other kids with behavior problems on the floor started to break lights,
he intervened and stopped them.

This story illustrates the behavior-changing power of giving children
responsibility for real-life tasks. In my informal survey of teachers' best
practical strategies for helping kids labeled A.D.D., one item that kept
showing up on their lists was "give them something practical to do";
things like collecting milk money, watering the plants, or rewinding the
film projector. From my own experience in teaching kids with behavior
and attentional problems, I can say with absolute certainty that such a
child confronted with a choice between doing a worksheet and setting
up a slide projector will almost always select the projector task. Of
course, there's the element of novelty to consider: they do worksheets
every day, but only every once in a while does the chance come around
to set up a projector. However, more significantly, the projector task is

real. People out in the real world don't do worksheets. But they *do* set up projectors.

When parents and teachers give children with attention and behavior difficulties real things to do, several things happen that serve to transform them. First, the child is treated with respect. The adult is essentially telling the child "Hey, I trust you to do this very important job." As a result, the child rises to this higher expectation and becomes responsible. Second, they're given an opportunity to interact with the real world. As children enter grade school, they start to take a special interest in the practical workings of the culture around them. Real-life jobs offer them the opportunity to discover the rules, routines, challenges, and difficulties that are part of being a full member of society. Finally, they're able to find out what they're good at. Psychoanalyst Erik Erikson says that children in the elementary school years are engaged in a struggle between the forces of inferiority and industry. They need to have experiences that make them feel like competent, industrious people, or risk emerging from this important life stage with a sense of deep inferiority.

Unfortunately, all too often, children who are labeled as A.D.D. or as having some other problem get placed in special education settings or take part in home-based behavior modification programs that are unreal. The adults around them are vigilant in tracking symptoms of hyperactivity, distractibility, and impulsivity. They're awarded points (or have them deducted), which they tally on pieces of graph paper. They receive smiley faces for doing neat worksheets and math problems. Nowhere else do these sorts of artificial activities occur in life. And not surprisingly, none of this has much relevance to the lives of most of these kids. This may be why the performance of A.D.D.-identified kids improves so much when they are *paid* for their work. At least in these situations they're getting some real money to do these dumb things. But when they're actually given *real* things to do, their performance and behavior often becomes virtually indistinguishable from that of so-called normal people. Perhaps this means kids labeled A.D.D. are normal people too!

There are many real-life jobs and tasks you can offer a child at home or at school that will help him develop competence, responsibility, and a feeling of membership in society. I use the word "offer" because no child should be *made* to do a real-life task just because a parent or teacher thinks it would be *good* for her. The following are only a few of the many possibilities:

At School:

- water the plants
- care for a pet
- tutor another student
- take notes to the office
- straighten the desks
- sharpen the pencils
- run the audio-visual equipment
- be the milk monitor
- collect money for lunch
- clean the gerbil cage
- fix a broken machine
- hand out or pick up student work
- open and close the windows
- take attendance
- be a playground monitor
- serve as a school mediator to resolve disputes
- be a student government officer
- do work in the community
- reshelve books in the library
- serve as a lab assistant in science class
- supervise the computer lab
- maintain the art supplies
- help rearrange desks and/or tables and chairs
- run errands between classrooms
- serve as a hallway monitor

♦ be a "buddy" to a younger child in school

♦ read the announcements over the intercom

♦ volunteer in the school cafeteria

♦ be a janitor's assistant

At Home:

♦ baby-sit

♦ volunteer in the community

♦ fix appliances

♦ take care of the yard

♦ repaint a portion of the house

♦ organize the book, tape, or CD collection

♦ make shelves or other household items

♦ cook regularly for the family

♦ be the "chauffeur" during family outings

♦ do special errands using a bike or car

♦ teach other family members (e.g., how to program the VCR)

♦ run the household's recycling effort

♦ set up a bank account

♦ learn CPR and first-aid skills

♦ specialize in cleaning tasks (e.g., polishing silver, vacuuming)

♦ put in a garden

♦ be the navigator (with map) during family trips

♦ take care of pets

♦ replace light bulbs or other consumables

♦ plan a family trip

♦ set up a sidewalk business

- preside at a family meeting

- repair or repaint furniture

- be the greeter at family parties

- be responsible for recording TV programs

- organize a family sports day or games night

- design greeting cards to send out at holiday time

- take photos for the family album (or videos for the family archives)

- help younger siblings with everyday tasks (e.g., feeding, toileting)

Make sure that the task is not beyond the skill level of your child, or he can end up feeling anxious, incompetent, and/or humiliated. If he really wants to do the job, however, help him learn the requisite skills he needs. Some kids have learned suddenly to read, for example, once they realize they need that skill in order to do something real, like passing a driver's exam or reading a motorcycle repair manual. If your child takes to the task and shows a special aptitude for it, you might want to help him find further opportunities to grow in this area. For example, if he enjoys taking care of the gerbil at school, perhaps you could help him get a volunteer job at a veterinarian's office. This kind of real-life experience as a child can pave the way for a full-fledged career in adulthood.

RESOURCES

Barbara A. Lewis, *The Kids' Guide to Social Action: How to Solve the Social Problems You Choose and Turn Creative Thinking into Positive Action* (Minneapolis: Free Spirit, 1991).

40

Use "Time Out" in a Positive Way

Everyone is familiar with the picture of Dennis the Menace sitting in his little rocking chair in a corner of the room as punishment for misbehavior. For many people, this image conjures up their own personal experiences of either giving or receiving "time out" as a discipline method. My own memories of time out come from when I was a teacher and had students go to an empty corner of the classroom after they had misbehaved. I remember negative experiences—students kicking chairs in the corner, smirking and making funny noises from behind the walled enclosure, and refusing to go, thus forcing me to drag them there. Yet there were also some positive experiences. I especially remember times when students chose to go to the time-out area voluntarily when they felt out of control. It seemed to me that when they actually chose to go to the "time-out" area—rather than being sent there as a punishment— they seemed to benefit the most. Sometimes I would even meet with them there, and we'd talk about the reasons for their misbehavior and try to come up with practical solutions for dealing with the problems that were causing them to act out.

Time out is currently a very popular discipline method used in the A.D.D. community. One best-selling book (and accompanying video) shows parents of A.D.D.-labeled kids how to count "1 . . . 2 . . . 3 . . . ," and if the child hasn't complied with the parent's command, they must go to the time-out area for five minutes. A typical dialogue runs like this: " 'Matt, stop poking the dog. That's 1.' Matt continues, enjoying himself. 'That's 2.' Matt continues, not looking up. 'That's 3, take 5.' Matt doesn't move, and is taken to his room yelling." Unfortunately, using time out as a punitive method with many of these kids may actually turn out to be counterproductive. Two prominent A.D.D. researchers noted as part of a broader study that "in general, time-out periods appear to be aversive to hyperactive children. If isolation really has a calming effect on hyperactive children one would expect to see reduced activity during time-out periods. However, [a previous study done by one of the researchers] . . . observed hyperactive children in time-out environments and noted increased rather than decreased activity levels." This may occur as a result of the need for many of these underaroused kids to create their own stimulation in environments that have low levels of stimulation. And even if punitive time out effectively controls a child's behavior in the short run, it may come at a cost to the child's self-respect and sense of dignity.

On the other hand, the time-out experience can be used in a positive way. It can serve as a "break in the action" in which children, after a fight, during a tantrum, or when caught up in a power struggle with authority, can get away from direct identification with the problem and on their own begin to come up with some proactive ways of dealing with their behavior. As Mary Sheedy Kurcinka, author of *The Spirited Child*, puts it, "Think of time out as a basketball coach does: an opportunity to take a break from the action, refresh the body, and pull the game plan back together."

Child discipline experts Jane Nelsen and H. Stephen Glenn counsel parents to explain to their children that all of us—adults and children alike—have times in our lives when we get angry, lose control, or find ourselves frustrated and confused. At such times, it can be helpful to have a place we can go to to sort things out, do things to make ourselves feel better, and put ourselves in a state of mind that will allow us to go back to the problem and face it in a more constructive manner. Nelsen and Glenn suggest that the *children* be the ones to decide when they need to go to a time-out area. They even recommend that parents get a timer that children can set themselves according to the amount of time they feel they need to get themselves together. Places for time out could be anywhere: a bedroom, a special chair, or a bench on the school playground are all suitable. Nelsen and Glenn even tell of a principal who took walks with kids as a way of getting them into a neutral space where problems could be ironed out. If students associate the words *time out* with punishment, you can rename the space. Some suggestions would be thinking corner, quiet space, home base, settling down room, energy place, and centering spot. One teacher called her area "the office" and let kids use it in other ways besides "time out" so that it was associated with positive learning experiences.

Since the purpose of time out has been changed from passive punishment (putting the child in a dull or painfully boring place) to active working out of problems, children can be shown things they can do in the time-out area to help them gain control and feel better inside. This is especially important for kids who *need* stimulation when they go to a time-out space. Some possibilities are self-talk, visualizing an image that helps them cope, meditating, doing physical-relaxation exercises, and thinking about solutions to their problem. I've known of some schools that have special corners equipped with punching bags for kids who need physical and emotional catharsis to help deal with a crisis. In any case, children must begin to see the time-out area as a place for renewal and not a place for pain.

Parents can help create this new mind-set by modeling time out in their own lives. When you're angry or frustrated about something your child has said or done, tell your child that you need time alone to get some distance and think things over. After all, time out can really help you as much as your child during power struggles. It offers an opportunity for a "cooling-down" period. Then, when you both are ready, you can come back from your time-out areas and be in a much better place to talk about problem behaviors and how best to deal with them. Chances are that if more parents took a time out themselves during parent-child conflicts, there would be fewer incidences of child abuse in our country. To those skeptical about positive time out, Nelsen and Glenn insist that it really can work if parents give it enough time (three to six weeks) and adopt a sincere attitude of encouragement and respect toward the child. "Where did we ever get the crazy idea," Nelsen and Glenn write, "that to make children do better, we must first make them feel worse?" Positive time out provides children with a way to get a grip on their own behavior and allows them to take a major role in becoming successful and capable people.

Resources

Jane Nelsen and H. Stephen Glenn, *Time Out: A Guide for Parents and Teachers Using Popular Discipline Methods to Empower and Encourage Children* (Fair Oaks, CA: Sunrise, 1991). The publishers can be contacted at Sunrise Books, P.O. Box B, Provo, UT 84603; 800-456-7770.

#41

Help Your Child
Develop Social Skills

Three kids are quietly playing a game of cards. Eddie walks into the room, quickly pushes one of the kids, and runs away laughing "Ha! Ha! I got you!" The boys glance up at Eddie and say, almost in unison, "Get lost!" Eddie is confused for a moment, and then runs off in another direction looking for someone else to bother. Eddie is having trouble developing social skills. He would like to make friends with the boys, but he doesn't know how. His own impulsiveness seems to act like a bludgeon on the delicately formed social network created by the boys through the medium of their card game.

Eddie's situation is not unlike that of some kids who've been labeled A.D.D. Their higher level of energy doesn't always agree with the social structures around them. Emotional outbursts, aggressiveness, and hyperactivity may cause peers to reject them. This rejection can create feelings of sadness, anger, and depression, which may in turn fuel more aggressiveness and more negative interactions with peers. It's estimated that as many as 60 percent of all kids identified as A.D.D. may experience some form of social rejection from their peer group.

Social skills are not given to us on a silver platter at birth. We learn them by having them modeled for us by parents, siblings, and others, and by practicing them in our own peer group. Clearly, kids labeled A.D.D. who chronically experience social rejection may greatly benefit from some kind of social-skills training to enable them to master the many different components involved in getting along with others, including such skills as taking turns, sharing, cooperating, communicating, dealing with anger, and abiding by social rules. In one study, conducted at the University of Pittsburgh School of Medicine, kids with attention and behavior problems were sorted into two groups. One group took part in open-ended games, tasks, and other activities. The other group was taught specific social skills through role play, watching videos of social interactions, and through direct instruction. The second group made the greatest gains in observed social interactions outside of the treatment setting.

You don't need to enroll your child in a structured social-skills treatment program, though, to help him develop his interpersonal abilities. There are several ways you can informally support him in getting along better with others. First, encourage your child to participate in social activities in the neighborhood and community. Non-competitive and low-stress settings like an arts-and-crafts program or a swimming class are generally preferable to highly competitive or high-stress environments like Little League or the community soccer team. It's especially helpful if the activity is supervised by an adult who is sensitive to group dynamics and interpersonal relationships and can help your child over the bumpy spots. You can even organize your own neighborhood get-togethers making non-competitive games (see Resources, below) as an excuse for a community event. Second, encourage your child to invite a friend home for an evening of games, snacks, and/or a movie. A child who has at least one good friendship can weather the storm of difficult peer relations in other parts of his life. Third, do role-playing together, using social troubles experienced at school or in the neighborhood as starting points. For example, if your child gets into fights when others tease him, talk with him about some other, nonviolent ways he could respond, and then practice these ways with one of you playing the teaser and the other playing the teased. Then switch roles. You can also use puppets to role-play if your child feels inhibited about dramatizing the events himself.

While role-playing and other forms of social-skills training have their value, it's out in the middle of his own peer-group network that your child will really practice what he's learned from you or others about how to get along. Take time to talk with him after school about any difficult times he had with others. If he describes conflicts, fights, rejection, taunting, or other social problems, ask him how he might deal with the difficulty in another way. Use the four-step problem-solving model shared on pages 208–209 as a framework. Then check back with him after he's had a chance to practice the newly learned skill and evaluate the results.

At school, find out if your child's teacher uses some kind of social-skill-building program, and if not, what sort of informal activities she uses to help build teamwork, caring, and sharing in the classroom. Schools increasingly are using a form of teaching called "cooperative learning" as a basis for instruction. In this approach, students work together in small groups to write papers, develop projects, and finish other assignments. Some schools have "buddy" programs, in which an older student takes a younger one under his wing and helps him deal with school difficulties. If your child's school has such a program, arrange for him to pair up with a "buddy" who has expert social skills and who can serve as an entryway into social circles your child may have been previously barred from entering. Remember that social skills are not instinctual. They are learned. And the more exposure your child has to models of appropriate and healthy social behavior, the more apt he'll be to develop his own people skills as he matures.

R E S O U R C E S

Leanne Domash with Judith Sachs, *Wanna Be My Friend? How to Strengthen Your Child's Social Skills* (New York: Hearst, 1994).

Naomi Drew, *Learning the Skills of Peacemaking* (Rolling Hills Estates, CA: Jalmar, 1987). This book deals with conflict resolution.

Judith B. Erickson, *1994–95 Directory of American Youth Organizations: A Guide to 500 Clubs, Groups, Troops, Teams, Societies, Lodges, and More for Young People* (Minneapolis: Free Spirit, 1994).

Jeanne Gibbs, *Tribes* (Santa Rosa, CA: Center-Source Publications, 1987). This book describes how to use small groups ("tribes") in classrooms for instilling a sense of cooperation, team spirit, and self-esteem in its members.

Terry Orlick, *The Cooperative Sports and Games Book* (New York: Pantheon, 1978).

Tips for Making and Keeping Friends, Poster available from Free Spirit Publishing, 400 First Avenue N., Suite 616, Minneapolis, MN 55401-1730.

Matt Weinstein and Joel Goodman, *Playfair: Everybody's Guide to Noncompetitive Play* (San Luis Obispo, CA: Impact Publications, 1980).

#42

Contract with Your Child

In Grimm's famous fairy tale "The Frog Prince," a princess loses her ball in a deep well. A frog appears who agrees to retrieve the ball if, in return, the princess will let him be her friend. She agrees and the frog brings up the ball. The rest of the story tells of how the princess attempts to renege on her "contract" with the frog but eventually is driven to accept it and take the frog into her life. Her decision proves fortuitous when he finally turns into a handsome prince.

This fairy tale delights children of all ages, but especially those who are starting to move into what German educator Rudolf Steiner called "the heart of childhood": the ages from seven to twelve. During this time, children are actively concerned with rules, responsibilities, and "contracts" of the kind made between the princess and the frog ("If you do this, then I'll do that"). In watching children at this age play ball or other games, we can observe their endless arguments, their fervent negotiations, and their careful determinations of what's "fair." And while some of these discussions seem rather pointless at first glance, it's really through these dialogues that children learn to internalize the social structures of the world around them and become active members of the culture.

I'm rather surprised to discover how infrequently A.D.D. books recommend the use of negotiated contracts as a strategy for improving behavior. For sure, some of these books do suggest using "contingency contracts." But these are usually imposed on the child with little dialogue. "Here's what I expect you to do," says the contract. "And here's what'll happen if you don't do it" (punishment) ... "or here's what'll happen if you do" (reward). Essentially, these are reward-and-punishment programs that masquerade as mutually agreed-upon contracts. If, as A.D.D. expert Russell Barkley suggests, children labeled A.D.D. have specific deficits in "rule-governed behavior," then they need plenty of practice in thinking about and grappling with matters related to the establishment of rules and their enforcement.

You can help provide your child with this valuable lesson in responsibility by contracting with your child on improving difficult behaviors that haven't been solved through the use of other discipline methods. Tell your child that you're concerned about the behavior in question and that you'd like to work out some kind of a solution in the form of a contract. For younger children, you might explain what a contract is by telling them the story of the Frog Prince. For older kids, give examples of the kinds of contracts people engage in during daily life, for example, to buy a house, to take out a loan, to marry, or to begin a job.

Explain that you'd like your child to do something for you, but that in return you'll do something for him. Explain what kind of behavior you currently see (e.g., a messy room) and what sort of behavior you'd like to see (e.g., a clean room). Ask your child if your description of the current state of affairs is accurate and if not, how he sees it. Dialogue until you are both in agreement about the nature of the problem and what a good outcome looks like. Then, tell your child that in return for an improvement in the specified behavior, you're willing to do something for him. Ask him what he'd like to receive as a reward for keeping his end of the bargain.

Most kids will have plenty of ideas for rewards, and you may find that your child needs to tone down his request to something you feel more comfortable with (e.g., maybe not a trip to Disney World, but perhaps a family outing at a miniature golf course). For children who can't think of anything they'd like, here are some possibilities: toys (e.g., action figures), sports equipment (e.g., a new catcher's mitt), arts and crafts supplies (e.g., a watercolor set), foods (e.g., pizza), family activities (e.g., a weekend trip), privileges (e.g., to go to bed later). For serious offenses, such as hurting other children or stealing things, you might also need to insist that a punishment be added to the contract specifying what will happen if the behavior continues. But make sure to involve your child in the determination of this as well. Usually I am against the use of rewards and punishments to improve behavior, but if the child is involved in their creation, then this process serves to empower and not control him.

Once you've come to an agreement, then draw up a contract. Work together on the wording so that it includes language of his own. Ask him what kind of paper he'd like it to be on (perhaps a huge sheet or one in his favorite color) and whether he'd like to write or type it up himself or whether you or a third party should do it. In drawing up the contract, you might want to suggest that it include photos or pictures of what the undesirable and desirable behaviors look like. Include a time frame so that you can sit down together and evaluate whether the terms of the contract have been fulfilled. Generally speaking, it's preferable to create short-term agreements with quick payoffs (at the end of the day or week) rather than a long-term agreement (end of the month or year). Once the contract is written up, make sure that it's signed by both parties and prominently posted for the both of you (but not others outside the family) to see. Then, when the evaluation time rolls around, sit down with your child and assess the results. Did your child do the desired behavior or continue to do the undesired one? Share any evidence you might have indicating the positive or negative results, and if there is a serious disagreement about the outcome, take it to a family meeting.

Some critics might think that this approach gives too much power over to the child. These disciplinarians would like to establish fixed rules and consequences that are determined and administered by the parent with no arguments. Unfortunately, this perspective ignores the fact that much of the world is built upon agreements and negotiations. A child who grows up in a family where rules are set down and must be obeyed without question moves into the world as an adult with a passive acceptance of life—a decidedly dangerous attitude during times of great change such as ours. On the other hand, a child who has the opportunity to take an active role in his own life moves into the world with strength, determination, and confidence. Don't we owe it to our kids to give them this?

#43

Use Effective
Communication Skills

Several years ago, a well-known comedian included a parent-child dialogue in his comedy routine that went something like this:

Parent: How many times do I have to tell you to pick up your room?
Child: Eight.

People laugh at this because they know that the parent really doesn't expect an answer to her question (or at least not an answer so precise). The question, in fact, was not even really a question; it was more like an "adultism"—one of the many one-liners that come tumbling out of an adult's mouth when she has reached a point of exasperation in dealing with her child's behavior.

When confronted with the disruptive or "mother-deaf" behaviors of a child, many parents have an almost irresistible impulse to nag, cajole, threaten, lecture, confront, judge, criticize, or ridicule in response. Research shows, in fact, that parents of kids labeled A.D.D. in particular tend to use significantly more commanding and negative statements and fewer neutral and positive communications with their children than the parents of so-called normal children. However, such communications rarely have the intended effect of better-behaved children. More likely, they may worsen an already fractured parent-child relationship. That's why the development of more positive communication patterns between parent and child represents a major ingredient in the effort to improve a child's behavior and a parent's peace of mind.

Unfortunately, it appears that in the A.D.D. community, the major focus thus far in improving family communication patterns has been in instructing parents to use more effective "commands" with their kids. Parents are counseled not to "argue" with children when they misbehave, but to state the desired behavior and the consequence of not behaving as succinctly as possible: for example, "If you don't pick up your toys right now, then you'll have to go to the time-out area." While this may be effective from a strictly behavioral point of view, it leaves out a world of communication. In fact, parents may find themselves confronted with this ultimatum precisely because they left out crucial communication steps leading up to it.

Discipline experts H. Stephen Glenn and Jane Nelsen suggest that the basis for a successful parent-child relationship is formed from "dialogue based on firmness with dignity and respect." They counsel parents to avoid five basic communication barriers to the development of closeness and trust with their kids:

♦ *Assuming*—"I didn't tell you that because I knew you'd get angry."

♦ *Rescuing*—"Now, remember to take your homework with you to school."

♦ *Directing*—"Pick up your clothes."

♦ *Expecting*—"I thought I could count on you to behave."

♦ *Adultisms*—"You know better than that!"

Instead, they suggest that parents can improve their relationships with their kids immeasurably by employing five communication "builders":

♦ *Checking*—"What were you thinking I wanted you to do?"

♦ *Exploring the what, why, and how*—"What could you do differently?" "Why were you so angry at me?" "How did that happen?"

♦ *Encouraging*—"I would really appreciate it if you could pitch in and get the garage cleaned up."

♦ *Celebrating*—"I think you did a terrific job on your homework assignment."

♦ *Respecting*—"I'd love to hear your ideas for solving this problem."

These positive communications help parents enter into the world of their children to determine what feelings, motivations, and intentions might be underlying their misbehaviors. In addition, these patterns of communication honor children for behavior that is positive. Instead of closing off dialogue through the five barriers to communication, the builders help open up meaningful talk between parent and child; talk that might well lead to the peaceful resolution of conflicts and cut short the need for an "if-then" ultimatum.

A major key to developing positive channels of communication with your child involves the use of *active listening*. This means putting your full attention into listening to your child's concerns, feelings, and needs, and letting him know that you understand. If your child comes bursting into the room in tears, for example, active listening means being able to make eye contact with your child, use a builder communication ("What's going on? Why are you so upset?"), listen carefully to his words ("Billy hit me and then Mary said I was a crybaby"), and then reflect back to him what you've heard and that his feelings are okay ("It sounds like Billy and Mary have been treating you badly. That must have been really upsetting for you."). When children discover that their feelings are acceptable and their experiences are valid, they are much less likely to act them out in undesirable ways. If they do act them out (e.g., your child runs off and pushes his baby sister), you can still acknowledge his feelings while letting him know that certain behaviors are unacceptable ("I know you're feeling hurt inside, but you still need to treat your baby sister with respect.").

Another important communication skill involves the use of "I" messages. When you precede a communication with "I," you personalize it so that your child doesn't feel judged or commanded by an arbitrary and impersonal third force ("I'm really upset with you for hitting your sister" rather than "You've just broken rule number four of the household that says no hitting"). There is a strong tendency when using "You" messages to blame or otherwise project negative feelings onto a child ("You're really acting like a brat" or "You just don't seem to listen" or "You never remember your homework"). Children are likely to respond to these projections with defensiveness and more acting-out behavior. "I" messages, on the other hand, allow kids to see the reasons why their misbehaviors are upsetting and places those problems in a human context where they can be resolved. Parent-training experts Don Dinkmeyer and Gary D. McKay recommend that "I" messages include three elements: a clear description of the behavior, the feeling it creates in you, and the consequences of the behavior. They use a simple formula for remembering how to phrase "I" messages:

1. "When ..." ("When you muddied up the kitchen floor ...")

2. "I feel ..." ("... I felt angry ...")

3. "... because ..." ("... because I had spent the whole morning cleaning and polishing it for the party this evening!")

This kind of communication allows children to see directly how their actions impact upon the environment, and more importantly, it does it without blaming or judging.

Finally, pay attention to non-verbal communication. Experts in the field of kinetics (body-motion studies) suggest that humans can produce almost three-quarters of a million different gestures, postures, and facial expressions in communicating messages from one person to another. Add vocal inflection and other non-verbal factors to the mix and you can see how complex the patterns of communication can be between people. Make sure that your non-verbal message matches your verbal one or your child may easily become confused (e.g., telling your child that "breaking the end table is not a big deal" while your face turns red with anger). To put you on the right track with your child, you might want to get help in developing communication skills. Many neighborhood organizations, such as schools, community centers, health centers, churches and synagogues, adult education programs, and civic groups, offer training in effective parent communication. Or you may want to work more intensively with a psychologist or other certified helping professional. Make sure that whomever you choose has special training and expertise in effective parenting strategies and communication skills. In any case, your efforts to develop positive communication patterns with your child are likely to be richly rewarded with a closer parent-child relationship—one that has fewer "kinks" and more "links" in it.

RESOURCES

Don Dinkmeyer and Gary D. McKay, *S.T.E.P. (Systematic Training for Effective Parenting): The Parent's Handbook* (Circle Pines, MN: American Guidance Services, 1989).

Adele Faber and Elaine Mazlish, *How to Talk So Kids Will Listen and Listen So Kids Will Talk* (New York: Avon, 1982).

H. Stephen Glenn and Jane Nelsen, *Raising Self-Reliant Children in a Self-Indulgent World* (Rocklin, CA: Prima, 1989).

Thomas Gordon, *P.E.T. (Parent Effectiveness Training)* (New York: Plume, 1991).

Shad Helmstetter, *What to Say When You Talk to Your Kids* (New York: Pocket Books, 1989).

44

Give Your Child Choices

One of the most heart-wrenching experiences I ever had as a teacher was sitting through a meeting at school in which one of my students was being confronted on a massive scale with his problem behavior. On one side sat the principal, myself, another teacher, and the boy's mother. On the other side was the boy. I could see the tension rise as the accusations flew. Finally, the boy couldn't stand it any longer and bolted from his chair. He ran into another administrative office, where he was cornered by everyone else in the meeting. At this point, he simply lost control and sobbed, struggled, and raged while four adults attempted to control him. This boy was like a wounded animal. Cornered and powerless, he fluttered and shuddered like a bird caught in the jaws of a cool predator.

This child acted as he did in part because he had lost the power to choose his destiny. No one had asked him whether he wanted to attend this meeting. No one had asked him what his own ideas were for dealing with the problems in the classroom. No one had even asked him years before whether he wanted to go to a special class or remain in the regular classroom. The boy's situation is not unlike that of many children who are given school labels and put in special classrooms. Few such children are ever given the opportunity of having an important say in the decision-making process that will affect their educational futures. Many children are not even given a chance to attend special school meetings at which their educational placement is being discussed. More to the point with children labeled as A.D.D., few if any of these children have the opportunity to have an important say in whether they're to be medicated (I know of no research study on psychoactive medications that have allowed children to have any role at all in their medical management) or in what other treatment approaches might be used to help them.

This loss of choice can have devastating consequences. Some children will respond with rage, as in the above example. However, many more children will quietly die a slow spiritual death as they find their personal voice ignored and forgotten. Externally, it will appear as if the child has "lost motivation," "become withdrawn," or is depressed (some of these kids are actually labeled as "A.D.D. without hyperactivity"), but essentially what has happened is that their inner flame has gone out. Their passion has been extinguished. Regrettably, many A.D.D.-type programs add insult to injury by providing these children with phony choices. One popular A.D.D. book advises parents of inattentive children to say something like this: "Johnny look at me! You have a choice! Either you clean this room up right now or you will have to go to time-out." That's not a choice! That's an adult dictating to a child the terms of his future behavior.

Giving children labeled A.D.D. choices can have quite a positive impact. Howard Adelman and his colleagues at the UCLA School Mental Health Project have demonstrated that when children with learning and behavior problems are given a say in the decision-making processes regarding their school careers, their motivation level increases and their behavior becomes more appropriate. Similarly, at Purdue University, when non-hyperactive "A.D.D. children" were presented with an opportunity to personally control the slide advance button while engaged in an attention task, their performance increased significantly over a more passive test condition.

When parents and teachers empower "A.D.D. kids" with choices, the children no longer need to manipulate their environment so much through symptoms of hyperactivity or inattention. After all, many of these undesirable behaviors are, at a deeper level, an attempt by these children to exert some kind of control over their surroundings. The act of choosing itself serves almost as a calming and stabilizing force for some kids. As psychotherapist Violet Oaklander observes, "I have watched the most fidgety, restless child stand endlessly in front of construction paper of a variety of colors, making his choice of the three colors he has been told he can choose."

The ability to choose is like a muscle. It gets stronger through use. You can help your child exert his "choice muscles" in several ways. At school, allow him to attend important school meetings at which his educational destiny is being charted, and give him the opportunity to ask questions, make comments, and have his ideas respected and included in the discussion. In the classroom, teachers should provide children with opportunities all through the day for making choices. Such choices might be what math problems to work on ("You can do the problems on page 54 or page 55"), what book to read ("You can read *Tom Sawyer* or *Huckleberry Finn*"), what type of homework to do ("You can write an essay or do a tape-recorded interview with an expert on the subject"), or what sort of long-term project to engage in ("You can do a photo essay, a diorama, a mural, or a play about the Civil War this term"). Also, parents and teachers should have educational materials available with choice built into them. For example, the *Choose-Your-Own-Adventure* reading series allows kids to stop at different points in the story and make choices about what the hero should do. Their choices lead them to any one of a number of story endings. Computer programs also allow kids to make choices. In one software package, the Oregon Trail, children have the opportunity to take a computer journey across the country, deciding what they'll take along and, when confronted with obstacles on the way, how they'll deal with each problem in turn.

At home, let your child choose the time, place, and method for doing chores or homework assignments. If you do use rewards and punishments in shaping your child's behavior, at least let your child be involved in deciding which ones they will be so that he will feel like a partner in his own rehabilitation. Involve him in making family decisions about where to go for dinner or a weekend or summer trip. And when it's time to go to bed, don't give him the false choice of "my way or the highway." Instead, offer him a real choice: "Do you want to go to bed in your blue PJs or your red PJs?" This approach maintains your child's dignity, allows him to flex his choice muscles, and does it all while keeping the "to bed or not to bed" question off the negotiating table. Remember that by giving your child the opportunity to make lots of little choices while he's young, you make it that much more likely he'll make the right decisions later on in life when the big decisions roll around!

Resources

Choose-Your-Own-Adventure series, published by Bantam. Currently there are over twenty volumes available in this fiction series geared to a fourth-grade reading level.

#45

Discover and Treat the Four Types of Misbehavior

The poet Kahlil Gibran, in his well-known poem about children, says, "Your children are not your children / They are the sons and daughters of life's longing for itself." By this, Gibran suggests, among other things, that children are not parents' "property," but rather have their own independent lives and destinies. And indeed, as separate human beings, children are deserving of our deepest respect. These watchwords are especially important when considering appropriate discipline methods for handling children's misbehaviors.

The approach to discipline that best embodies this kind of respect for children is one that has its origins in the work of Alfred Adler, an Austrian psychiatrist who was at one time a disciple of Sigmund Freud. Adler, and his colleague Rudolf Dreikurs, an American psychiatrist, believed that all children's behavior was bent on achieving two goals: to feel a sense of belonging and to be significant. Children who misbehave are trying to reach these two objectives, but they mistakenly believe that they can attain these goals by engaging in activities that those around them experience as troublesome and disturbing. An important step in helping children learn more appropriate ways of behaving involves parents and teachers in a process of discovering the real reasons behind a child's misbehavior and then treating the underlying need.

Rudolf Dreikurs suggests that instances of misbehavior are apt to fall primarily into one of four types:

1. *Children misbehave to gain attention.* When children misbehave in this way, they're trying to feel significant and a sense of belonging by drawing attention to themselves ("You haven't been paying enough attention to me! I want you to notice me and care about me!").

2. *Children misbehave to achieve power.* Here, children are trying to feel important and connected to others by asserting themselves in a strong way ("I can do *what* I want, *where* I want, *when* I want! So there!).

3. *Children misbehave to seek revenge.* Here, children want compensation for the hurt of feeling deprived of importance or a sense of belonging ("So you don't think I matter much, do you? Well, I'll show you a thing or two!").

4. *Children misbehave to assume an attitude of inadequacy.* In this case, children are reacting to perceived loss of importance and belonging by simply giving up. ("Nothing I do makes any difference to you! Well, you can just forget about it! I'm not doing anything anymore!").

It's important to realize that any specific instance of misbehavior a child commits can appear to be of one or more of these four types. So, for example, when Susie knocks the flowerpot off the table, she could be saying "Pay attention to me!" or "I'm more powerful than you!" or "That's what you get for punishing me!" or "I don't care anymore!" If it isn't readily apparent whether the misbehavior is of one type or another, parents and teachers need not despair. There are two main ways Dreikurs suggests that you can uncover the hidden meaning of a child's inappropriate actions.

The first way is to pay attention to your reaction to your child's misbehavior. If you react with irritation or annoyance, chances are the child is looking for attention. If you feel threatened, then power may be the motive. If you feel hurt, then it could be that your child is seeking revenge. And if you start to feel inadequate during or after your child's misbehavior, then you might be dealing with feelings of inadequacy in your child as well.

The second way is to take note of your child's response when you tell her to stop misbehaving. If she stops, then resumes the behavior (or a similar one) later on, it could indicate a desire for attention. If she defies or resists your request to stop, and especially if it continues to escalate, then you could be locked in a power struggle. If she retaliates to your request by saying or doing something hurtful, then revenge could be at work here. And if she adopts a passive-aggressive strategy, trying to wear you down, then feelings of inadequacy might be the underlying issue.

Once you've identified the type of misbehavior, you need to take practical steps to deal with it. Each of the four types requires a somewhat different approach. So, for example, when the issue is attention, you might ignore the behavior or do something unexpected (e.g., sing a funny song in response to a child's attention-getting whining). If, however, the underlying motive is power, then you might need a cooling-off period followed by a problem-solving session to resolve the struggle. If your child seeks revenge, then curbing the urge to retaliate and welcoming cooperation might be ways you could handle the problem. Finally, if your child misbehaves because of feelings of inadequacy, then teaching her the skills in the area of perceived inadequacy, as well as setting up opportunities for her to experience small successes, can go a long way toward redirecting her in a more positive direction. In each of these four cases, children have become discouraged in their attempts to feel important and connected: "A misbehaving child is a discouraged child," says Dreikurs. Consequently, another important strategy, especially when revenge or perceived inadequacy is a motive, involves providing children with gentle encouragement through a friendly, caring, and respectful attitude.

According to Dreikurs, rewards and punishments are not effective ways of helping children achieve their primary goals of feeling significant and a sense of belonging. Punishments violate the dignity of children and breed resentment, a desire for revenge, and a retreat into feelings of low self-worth. Rewards, on the other hand, show a lack of trust and thereby also undermine the dignity of the child. Giving rewards conveys the notion to children that "you can't behave on your own so I have to give you this material incentive." As a result, and as we've seen earlier in this book, children focus their efforts on striving for external rewards rather than dealing with the feelings and needs that gave rise to the misbehavior in the first place.

Some parents might think, "Well, my child is misbehaving because he's A.D.D., not because of these other things, and so he needs medication and behavior modification to control his medical condition." However, just because your child might have a diagnosis of A.D.D. doesn't mean that he's any less human or any less subject to the same need to feel significant and a sense of belonging as any other child. This approach to discipline works as well with children labeled A.D.D. as it does with so-called normal children. Positive-discipline consultant Jane Nelsen shares the story of a teacher named Mr. Gilbert, who teaches children labeled A.D.D. Mr. Gilbert has taught his class about the four types of misbehavior. Each student has signs for the four types attached to the end of popsickle sticks. If a child notices another student misbehaving, he holds up the appropriate sign as a friendly reminder to his classmate. Mr. Gilbert comments that "misbehavior has decreased significantly in my class. The more I get students involved in understanding themselves and each other, and in helping each other in respectful ways, the more belonging and significance they feel. When kids feel belonging and significance, they don't feel the need to misbehave."

RESOURCES

Rudolf Dreikurs and Vicki Soltz, *Children: The Challenge* (New York: Hawthorn, 1964).
Jane Nelsen, *Positive Discipline* (New York: Ballantine, 1987).

46

Establish Consistent Rules, Routines, and Transitions

Probably the hardest thing I had to learn as a teacher was how to be consistent. Students misbehaved and I reacted in knee-jerk fashion, using whatever method came to me in the moment: yelling, arguing, pleading, reasoning, cajoling, humoring, or even giving "the evil eye." If the misbehavior continued, I brought out the big guns and inconsistently applied such approaches as keeping students after school, referring them to the principal, calling parents, or sending them to a time-out area. During my first two years in the classroom, I bounced like a Ping-Pong ball between the extremes of being an overly permissive teacher on the one side, and a rigidly conservative disciplinarian on the other. About the beginning of the third year, I began to discover the joys of consistency, and one of the greatest compliments I ever received was in response to something I said I was going to do to follow up a misbehavior. I overheard a thirteen-year-old boy in a special day class whisper to a friend, "I really believe that he's going to do it!"

I later discovered that what I was going through in my efforts to provide consistency in the classroom had parallels in the dynamics of family discipline. Some of the best research we have on what makes for healthy parenting comes to us from the Institute for Human Development at the University of California at Berkeley. Work done by Diana Baumrind and her colleagues suggest that there are three primary parenting styles. First, there is an *authoritarian* style (what parenting expert Barbara Colaruso calls the "rigid brick wall family"), consisting of dictatorial parents who demand blind obedience from their kids. Such families combine high expectations and high control with low levels of warmth and communication. Second, there is the *permissive* child-rearing style (the "jellyfish family") that is essentially the opposite: high warmth and communication but without much control or clear expectations Finally, the *authoritative* parenting style (the "backbone family") combines the best aspects of both of the first two patterns. These parents provide clear and consistent rules and expectations within the context of a caring and loving family.

Baumrind's research suggests that children who are raised in "backbone families" show the greatest independence, leadership, social responsibility, originality, self-confidence, and achievement orientation. Kids from "rigid brick wall families," on the other hand, tend to be obedient but less independent or confident of themselves, while children in "jellyfish families" seemed worst off of all: they lacked social responsibility, weren't particularly independent, were low in self-confidence, and were high in anxiety.

All children need clear limits and consistent boundaries. But children who themselves are inconsistent in their behavior may need them even more. If a child who already feels like a cue ball caroming around on a pool table has to live in a family where meals are haphazard, rules are inconsistently enforced, and events arise without warning, then he's likely to bounce clear off the table. Consequently, a primary responsibility for parents and teachers of kids who already have behavior difficulties is to provide a safe and protected space at home and at school, a space with consistent rules, regular routines, and efficient transitions to help clear a path through the day.

A look at some of the most successful American businesses reveals that they steer their course using what are called "mission statements" to provide coherence, direction, and inspiration to their employees. Parents and teachers might consider doing the same thing: establish a mission statement that embodies fair rules to govern behavior in the family. Involve your child or student in deciding what rules there should be in the household or classroom. Frame the rules in a positive way (not "No breaking things," but "Respect the property of others"). It's better to have fewer broader rules that encompass many possible incidents than to have many smaller rules to cover every possible contingency. Your family or classroom mission statement should look and sound more like the Constitution than your state's current penal code. Post the statement in a colorful eye-catching way in a common area of the house, like the kitchen or family room. Then make sure violations are consistently dealt with through one or more of the discipline approaches you currently use (e.g., logical consequences, time out, problem-solving, contracting, family meeting).

Kids need consistency in their daily routines as well. At home, see that your child gets up at about the same time every morning, has regularly scheduled meals (preferably with other family members), and goes to bed about the same time every evening. Create a special daily and/or weekly calendar with your child where he can write in or draw events that are coming up. Keep this calendar posted near the mission statement or in the child's bedroom. If your child has trouble anticipating these events, use music to help signal their coming. For example, you might have a special "getting up" piece of music (e.g., Irving Berlin's "Oh, How I Hate to Get Up in the Morning"), a "going to eat" music (e.g., "Food, Glorious Food" from the musical *Oliver!)*, and a "time for bed" music (e.g., "Goodnight" from the Beatles' "White Album"). To remind him that it's time to do his chores, you could put on a song like "Heigh-Ho" ("It's off to work we go!") from *Snow White and the Seven Dwarfs*.

At school, similar principles apply. Let children know five to ten minutes in advance that it's going to be time to put away materials and prepare for the next class or assignment. You can tell them this verbally, or by using music, a physical gesture, a picture, or by playing "telephone" (e.g., whisper "start to get ready for lunch" to one child, who then must whisper it to another child and so on down the line). It's also helpful to provide children with gradual transitions in moving from highly active events to quieter tasks. So, for example, it might be difficult for kids to come in from a rough ballgame on the playground and have to immediately sit quietly for a test. So, when kids come in from recess, plan a cooperative game or group-sharing activity first to allow some space for gradual calming down, and then follow that with a quiet time for study.

If unpredictable events are brewing on the horizon, prepare your child for them with a few words ("Today when I pick you up at school, we won't be going home. We're going to the airport to welcome Grandma for a visit"). It might be helpful to suggest that your child visualize the new event so that when it comes it won't be so upsetting to his daily routine. If your child's life has been unstable up until now and/or rules have been inconsistently enforced, he may initially respond to the "new consistency" with irritation, anger, or other negative feelings. However, when your consistency is accompanied by a sense of respect and caring for your child, you can rest assured that you're providing him with the "backbone" he'll need in order to make his own way in the world as an adult.

R ESOURCES

Children's Television Workshop, *Parent's Guide to Understanding Discipline*, Family Living Series (New York: Prentice-Hall, 1990).
Robert J. MacKenzie, *Setting Limits: How to Raise Responsible, Independent Children by Providing Reasonable Boundaries* (Rocklin, CA: Prima, 1993).

#47

Hold Family Meetings

When I was a child, my father explained to us one day that he'd like us to participate in a family council. He said that we would meet as a family on a regular basis to discuss issues of concern to everyone. I remember two meetings in particular. At the first meeting, my father shared a grievance: we kids had held a dance party in the basement recreation room and the dancers managed to scuff up the linoleum floor. It was decided that we would have to polish up the floor and not be able to go downstairs (where the television was) for a week. The second meeting I remember was when one of us kids brought up a similar grievance: our parents had held a party downstairs and had done the same thing—they had scuffed up the floor. The decision: they had to polish the floor and no TV for a week.

What stands out for me in these memories is the experience of equality. We children now had a voice in the management of the household and could hold our parents accountable just as they did with us. I didn't know it at the time, but this family council idea was the brainchild of discipline pioneer Rudolf Dreikurs and today is being used more widely than ever. Because family councils (or family meetings, as they are now called) empower children to take responsibility for their own behavior, they represent an attractive non-controlling alternative to the use of behavior modification programs with children who have been labeled A.D.D.

Basically, a family meeting is a regularly scheduled coming-together of all family members to discuss issues of mutual importance. Such meetings function as a place where parents and children alike can share positive experiences, express feelings, plan fun things to do together, establish family rules, settle conflicts, deal with recurring issues, and problem-solve in a cooperative climate. Parents and children function as equals in a family meeting. This democratic structure helps ensure that parents aren't perceived as dictators or autocrats by children in the family, and provides children with opportunities for problem-solving, decision-making, consensus-building, and many other skills important for getting along together in life.

Family meetings work by having members agree to meet at a regularly scheduled time (usually once a week) for a set length of time. (Twenty to thirty minutes is recommended for younger children, one hour for older kids). At the first meeting, a chairperson should be appointed. A parent usually can take on this role initially to model the behaviors for their kids. But the chairperson's role should rotate every week so that each family member has the opportunity to experience being a facilitator. A "scribe," or secretary who is responsible for writing up a summary of the meeting, should also be appointed, and this role should also rotate each week (very young children who haven't developed writing skills yet can keep records using a tape recorder). The basic structure of a meeting looks something like this:

- ◆ summarize previous meeting (e.g., reading of minutes)
- ◆ discuss old business
- ◆ bring up new business
- ◆ summarize the meeting and any decisions made

Minutes of the meeting can be posted during the week so that family members have a reference point for the decisions and agreements made.

In a family meeting, decisions and agreements are usually made by consensus rather than majority rule. The problem with using a majority to make decisions is that the losers are likely to feel disenchanted, may lose interest in the process, and could even seek to sabotage agreements made. Consensus means that family members need to work actively to find a cooperative solution to family issues. Any agreements made through a family meeting are effective until the next meeting. If parents or children are dissatisfied with the results of the agreement at any time during the week, they need to "table" their dissatisfaction until the meeting. (A brief reminder, such as "save it for the meeting" or "bring it up at the meeting," might need to be used.) A special meeting book, however, can be set up where family members can record their feelings and put issues of concern on the agenda for the next meeting.

The structure of family meetings has been successfully transplanted into many schools, where they are called "class meetings." Class meetings were instrumental for me in changing my discipline system over from an externally controlling behavior modification program to an internally empowering mutual problem-solving program. At class meetings, students can share a wide range of issues from dealing with playground bullies and coping with a shortage of art supplies to planning an end-of-semester picnic and questioning the fairness of a class rule. Class meetings work best when students are seated in a circle rather than in rows of desks. As with family meetings, chairperson and secretary roles should rotate. If consensus is difficult to achieve with such a large number of students, then majority rule can serve as the method for coming to agreement.

It's very important, especially at the early stages of holding family meetings, to encourage the involvement of the kids. Parents can easily overwhelm the meeting with their advice, lecturing, ideas, and judgments. Make a conscious effort to hold back at the start and let your children propose suggestions, bring up issues, and plan events. Make sure that the family meeting is upbeat and proactive. If all you do at the meeting is bring up problems, make criticisms, and dole out consequences for misbehavior, your children are likely to lose interest fast. Start your meetings on a positive note by sharing positive experiences and complimenting or appreciating other family members for things that happened during the week. End your meetings with a fun activity such as a game, a sport, or a movie.

Above all, keep the focus on the family. If you have a child who's been labeled A.D.D., then it's likely he's used to being singled out for disruptive or disturbing behaviors. Try very hard not to make family meetings a time of focusing on his problems. As Rudolf Dreikurs says, "The secret of the success of the Family Council lies in the willingness of all members of the family to approach a problem as being a *family* problem." Consequently, if your A.D.D.-identified child's behaviors keep showing up frequently on the meeting agenda, remember to frame his problems as a family issue, seek out his advice in coming up with solutions, put in enough agenda items related to other family members so that he doesn't feel picked on, and give him regular experiences of serving as chairperson and secretary. As your child begins to experience himself more as an equal in the family meetings, his own inner powers of self-control and self-discipline are likely to be activated and used to help solve not only his difficulties but those of other family members as well.

R ESOURCES

Betty Lou Bettner and Amy Lew, *Raising Kids Who Can: Using Family Meeting to Nurture Responsible, Cooperative, Caring, and Happy Children* (New York: HarperCollins, 1992).

Rudolf Dreikurs, R. Corsini, and S. Gould, *Family Council* (Chicago: Henry Regnery, 1974).

Jane Nelsen, Lynn Lott, and H. Stephen Glenn, *Positive Discipline in the Classroom* (Rocklin, CA: Prima, 1993).

Robert Slagle, *A Family Meeting Handbook: Achieving Family Harmony Happily* (Sebastopol, CA: Family Relations Foundation, 1985). The Family Relations Foundation can be contacted at P.O. Box 462, Sebastopol, CA 95472.

#48

Have Your Child Teach
a Younger Child

One of the classic images of American education is the one-room school-house. Although there are few of them left in the country, one aspect of these self-contained educational institutions remains with us as a potent learning and teaching method: cross-age tutoring. Older kids teaching younger ones provides benefits for both, according to the latest research. And for children who have had learning or behavior problems, cross-age tutoring can offer a means of taking on a more responsible role for a welcome change.

Although it may seem as if older tutors have little to gain from the experience of teaching their younger charges, several studies provide support for the old Latin dictum *qui docet dicet* ("One who teaches, learns"). In fact, tutors actually get *more* out of the experience than the tutees. In one program in which a group of high school students with academic deficits and behavior problems worked regularly with young-sters identified as mentally retarded in a nearby elementary school, test results increased from 60 to 85 percent in the high schoolers (compared with 69 to 84 percent for the younger students). In addition, absences of the high school students dropped from once a week to once a month, completion of assignments rose from 66 percent to over 90 percent and most of the tutors chose to continue tutoring after the study was completed.

Cross-age tutoring seems to help the older child for many different reasons. It requires the student to review basic material that may not have been fully mastered the first time around. Also, tutors must think through the processes they teach before presenting them to their younger charges. This helps awaken mental processes that can be applied to course work at their own level. Most importantly, for kids with behavior problems, cross-age tutoring puts them in the "adult" role and thus elicits from them their most responsible social and behavioral skills. It also enhances self-esteem by acknowledging that the tutor is someone who knows something worth teaching.

The literature on cross-age tutoring is full of examples of students who were wild and rebellious in a typical teacher-led classroom, only to show opposite qualities of patience, caring, and authority when helping a younger child learn something new. In one study done at the Fernald Child Study Center at UCLA, researchers compared kids identified as hyperactive with those considered normal in terms of how well they acted as "leaders" for small groups of younger children. The researchers noted that "one boy who was often disruptive and uncooperative told the task coordinator, 'I sure hope the younger kids like me and that I'm able to help them do good [sic] on their projects.' He then went on to be extremely cooperative and task-oriented." In Utah, a group of fifth- and sixth-grade students who had learning and behavior problems successfully taught phonics to a group of first graders who were behind in reading, and improved their own reading skills in the process. And finally, in a program that turned the tables on school labels, a class of twelve "behaviorally disabled" students successfully taught sign language to a group of twenty-four "gifted and talented students" twice each week.

Encourage your child's school to set up a program similar to one of those described above. If a program isn't feasible for financial or logistical reasons, then talk with your child's teacher and see if an informal arrangement can be made for him to leave class for twenty minutes during the day to work with a child in the kindergarten program. It would probably work best if a number of students participated so that your child didn't feel singled out (and possibly feel embarrassed being seen as the only older kid in a kindergarten classroom). Tutoring programs work best when teachers supervise tutors and provide them with simple guidelines in helping their younger students, including avoiding criticism, making the task specific, and giving immediate feedback. Teachers should also think about using other approaches in which students teach other students, including a "buddy system" (in which older kids provide informal assistance for younger students in school-related tasks such as how to use the library or a school computer), peer teaching (in which same-age students teach each other), and cooperative learning (in which small groups of students work together on collaborative projects).

Parents can support cross-age tutoring at home by encouraging their children to work with younger neighborhood friends or younger siblings. Kids can help younger kids with their homework or with simple tasks like learning how to ride a bike, draw a picture, or do a cartwheel. These activities offer your child a chance to share his unique gifts and talents with others. The more opportunities he has to experience himself in the role of "teacher," "expert," or "authority," the easier it will be for him to slough off the negative labels that have accumulated over the years due to behavior and attention problems. Cross-age tutoring suggests that one of the best ways to develop maturity and responsibility isn't by striving to become a model student, but by becoming a model teacher.

#49

Use Natural and
Logical Consequences

Joey is playing roughly with his toy truck and breaks it. Mom comes into the room and yells, "How many times have I told you to be gentle with your things? Go to your room!" Joey runs off crying while mom picks up the toy and throws it in the garbage. A half hour later, mom comes into Joey's room and says, "I hope you've learned your lesson! Tomorrow we'll go to the mall and get you another truck if you're good the rest of the day."

Has Joey learned his lesson? Probably not. More likely, Joey has learned to associate breaking things with anger toward mom for punishing him, and gratefulness toward mom for getting him a new toy. There's nothing in the "lesson" that helps Joey relate the manner in which he plays with toys to their breaking and subsequent loss. In the above scenario, Joey appears to have been disciplined. However, if you look up the word *discipline* in a big dictionary, you'll see that it's derived from the Latin word *discipulus*, meaning "a learner." In other words, *real* discipline implies that a (useful) learning experience has taken place. Joey has only learned that if he breaks another toy, he'll be sent to his room and then be taken to the mall to buy a new one.

The use of natural or logical consequences, on the other hand, is much closer to the true meaning of the word *discipline*. Natural consequences refers to things that happen as a result of the natural flow of events. In the case above, the natural consequence of Joey playing

roughly with the toy is that the toy breaks. A further natural consequence of the toy breaking is that Joey no longer has a functioning toy.
In this case, nature supplies its own consequence and mom really
doesn't have to do anything at all, other than to say something like
"Gee, Joey, I'm sorry your toy broke" and leave it at that. No yelling,
no punishment, and no new toy. Logical consequences are a little bit different. These refer to events created by a parent that are logically related to the child's actions. So, if Joey had been playing roughly with his
sister's toy truck and broke it, then mom might arrange a logical consequence that required Joey to buy his sister a new one using his allowance money.

Natural and logical consequences have several advantages over the
punishment or "response cost" (withdrawal of rewards) approaches that
are commonly used in behavior management programs with kids labeled
A.D.D. First, natural and logical consequences are directly related to a
child's behavior. If a child misses dinner, he'll go hungry. On the other
hand, punishment is rarely related to the child's behavior. A child hits
another child and has TV privileges taken away. While this may stop
the behavior, it provides no lesson for the child concerning why he
needs to stop hurting others. Second, natural and logical consequences
make life the teacher. After leaving his lunch at home and going hungry
at school three days in a row, Paul learns to remember his lunch bag. If
Paul is punished for forgetting his lunch, however, parents become the
"bad guys," and all that likely will happen is that Paul will begin to resent his parents or start to feel bad about himself. Finally, natural and
logical consequences put the child in the driver's seat and allow him to
make the choices. If Susan leaves clothes around her room, they don't
get washed and she has to wear dirty, smelly clothes. It's her choice to
continue this behavior or to begin putting them in the hamper. With
punishment, Susan has no choice—she either has to pick up her room or
get points deducted from her behavior modification program.

The use of natural consequences is the preferred approach of the
two, since the impersonal force of nature or the social order do all the
disciplining. Logical consequences, on the other hand, seem to work best
primarily with behavior motivated by a need for attention. If you're
locked in a power struggle with your child, or your child seeks revenge
for some perceived wrong, he's apt to interpret your efforts to arrange
a "logical" consequence as another example of how you're out to get
him. And if he already feels angry or hurt, he's likely not to care what
consequences you may concoct for him, logical or otherwise.

To apply natural consequences, Rudolf Dreikurs recommends that parents simply ask the question "What would happen if I didn't interfere?" If the toy is lost, there is no toy. If the child misses dinner, he gets hungry. These are inevitable consequences that don't require the intervention of the parent. Of course, if the child is likely to hurt himself with no parental interference (e.g., playing out in traffic), then immediate action in the form of logical consequences may be warranted (e.g., being put in the back yard, where it's safer). To create effective logical consequences, parenting expert Jane Nelsen recommends parents apply the criteria of the 3 Rs: is the proposed consequence *related, respectful,* and *reasonable*? If the child is sent to bed for throwing a tantrum, the consequence is not related to the child's original behavior. If the parent tells a child who just broke a toy, "There! I hope you're satisfied with what you just did!" there's no real respect for the child. And if the child marks up her desk with graffiti and she has to clean every class member's desk as a result, then that's not reasonable.

When employing natural or logical consequences, it's especially important for parents to use a friendly but firm tone when talking with their kids. Avoid threats, sermons, lectures, or other judging or disparaging remarks. "I'm sorry you're hungry, but I can't make an extra meal for you" is much better than: "I told you to come to dinner, but did you listen to me? No! So now you'll just have to learn to live with the consequences of your actions, young lady!" This condemning parental tone turns a natural consequence into a punishment. Rudolf Dreikurs advises that the most important thing to remember in using this method is that the child experience the sense or logic of what he's done. Then it becomes a learning experience. On the other hand, if he feels he's a victim of a punitive parent, even when the consequence is natural or logical, he's unlikely to get the message and may continue to repeat his mistakes. Remember that the real purpose of discipline is not to "teach your kid a lesson!" but to help your child learn new and more positive behaviors for living more responsibly in the world.

RESOURCES

Rudolf Dreikurs and Loren Grey, *Logical Consequences: The New Approach to Discipline* (New York: Plume, 1993).

#50

Hold a Positive Image
of Your Child

Goethe once said, "Treat people as if they were what they ought to be and you help them to become what they are capable of being." This means that we ought to hold in our mind's eye the most positive vision possible of an individual. Our affirmative thoughts serve as a kind of "hope magnet" helping to pull the person closer to her highest potential. One of the biggest problems I have with the A.D.D. myth is that it creates an image of the child based on disease, damage, and deficit—not on asset, affirmation, and advantage. We speak of the "A.D.D. child" as if he had a little A.D.D. virus running around in his brain, or an A.D.D. tattoo somewhere hidden on his anatomy. Soon, the child begins to wear a kind of negative halo that others use to judge his character.

A.D.D. proponents attempt to do some "damage control" by telling labeled kids that they are okay but have a chemical imbalance that makes it hard for them to pay attention or sit still. Children may cooperate with this re-education strategy, but still, many of them are troubled by the labels—both the informal ones that have been used by peers and adults before diagnosis (e.g., "stupid," "wild," "crazy," "space cadet"), as well as the formal label of A.D.D. and others (like LD) that might also be applied to them.

That's why I recommend that parents and professionals avoid using deficit-oriented terms like LD or A.D.D. to describe a child who's experiencing learning or behavior problems. If a child is having trouble at home or in school, the last thing he needs is to be saddled with a new label. What he requires most of all is to be surrounded by adults who see the best in him.

Fortunately, there are a number of new models that can help parents view their children in a much more positive light. St. Paul psychologist Linda Budd has developed a new way of looking at high-energy children she calls *active alert* kids. According to Budd, "active-alerters" possess several characteristics that distinguish them from other kids. These traits include

♦ a high degree of physical activity
♦ a high degree of alertness to the surrounding environment
♦ a bright mind
♦ a tendency to be controlling
♦ fearfulness
♦ intensity
♦ hunger for attention
♦ a fluctuating self-esteem
♦ trouble getting along with others
♦ a tendency to be a performer
♦ an ability to empathize

Budd writes that "although active alert children share the eleven characteristic traits ... they do not all look the same.... One active alert child may be more active than another, one may be more intrusive, and another may need to be the center of attention all the time.... The characteristics that sometimes try your patience and stretch you to the limits of your endurance will at other times intrigue and delight you." While Budd at times seems to differentiate an A.D.D. diagnosis from her active alert term ("a child who has an attention deficit exhibits behavior so extreme that it can only derive from a physiological problem or deficit"), the examples and advice she uses are in many cases quite applicable to a large number of children who have been labeled A.D.D.

Similarly, educator Mary Sheedy Kurcinka uses the term *spirited child* to talk about kids who are more intense, sensitive, perceptive, persistent, and energetic than average. Kurcinka developed the term after being dissatisfied with existing terms when she was looking around for help with her son Joshua. "In fact," says Kurcinka, "the only information I could find that described a kid like him used words such as difficult, strong-willed, stubborn, mother killer, or Dennis the Menace."

Again, Kurcinka is unwilling to meddle with the medical model and won't incorporate A.D.D. into this new term. The distinction she makes between "spirited child" and "A.D.D child" is not very clear though. For example, "the six-year-old who wiggles around and jumps in and out of his chair while he completes his worksheet is a child with an active temperament. The child who pings around the room and never completes his worksheet may be experiencing A.D.D." But there is much in her book *The Spirited Child* that parents of children who've been labeled A.D.D. will find relevant and useful, including making transitions easier, helping kids hear your instructions, choosing your battles in power struggles, spotting the triggers of tantrums, and dealing with mealtime and bedtime problems.

Another intriguing metaphor to characterize children and adults who've been labeled A.D.D. was developed by Thom Hartmann, the director of a residential treatment facility for children and author of the book *Attention Deficit Disorder: A Different Perception*. Looking back into humanity's origins in hunting and farming societies, Hartmann speculates that A.D.D. represents a kind of residual collection of natural adaptive traits developed by the hunters. He contrasts them with their more "responsible" counterparts, the farmers of society (e.g., so-called normal people). He writes that "people with A.D.D. are the leftover hunters, those whose ancestors evolved and matured thousands of years in the past in hunting societies." While it's difficult to take this idea seriously as a historical precedent or genetic trend, the metaphor that Hartmann weaves puts A.D.D. behaviors in a new and more constructive context. According to Hartmann, today's "hunters" constantly monitor the environment just as their ancestors did. Once they see where the action is, they "throw themselves into the hunt." They're flexible and invest incredible bursts of energy into the "hunt." They also think visually and concretely. "Farmers," on the other hand, are not easily distracted, are able to sustain a steady dependable effort, are conscious of time, have patience, and are quite organized. People labeled A.D.D., according to Hartmann, are "hunters in a farmer's world."

While Hartmann's metaphor has us looking backward in time at the remnants of an older society, another positive perspective involves looking at children who have been labeled A.D.D. as part of the vanguard of a new world. One of the most intriguing aspects of kids who've been labeled A.D.D. is the extent to which they, at times, act like much younger children. At the start of the book I mentioned twelve-year-old Manny, who had the curiosity and impulse-control of a toddler. It has been speculated by some researchers that kids who are labeled A.D.D. have a *maturational lag,* or are slower to develop than other kids. Another way of putting this is that these children retain more youthful characteristics than other kids as they grow up. Anthropologists call this tendency *neoteny* (literally, "stretching youth"), and regard it as an evolutionary advance. Princeton anthropologist Ashley Montagu writes in his book *Growing Young* that our society badly needs more people who exhibit a high degree of certain characteristics of very young children, including creativity, playfulness, spontaneity, sensitivity, curiosity, imagination, and a sense of humor. Set in this perspective, many children labeled A.D.D. may actually be carrying characteristics of early childhood up into later childhood and adulthood, where such traits can be incorporated into the culture. This makes it very important that we treat these children with great respect and nurture them so they can make their important contributions to society.

Proponents of the A.D.D. myth sometimes say that the use of the A.D.D. label itself is liberating for many parents and children. Having a name to put to something that has been troubling them for years provides a means of controlling and to some extent triumphing over that experience. It's not unusual for a parent to say, "I used to think my child was crazy ... that I was crazy ... or that my child was lazy and unmotivated.... Now I realize it's all because he's A.D.D.!" I would agree that the use of the term *A.D.D.* is a step up from informal labels like "stupid," "crazy," "brat," "nincompoop," and "menace to society." However, I believe there are further steps up the "label ladder" that one needs to make in constructing a more positive image of these kids. Here is a four-step hierarchy of labels that moves from global-negative views of a child to specific-positive perspectives. Examples of the kinds of terms that exist in each step are as follows:

Step 1. *Informal-judgmental:* stupid, lazy, idiot, jerk, unmotivated

Step 2. *Formal-diagnostic:* school labels, including A.D.D., ADHD, LD, ED, EMR

Step 3. *Informal-positive:* spirited, active-alerter, hunter, right-brained, visual-spatial

Step 4. *De-labeling:* the particular combination of positive traits that makes your child uniquely special

The movement in this model is from essentially negative images to fundamentally positive ones. It also suggests that descriptions that are specifically tailored to an individual child are superior to global formulations that leave plenty of room for stereotyping (e.g., even some of the positive labels like "active-alerter" and "hunter" can lead to stigmas and confining categories that mask the real child). Ideally, the movement should be toward the elimination of *all* labels so that what remains is simply the child himself in all his wonderful uniqueness.

I realize that some parents might have difficulty initially creating a positive image of their children. If you've had to endure years of tantrums, power struggles, defiance, and other difficulties, then positive traits might not spring easily into your mind. However, I'd like to invite you to reframe some of the negative terms you might be using to describe your child into positive terms that can serve as "hope magnets" toward which your child can be pulled. Here are some examples:

Instead of thinking of your child as . . .	*Think of him as . . .*
hyperactive	energetic
impulsive	spontaneous
distractible	creative
a daydreamer	imaginative
inattentive	global thinker with a wide focus
unpredictable	flexible
argumentative	independent
stubborn	committed
irritable	sensitive
aggressive	assertive
attention deficit disordered	unique

Remember that a hyper*active* child is an *alive* child. The energies that many kids labeled A.D.D. possess represent a valuable natural resource that, properly channeled, can really make a difference in the world!

RESOURCES

The Active Alerter. Dr. Linda Budd, 2301 Como Avenue, Suite 204, St. Paul, MN 55108. This newsletter is issued three times a year to update parents on support groups, events, and helpful hints regarding the active alert child.

Linda S. Budd, *Living with the Active Alert Child* (New York: Prentice-Hall, 1990).

Thom Hartmann, *Attention Deficit Disorder: A Different Perception* (Lancaster, PA: Underwood-Miller, 1993). Contact the publisher at Underwood-Miller, 708 Westover Drive, Lancaster, PA 17601.

Mary Sheedy Kurcinka, *Raising Your Spirited Child* (New York: HarperCollins, 1991).

Ashley Montagu, *Growing Young* (New York: McGraw-Hill, 1983).

To contact Thomas Armstrong about doing a presentation on this material, write:

Thomas Armstrong, Ph.D.
P.O. Box 548
Cloverdale, CA 95425

Notes

Preface to the Paperback Edition

Page xiii. The *Washington Post Magazine* article is in Anne Glusker, "Deficit Selling," *The Washington Post Magazine*, March 30, 1997, p. 14.

Page xiii. The link to the "thrill-seeking" gene was reported in G. J. LaHoste et al., "Dopamine D4 Receptor Gene Polymorphism Is Associated with Attention Deficit Hyperactivity Disorder," *Molecular Psychiatry*, 1996, 1, 121–124.

Page xiii. Questions about the "thrill-seeking" gene were raised in A. K. Malhotra et al. "The Association Between the Dopamine D4 Receptor (D4DR) 16 Amino Acid Repeat Polymorphism and Novelty Seeking," *Molecular Psychiatry*, 1996, 1, 388–391.

Page xiv. McGill University research is discussed in Sharon Begley, "Holes in Those Genes," *Newsweek*, January 15, 1996, p. 57.

Page xiv. The correlation between home environment and A.D.D. diagnoses is examined in Joseph Biederman et al. "Family-Environment Risk Factors for Attention-Deficit Hyperactivity Disorder," *Archives of General Psychiatry*, vol. 52, June 1995, pp. 464–469.

Page xiv. Bonnie Cramond's findings on creativity and A.D.D. appear in Bonnie Cramond, "Attention-Deficit Hyperactivity Disorder and Creativity—What Is the Connection?" *The Journal of Creative Behavior*, vol. 38, no. 3, 1994, pp. 193–210.

Page xv. The study of the corpus collosum is summarized in Jay N. Giedd et al. "Quantitative Morphology of the Corpus Collosum in Attention Deficit Hyperactivity Disorder," *American Journal of Psychiatry*, May 1994, pp. 665–668.

Page xv. The quotation about phrenology is by F. Xavier Castellanos, quoted in Kristin Leutwyler, "Paying Attention," *Scientific American*, August 1996, p. 14.

Page xvi. *Forbes* magazine's article appears in Dyan Machan, "An Agreeable Affliction," *Forbes*, August 12, 1996, pp. 148–151.

Page xvii. The DEA report on methylphenidate is in Drug Enforcement Administration, "Methylphenidate: A Background Paper," October 1995, pp. 24–25. To obtain a free copy of this report, write: Drug and Chemical Evaluation Section, Office of Diversion Control, DEA, Washington, D.C. 20537.

Preface

Page xix. For the story of Prince Rilian and the Queen of Underland, see C. S. Lewis, *The Silver Chair* (Book 4 in the *Chronicles of Narnia*) (New York: Macmillan, 1953), pp. 146–158.

In this book, I've chosen to use the generic term "attention deficit disorder" (A.D.D.) rather than the American Psychiatric Association's current diagnostic category of attention deficit hyperactivity disorder (ADHD), because *A.D.D.* is the informal label most commonly understood and used by parents and teachers. When quoting other sources, however, the term *ADHD* may occasionally appear. For a complete description of ADHD and its various subtypes, see *Diagnostic and Statistical Manual of Mental Disorders, Fourth Edition* (Washington, DC: American Psychiatric Association, 1994), pp. 78–85.

Because I do not accept the validity of A.D.D. or hyperactivity as real diagnostic classifications, I usually qualify references to the diagnosis by using quotation marks (e.g., "the 'A.D.D. child,'" "a 'hyperactive child'") or by referring to the identification process itself (e.g., "the A.D.D.-identified child," "the child with the A.D.D. label," etc.).

Chapter 1—America's New Learning Disease

Page 4. Some of the more popular books on A.D.D. for parents include Barbara Ingersoll, *Your Hyperactive Child* (New York: Doubleday, 1988); Robert A. Moss, *Why Johnny Can't Concentrate: Coping with Attention Deficit Problems* (New York: Bantam, 1990); Lisa J. Bain, *A Parent's Guide to Attention Deficit Disorders* (New York: Delta, 1991); and Mary Cahill Fowler, *Maybe You Know My Kid: A Parents' Guide to Identifying, Understanding, and Helping Your Child with Attention Deficit Hyperactivity Disorder* (New York: Carol, 1990).

Page 6. Hoffmann's doggerel is quoted in *The Struwwelpeter: Pretty Stories and Funny Pictures for Little Children* (Munich, ars Edition, 1994).

Still's lectures are found in *Lancet*, April, 1902, pp. 1008–1012, 1077–1082, 1163–1168.

For the impact of the post–World War I encephalitis epidemic on children, see Oliver Sacks, *Awakenings* (New York: Harper Perennial, 1990), p. 17.

Page 7. See Alfred Strauss and Laura Lehtinen, *Psychopathology and Education of the Brain-Injured Child* (New York: Grune & Stratton, 1947).

One of the key books to discredit MBD as a disorder was H. E. Rie and E. D. Rie (eds.), *Handbook of Minimal Brain Dysfunction: A Critical View* (New York: Wiley, 1980). See pp. 18–51 for a good history of the early years leading up to A.D.D.

Virginia Douglas's speech and other details about the history of A.D.D. are cited in Russell A. Barkley, *Attention Deficit Hyperactivity Disorder: A Handbook for Diagnosis and Treatment* (New York: Guilford, 1990), pp. 3–38.

Page 8. See Edward M. Hallowell and John J. Ratey, *Driven to Distraction: Recognizing and Coping with Attention Deficit Disorder from Childhood Through Adulthood* (New York: Pantheon, 1994); and *Answers to Distraction* (New York: Pantheon, 1994).

The *Time* cover story is in Claudia Wallis, "Life in Overdrive," *Time*, July 18, 1994, pp. 43–50.

Page 9. An excellent historical account of psychiatry's use of "moron" and other denigrating terms can be found in Stephen Jay Gould's *The Mismeasure of Man* (New York: W. W. Norton, 1981). See also James W. Trent, *Inventing the Feeble Mind: A History of Mental Retardation in the United States* (Berkeley, CA: University of California Press, 1994).

For a description of the evolving diagnostic categories used by the American Psychiatric Association over the past twenty-five years to designate A.D.D.-type behaviors, see Keith McBurnett, Benjamin Lahey, and Linda Pfiffner, "Diagnosis of Attention Deficit Disorders in *DSM-IV*: Scientific Basis and Implications for Education," *Exceptional Children*, vol. 60, no. 2, pp. 108–117.

Goodman and Poillion are quoted in Gay Goodman and Mary Jo Poillion, "A.D.D.: Acronym for Any Dysfunction or Difficulty," *The Journal of Special Education*, vol. 26, no. 1, 1992, p. 38.

For a description of the public opposition to A.D.D.'s inclusion in federal law as a handicapping condition, and the subsequent issuance of government guidelines, see Susan Moses, "Unusual Coalition Nixes Inclusion of A.D.D. in Bill," *APA Monitor*, November 1990, p. 37; and Susan Moses, "Letter on A.D.D. Kids Gets Mixed Reactions," *APA Monitor*, December 1991, pp. 36–37. (The *APA Monitor* is a publication of the American Psychological Association.)

Page 10. The three ways children labelled A.D.D. could receive services under the Department of Education directive included: 1. if they also had another disability (e.g., LD) that qualified for special services; 2. under the catagory "other health impaired" within current disability laws; 3. under Section 504 of the Rehabilitation Act of 1973.

Costs for diagnosis and evaluation of children for A.D.D. provided in "Attention Deficit Hyperactivity Disorders, A Resource Handbook Prepared for the Board of Directors of the National Association of State Directors of Special Education," January 1991, p. 2.

A recent copy of CH.A.D.D.'s new magazine *Attention!* contains fifty ads (the magazine is only forty-nine pages long) for books, videos, tests, programs, catalogs, camps, lecture schedules, schools, newsletters, audio tapes, and other resources.

One book advertised is Michael Gordon's *How to Operate an ADHD Clinic or Subspecialty Practice* (Dewitt, NY: GSI Publications).

For a description of psychiatry's movement away from psychoanalysis and toward psychopharmacology, see Paul H. Wender and Donald F. Klein, *Mind, Mood, and Medicine: A Guide to the New Biopsychiatry* (New York: Farrar, Straus, Giroux, 1981). For a critique of psychiatry's use of psychoactive drugs, see Peter R. Breggin, *Toxic Psychiatry: Why Therapy, Empathy, and Love Must Replace the Drugs, Electroshock, and Biochemical Theories of the "New Psychiatry"* (New York: St. Martin's, 1991).

For a history of the cognitive movement in psychology, see Howard Gardner, *The Mind's New Science: A History of the Cognitive Revolution* (New York: Basic Books, 1985). For a survey of some of the key topics in cognitive psychology (including attention), see John B. Best, *Cognitive Psychology* (New York: West, 1986).

Chapter 2—A.D.D.: Now You See It, Now You Don't

Page 12. For research on the lack of A.D.D. symptoms in one-to-one relationships with physicians and fathers, see E. K. Sleator and R. L. Ullmann, "Can the Physician Diagnose Hyperactivity in the Office?" *Pediatrics*, vol. 67, 1981, pp. 13–17; and Russell A. Barkley, *Attention Deficit Hyperactivity Disorder: A Handbook for Diagnosis and Treatment* (New York: Guilford, 1990), pp. 56–57.

Page 13. For studies suggesting a lack of differentiation between hyperactive and "normal" kids in self-regulating settings, see R. G. Jacob, K. D. O'Leary, and C. Rosenblad, "Formal and Informal Classroom Settings: Effects on Hyperactivity," *Journal of Abnormal Child Psychology*, vol. 6, no. 1, 1978, pp. 47–59; and Donald H. Sykes, Virginia I. Douglas, and Gert Morgenstern, "Sustained Attention in Hyperactive Children," *Journal of Child Psychology and Psychiatry*, vol. 14, 1973, pp. 213–220.

On paying "hyperactive" children to do assessment tasks, see Diane McGuinness, *When Children Don't Learn* (New York: Basic Books, 1985), p. 205.

On "hyperactive" children's positive responses to novelty and high stimulation, see Sydney S. Zentall, "Behavioral Comparisons of Hyperactive and Normally Active Children in Natural Settings," *Journal of Abnormal Child Psychology*, vol. 8, no. 1, 1980, pp. 93–109; and Sydney S. Zentall and Thomas R. Zentall, "Optimal Stimulation: A Model of Disordered Activity and Performance in Normal and Deviant Children," *Psychological Bulletin*, vol. 94, no. 3, 1983, pp. 446–471.

For research showing the disappearance of hyperactive symptoms in adulthood, see Gabrielle Weiss, Lily Hechtman, Terrye Perlman, Joyce Hopkins, and Albert Wener, "Hyperactives as Young Adults," *Archives of General Psychiatry*, vol. 36, June 1979, pp. 675–681.

Barkley is quoted from Russell A. Barkley, *Attention Deficit Hyperactivity Disorder: A Handbook for Diagnosis and Treatment* (New York: Guilford, 1990), p. 61.

Page 14. The British epidemiological survey is cited in Eric Taylor and Seija Sandberg, "Hyperactive Behavior in English Schoolchildren: A Questionnaire Survey," *Journal of Abnormal Child Psychology*, vol. 12, no. 1, 1984, pp. 143–155.

Figures on prevalence of hyperactivity in Israel are taken from Malka Margalit, "Diagnostic Application of the Conners Abbreviated Symptom Questionnaire," *Journal of Clinical Child Psychology*, 1983, vol. 12, no. 3, pp. 355–357.

U.S. teacher survey of A.D.D.-type symptoms is taken from J. S. Werry and H.C. Quay, "The Prevalence of Behavior Symptoms in Younger Elementary School Children," *American Journal of Orthopsychiatry*, vol. 41, 1971, pp. 136–143.

Parent, teacher, and physician group surveys of hyperactive behavior in children reported in Nadine M. Lambert, Jonathan Sandoval, Dana Sassone, "Prevalence of Hyperactivity in Elementary School Children as a Function of Social System Definers," *American Journal of Orthopsychiatry*, vol. 48, July 1978, pp. 446–463.

Lack of agreement about children's hyperactivity symptoms between mothers and fathers and between parents and teachers is cited in Diane McGuinness, *When Children Don't Learn*, pp. 188–189.

Page 16. Barkley's testimonial on the Gordon Diagnostic System appears in Russell A. Barkley, *Attention Deficit Hyperactivity Disorder*, p. 329.

For criticisms of these and other assessment approaches used to diagnose hyperactivity and/or A.D.D. in children, see Susan Kroener, "Concept Attainment in Normal and Hyperactive Boys as a Function of Stimulus Complexity and Type of Instruction," *Dissertation Abstracts International*, vol. 36, 1975, p. 1913; Lisa S. Fleisher, Leslie C. Soodak, and Marjorie A. Jelin, "Selective Attention Deficits in Learning Disabled Children: Analysis of the Data Base," *Exceptional Children*, vol. 51, no. 2, 1984, pp. 136–141; Richard A. Gardner, *Hyperactivity, the So-called Attention-Deficit Disorder, and the Group of MBD Syndromes* (Cresskill, NJ: Creative Therapeutics, 1987); Russell A. Barkley, *Attention Deficit Hyperactivity Disorder*, pp. 330–332.

Page 17. The Toronto study that failed to find a sustained attention deficit in children labeled A.D.D. is reported in R. Schachar, G. Logan, R. Wachsmuth, and D. Chajczyk, "Attaining and Maintaining Preparation: A Comparison of Attention in Hyperactive, Normal, and Disturbed Control Children," *Journal of Abnormal Child Psychology*, vol. 16, no. 4, 1988, pp. 361–378.

On the Dutch study failing to find evidence for a focused attention deficit in children labeled A.D.D., see Jaab van der Meere and Joseph Sergeant, "Focused Attention in Pervasively Hyperactive Children," *Journal of Abnormal Child Psychology*, vol. 16, no. 6, 1988, pp. 627–639.

For studies that failed to find other attention deficit problems in children labeled A.D.D., see Esther Benezra and Virginia I. Douglas, "Short-Term Serial Recall in ADHD, Normal, and Reading-Disabled Boys," *Journal of Abnormal Child Psychology*, vol. 16, no. 5, 1988, pp. 511–525; and Robert A. Rubinstein and Ronald T. Brown, "An Evaluation of the Validity of the Diagnostic Category of Attention Deficit Disorder," *American Journal of Orthopsychiatry*, vol. 54, 1984, pp. 398–414.

Page 18. For researcher's questioning of the existence of attention deficits and Russell Barkley's proposing of deficits in "rule-governed behavior," see Russell A. Barkley, *Attention Deficit Hyperactivity Disorder*, pp. 26–27.

Pages 18–19. Stanley Milgram's famous experiment on obedience is reported in S. Milgram, "Behavioral Study of Obedience," *Journal of Abnormal and Social Psychology*, vol. 67, 1963, pp. 371–378.

Page 19. For a look at the image of the machine as it affects special education perspectives in general, see L. Heshusius, "At the Heart of the Advocacy Dilemma: A Mechanistic World View," *Exceptional Children*, vol. 49, 1982, pp. 6–11.

See Matthew Galvin, *Otto Learns About His Medicine: A Story About Medication for Hyperactive Children* (New York: Brunner/Mazel, 1988).

Pages 19–20. For a description of how parents are advised to "accept the diagnosis" of A.D.D., see, for example, Lisa J. Bain, *A Parent's Guide to Attention Deficit Disorders*, pp. 150–151.

Page 20. This mechanistic view of the brain is hopelessly outdated and doesn't even make use of longstanding perspectives that use the computer as a model for neuropsychological processes. In fact, current thinking suggests that the brain may function more like a rain forest than a computer. See, for example, Gerald M. Edelman, *Bright Air, Brilliant Fire: On the Matter of the Mind* (New York: Basic Books, 1992).

The Russell Barkley quotation was from a keynote address entitled "Help Me, I'm Losing My Child!" The text is included in the *Proceedings of the CH.A.D.D. Fourth Annual Conference* (Fairfax, VA: Caset Associates, Ltd., 1993), p. 1.

For a survey of some of the proposed causes of hyperactivity, see Dorothea M. Ross and Sheila A. Ross, "Etiology," in *Hyperactivity: Current Issues, Research, and Theory* (New York: John Wiley, 1982). For a rundown of some of the proposed neurological causes of A.D.D., see Cynthia A. Riccio, George W. Hynd, Morris J. Cohen, and Jose J. Gonzalez, "Neurological Basis of Attention Deficit Hyperactivity Disorder," *Exceptional Children*, vol. 60, no. 2, pp. 118–124.

For the much heralded 1990 Zametkin study, see A. J. Zametkin et al., "Cerebral Glucose Metabolism in Adults with Hyperactivity of Childhood Onset," *New England Journal of Medicine*, November 15, 1990, vol. 323, pp. 1361–1366. Interestingly, there were no significant differences between "hyperactive" and "normal" groups on the performance task used in the study, and the "hyperactive" group actually made fewer errors overall!

The national media articles highlighting the Zametkin study include the following: Philip Elmer-DeWitt, "Why Junior Won't Sit Still," *Time*, November 26, 1990, p. 59; Gina Kolata, "Hyperactivity Is Linked to Brain Abnormality," *New York Times*, November 15, 1990, p. A1; Sally Squires, "Brain Function Yields Physical Clue That Could Help Pinpoint Hyperactivity," *The Washington Post*, November 15, 1990, p. A18.

"In November, 1990, parents of children with A.D.D. heaved a collective sigh of relief . . ." is quoted from Jeanne Gehret, "Parent Resource Guide," in *Eagle Eyes: A Child's Guide to Paying Attention* (Fairport, NY: Verbal Images, 1991).

Pages 20–21. Zametkin's study with adolescents was reported in Alan J. Zametkin et al., "Brain Metabolism in Teenagers with Attention Deficit–Hyperactivity Disorder," *Archives of General Psychiatry*, vol. 50, May 1993, pp. 333–340. Strangely, the one major positive finding of this study was that it was now considered feasible to inject adolescent subjects with a radioactive substance to monitor their cerebral processes! More recently, a study by Zametkin and colleagues to see if psychostimulants actually *improved* glucose metabolism in the brains of "ADHD adults" showed no significant effects either. See John A. Matochik et al., "Cerebral Glucose Metabolism in Adults with Attention Deficit Hyperactivity Disorder After Chronic Stimulant Treatment," *American Journal of Psychiatry*, vol. 151, no. 5, May 1994, pp. 658–663.

Page 21. For the University of Nebraska critique of the 1990 Zametkin study, see Robert Reid, John W. Maag, and Stanley F. Vasa, "Attention Deficit Hyperactivity Disorder as a Disability Category: A Critique," *Exceptional Children*, vol. 60, no. 3, p. 203. See also Katherine Tyson, "The Understanding and Treatment of Childhood Hyperactivity: Old Problems and New Approaches," *Smith College Studies in Social Work*, vol. 61, no. 1, March 1991, pp. 137–141.

Page 22. The federal commission on the needs of children is quoted in Nicholas Hobbs, *The Futures of Children* (San Francisco: Jossey-Bass, 1975), p. 81.

For an account of a recent Supreme Court decision upholding a parent's right to sue a school district for reimbursement of private school expenses to treat A.D.D., see Wade F. Horn, "Report from the National Executive Director," *Chadder Box*, January 1994 (*Chadder Box* is a publication of CH.A.D.D.).

Studies on the "self-fulfilling prophecy" are reported in Robert Rosenthal and Lenore Jacobson, *Pygmalion in the Classroom* (New York: Holt, Rinehart, & Winston, 1968); and Robert Rosenthal, "Interpersonal Expectancy Effects: The First 345 Studies," *The Behavioral and Brain Sciences*, vol. 3, 1978, pp. 377–415.

Page 23. For the negative impact of teacher bias on student performance, see J. Sutherland and B. Algozzine, "The Learning Disabled Label as a Biasing Factor in the Visual Motor Performance of Normal Children," *Journal of Learning Disabilities*, vol. 12, 1979, pp. 17–23.

For the negative impact of labels on peer relationships, see Monica J. Harris, Richard Milich, Elizabeth M. Corbitt, Daniel W. Hoover, and Marianne Brady, "Self-Fulfilling Effects of Stigmatizing Information on Children's Social Interactions," *Journal of Personality and Social Psychology*, vol. 63, no. 1, 1992, pp. 41–50.

NASP president Peg Dawson is quoted in the *APA Monitor*, November 1990.

Debra DeLee is quoted from a March 29, 1991, letter to the Office of Special Education Programs by the National Educational Association in response to the federal government's Notice of Inquiry regarding A.D.D.

Chapter 3—Why A.D.D. Is a Simplistic Answer to the Problems of a Complex World

Page 26. Samuel Cartwright is quoted in Samuel A. Cartwright, "Report on the Diseases and Physical Peculiarities of the Negro Race," *The New Orleans Medical and Surgical Journal*, May 1851, p. 707. "Drugging Children: Child Abuse by Professionals," in Gerald P. Koocher (ed.) *Children's Rights and the Mental Health Professions* (New York: Wiley, 1976), p. 219.

Ivan Illich is quoted from Ivan Illich, *Medical Nemesis* (New York: Bantam, 1976), p. 112. For a similar social perspective specifically focusing on hyperactivity, see Peter Conrad, "The Discovery of Hyperkinesis: Notes on the Medicalization of Deviant Behavior," *Social Problems*, vol. 23, 1975, pp. 12–21.

For a classic description of the Protestant work ethic see Max Weber, *The Protestant Ethic and the Spirit of Capitalism* (New York: Macmillan, 1980).

Pages 26–27. Nicholas Hobbs is quoted from Nicholas Hobbs, *The Futures of Children* (San Francisco: Jossey-Bass, 1975), p. 24.

Page 27. Terry Orlick is quoted from Terry Orlick, *Second Cooperative Sports and Games Book* (New York: Pantheon, 1982), p. 128.

For research showing cultural bias in the United States, Japan, China, and Indonesia in diagnosing hyperactivity, see Eberhard M. Mann et al., "Cross-Cultural Differences in Rating Hyperactive-Disruptive Behaviors in Children," *American Journal of Psychiatry*, vol. 149, no. 11, November 1992, pp. 1539–1542.

Pages 27–28. Lester Grinspoon and Susan B. Singer are quoted from Lester Grinspoon and Susan B. Singer, "Amphetamines in the Treatment of Hyperkinetic Children," *Harvard Educational Review*, vol. 43, no. 4, November 1973, pp. 546–547.

Page 28. Statistics on the growth of single-parent households are cited in *Newsweek*, January 10, 1994, p. 44, and are from U.S. Bureau of the Census and U.S. Bureau of Labor Statistics data.

Child-abuse figures are cited in Robert E. Emery, "Family Violence," *American Psychologist*, February 1989, p. 321.

Mental health statistics on children are cited in June M. Tuma, "Mental Health Services for Children," *American Psychologist*, February 1989, p. 188.

Antoinette Saunders and Bonnie Remsberg are quoted from Antoinette Saunders and Bonnie Remsberg, *The Stress-Proof Child* (New York: Signet, 1986), p. 25.

Figures on the incidence of depression and anxiety in children labeled A.D.D. are cited in Joseph Biederman, Jeffrey Newcorn, and Susan Sprich, "Comorbidity of Attention Deficit Hyperactivity Disorder with Conduct, Depressive, Anxiety, and Other Disorders," *American Journal of Psychiatry*, vol. 148, no. 5, May 1991.

On depression possibly playing the major underlying role in hyperactivity, see R. Dennis Staton and Roger A. Brumback, "Non-specificity of Motor Hyperactivity as a Diagnostic Criterion," *Perceptual and Motor Skills*, vol. 52, 1981, p. 220.

Page 29. On the CBS sound-bite experiment, see Richard L. Berke, "Sound Bites Grow at CBS, Then Vanish," *New York Times*, July 11, 1992, p. L7.

Marshall McLuhan's views can be found in Marshall McLuhan and Quentin Fiore, *The Medium Is the Message* (New York: Bantam, 1967), p. 18.

Film critic Arthur Knight was quoted from his book *The Liveliest Art: A Panoramic History of the Movies* (New York: Mentor, 1979), p. 337.

Tony Schwartz was quoted from his book *The Responsive Chord* (Garden City, NY: Doubleday, 1973) pp. 110–111.

Page 30. For research suggesting that kids labeled A.D.D. have difficulty in boring, repetitive, authority-controlled, or maternal-dominated environments, see S. S. Zentall, "Optimal Stimulation as Theoretical Basis of Hyperactivity," *American Journal of Orthopsychiatry*, vol. 45, 1975, pp. 549–563; D. H. Sykes, V. I. Douglas and G. Morgenstern, "Sustained Attention in Hyperactive Children," *Journal of Child Psychology and Psychiatry*, vol. 14, 1973, pp. 213–221; and Russell A. Barkley, *Attention Deficit Hyperactivity Disorder: A Handbook for Diagnosis and Treatment* (New York: Guilford, 1990), pp. 56–57.

Russell Barkley is quoted in Susan Moses, "Hypotheses on ADHD Debated at Conference," *APA Monitor*, February 1990, p. 34.

A very readable account of the Goodlad study can be found in John I. Goodlad, *A Place Called School* (New York: McGraw-Hill, 1984). Quoted material is from pp. 114–115 and 231. Even more telling of the schools' failure to engage all children—thus creating a kind of universal distractibility—is a study done by University of Chicago professor Mihaly Csikszentmihalyi. He rigged up a group of non-labeled (e.g. "normal") high school students with beepers and randomly signaled them throughout the school day. On hearing the beeper, students were instructed to write down what they were thinking of at the moment they were paged. Csikszentmihalyi writes "... in a typical history classroom where the teacher was lecturing about Genghis Khan's invasion of China and conquest of Beijing in 1215, only two out of twenty-seven students were thinking about China when they were signaled. One of the two was remembering the meal he had when he last ate out with his family at a Chinese restaurant, and the other was wondering why Chinese men wore their hair in a ponytail. None mention Genghis Khan or Beijing or 1215." Mihaly Csikszentmihalyi, Kevin Rathunde, and Samuel Whalen, *Talented Teenagers: The Roots of Success and Failure* (New York: Cambridge University Press, 1993), p. 196, n. 2. Quoted in Blythe McVicker Clinchy, "Goals Zoo: The Student as Object," in *Phi Delta Kappan*, Jan. 1995, vol. 76, no. 5, p. 390.

Page 31. Ratios on the proportion of boys to girls identified as A.D.D. are taken from Russell A. Barkley, *Attention Deficit Hyperactivity Disorder*, p. 65.

Pages 31–32. Diane McGuinness's research is described in Diane McGuinness, *When Children Don't Learn*, pp. 190–192; see also J. E. Goggin, "Sex Differences in the Activity Level of Preschool Children as a Possible Precursor of Hyperactivity," *Journal of Genetic Psychology*, vol. 127, 1975, pp. 75–81. Additional research cited by McGuinness is included in Diane McGuinness, *When Children Don't Learn*, p. 84.

Page 32. For more about the theory of temperament, see Alexander Thomas and Stella Chess, *Temperament and Development* (New York: Brunner/Mazel, 1977).

Stanley Turecki was quoted from his book *The Difficult Child* (New York: Bantam, 1989), p. 18.

James Cameron's conclusions are contained in James R. Cameron, "Parental Treatment, Children's Temperament, and the Risk of Childhood Behavioral Problems," *American Journal of Orthopsychiatry*, vol. 48, no. 1, January 1978, p. 146.

Page 33. Cornell University research on incidental memory and hyperactivity is reported in Stephen J. Ceci and Jayne Tishman, "Hyperactivity and Incidental

Memory: Evidence for Attention Diffusion," *Child Development*, vol. 55, no. 6, December 1984, pp. 2192–2203.

Purdue University research on spontaneous talking is presented in Sydney S. Zentall, "Production Deficiencies in Elicited Language but Not in the Spontaneous Verbalizations of Hyperactive Children," *Journal of Abnormal Child Psychology*, vol. 16, no. 6, 1988, pp. 657–673; for a study of the value of spontaneous talk in learning, see Anne Haas Dyson, "The Value of 'Time Off Task': Young Children's Spontaneous Talk and Deliberate Text," *Harvard Educational Review*, vol. 57, no. 4, November 1987, pp. 396ff.

For estimates of the prevalence of "learning disabilities" among children identified as A.D.D., see Joseph Biederman, Jeffrey Newcorn, and Susan Sprich, "Comorbidity of Attention Deficit Hyperactivity Disorder with Conduct, Depressive, Anxiety, and Other Disorders," *American Journal of Psychiatry*, vol. 148, no. 5, May 1991, pp. 571–572.

Pages 33–34. For more on the role that learning problems have in causing attention problems and hyperactivity, see Charles E. Cunningham and Russell A. Barkley, "The Role of Academic Failure in Hyperactive Behavior," *Journal of Learning Disabilities*, vol. 11, no. 5, May 1978, p. 20; and Rob McGee and David L. Share, "Attention Deficit Disorder–Hyperactivity and Academic Failure: Which Comes First and What Should be Treated?" *Journal of the American Academy of Child and Adolescent Psychiatry*, vol. 27, no. 3, 1988, pp. 318–325.

Page 34. On the indistinguishability of "A.D.D. students" from "normal" students in high-stimulation, self-paced classrooms, see Sydney S. Zentall, "Behavioral Comparisons of Hyperactive and Normally Active Children in Natural Settings," *Journal of Abnormal Child Psychology*, vol. 8, no. 1, 1980, pp. 93–109; and Rolf G. Jacob, K. Daniel O'Leary, and Carl Rosenblad, "Formal and Informal Classroom Settings: Effects on Hyperactivity," *Journal of Abnormal Child Psychology*, vol. 6, no. 1, 1978, pp. 47–59.

Chapter 4—What's Good (and Not So Good) About the Good Pill

Pages 36–37. For a brief history of drug use with children, see Dorothea M. Ross and Sheila A. Ross, *Hyperactivity: Current Issues, Research, and Theory* (New York: John Wiley & Sons, 1982), pp. 179–181; see also, Carole Wade Offir, "Are We Pushers for Our Own Children?" *Psychology Today*, December 1974, p. 49; and Peter Schrag and Diane Divoky, *The Myth of the Hyperactive Child: And Other Means of Child Control* (New York: Pantheon, 1975).

Page 38. Charles Bradley's research is reported in Charles Bradley, "The Behavior of Children Receiving Benzedrine," *American Journal of Psychiatry*, vol. 94, November 1937, pp. 577–585.

DEA figures on production quotas of Ritalin came from a telephone communication with the DEA's office of public affairs.

On CH.A.D.D.'s efforts to avert a perceived 1993 Ritalin shortage, see "Nationwide Ritalin Shortage: Delay Sends Parents Scurrying, CH.A.D.D. into Action," *Chadder Box*, November 1993, p. 1.

For information on other medications used to treat A.D.D., see Edna D. Copeland, *Medications for Attention Disorders (ADHD/ADD) and Related Medical Problems* (Atlanta: Southeastern Psychological Institute Press, 1991).

Pages 38–39. For the Baltimore County Health Department's survey of medication use, see Daniel J. Safer and John M. Krager, "A Survey of Medication Treatment for Hyperactive/Inattentive Students," *Journal of the American Medical Association*, vol. 260, no. 15, October 21, 1988, p. 2256.

The report on the surge in variety and acceptance of medications, and the one million children medicated figure, are found in Nina Youngstrom, "Most Child Clinicians Support Prescribing," *APA Monitor*, March 1991, p. 21.

Page 39. Carol Whalen and Barbara Henker are quoted from Carol K. Whalen and Barbara Henker, (eds.), *Hyperactive Children: The Social Ecology of Identification and Treatment* (New York: Academic Press, 1980), p. 45.

For side effects of Cylert, see *Physicians' Desk Reference* (Oradell, NJ: Medical Economics, 1993), pp. 511–512; for side effects of antidepressants, see S. H. Preskorn and G. A. Fast, "Therapeutic Drug Monitoring for Antidepressants: Efficacy, Safety, and Cost Effectiveness," *Journal of Clinical Psychiatry*, vol. 52 (suppl. 6), 1991, pp. 23–33.

On the positive influence of psychostimulants in mother-child interactions: Russell A. Barkley, "Hyperactive Girls and Boys: Stimulant Drug Effects on Mother-Child Interactions," *Journal of Child Psychology and Psychiatry*, vol. 30, no. 3, pp. 379–390.

On the positive influence of Ritalin and teacher-student interactions: Carol K. Whalen, Barbara Henker, and Sharon Dotemoto, "Methylphenidate and Hyperactivity: Effects on Teacher Behaviors," *Science*, vol. 208, June 13, 1980, pp. 1280–1282.

On the positive influence of Ritalin on peer relationships, see Charles E. Cunningham, Linda S. Siegel, and David R. Offord, "A Developmental Dose-Response Analysis of the Effects of Methylphenidate on the Peer Interactions of Attention Deficit Disordered Boys," *Journal of Child Psychology and Psychiatry*, vol. 26, no. 6, 1985, pp. 955–971.

Pages 39–40. For the impact of Ritalin on motor movements, attentiveness, compliance, aggressiveness, and oppositional behavior, see Howard Abikoff and Rachel Gittelman, "The Normalizing Effects of Methylphenidate on the Classroom Behavior of ADD-H Children," *Journal of Abnormal Child Psychology*, vol. 13, no. 1, 1985, pp. 33–44.

For research pointing to the benefits of psychostimulants on "normal" children's thinking and behavior, see J. L. Rapoport et al., "Dextroamphetamine: Cognitive and Behavioral Effects in Normal Prepubertal Boys," *Science*, vol. 199, 1978, pp. 560–563; and H. Weingartner et al., "Cognitive Processes in Normal and Hyperactive Children and Their Response to Amphetamine Treatment," *Journal of Abnormal Psychology*, vol. 89, 1980, pp. 25–37.

Page 40. For the impact of Ritalin on short-term academic and memory skills, see William E. Pelham et al., "Methylphenidate and Children with Attention Deficit Disorder: Dose Effects on Classroom Academic and Social Behavior," *Archives of General Psychiatry*, vol. 42, October 1985, pp. 948–952; and "Methylphenidate and Memory: Dissociated Effects in Hyperactive Children," *Psychopharmacology*, vol. 90, 1986, pp. 211–216.

At the time of this printing, the parent advocacy group CH.A.D.D. was involved in a campaign to get the DEA to change Ritalin to a Schedule III drug, so that it can be more easily made available through physicians to consumers. See "Petition to Reclassify Methylphenidate Field by C.H.A.D.D." *Chadder Box*, January–February 1995.

For a description of the types of drugs contained on the DEA Schedules I–V, see Scott E. Lukas, *Amphetamines: Danger in the Fast Lane* (New York: Chelsea House, 1985), pp. 77–78.

NCAA and U.S. Olympic Committee restrictions on Ritalin are reported in Paul G. Dyment, "Hyperactivity, Stimulants, and Sports," *The Physician and Sportsmedicine*, vol. 18, no. 4, April 1990, p. 22.

The rarity of psychoactive medication use to control children's behavior in Britain is reported in Gabrielle Weiss, "Hyperactivity in Childhood," *The New England Journal of Medicine*, vol. 323, no. 20, November 15, 1990, p. 1414.

Page 41. Side effects of Ritalin are provided by the drug manufacturer, Ciba Geigy, and are reported in the *Physicians' Desk Reference* (Oradell, NJ: Medical Economics, 1994), pp. 835–836.

For information about the dysphoric and socially isolating effects of psychostimulant drug use, see Duane Buhrmester et al., "Prosocial Behavior in Hyperactive Boys: Effects of Stimulant Medication and Comparison with Normal Boys," *Journal of Abnormal Child Psychology*, vol. 20, no. 1, 1992, p. 116.

For the influence of Ritalin on creative behavior in adults, see Thom Hartmann, *Attention Deficit Disorder: A Different Perception* (Novato, CA: Underwood-Miller, 1993), pp. 60–61.

On the "rebound" effect with psychostimulants, see Lisa J. Bain, *A Parent's Guide to Attention Deficit Disorders* (New York: Delta, 1991), p. 97.

Less common side effects are taken from the *Physicians' Desk Reference*, 1994 edition, pp. 835–836.

Recent studies on the impact of Ritalin on physical growth include the following: Rachel Gittelman Klein et al., "Methylphenidate and Growth in Hyperactive Children," *Archives of General Psychiatry*, vol. 45, December 1988, pp. 1127–1130; and Rachel Gittelman Klein and Salvatore Mannuzza, "Hyperactive Boys Almost Grown Up. III. Methylphenidate Effects on Ultimate Height," *Archives of General Psychiatry*, vol. 45, 1988, pp. 1131–1134.

On the ability of Ritalin to activate or aggravate latent or existing conditions, see *Physicians' Desk Reference*, 1994 edition, pp. 835–836.

For case studies of children with serious emotional reactions to Ritalin, see Allan S. Bloom et al., "Methylphenidate-Induced Delusional Disorder in a Child with Attention Deficit Disorder with Hyperactivity," *Journal of the American Academy of*

Child and Adolescent Psychiatry, vol. 27, no. 1, 1988, pp. 88–89; and Troy C. Koehler, M. Strober, and R. Malenbaum, "Methylphenidate-Induced Mania in a Prepubertal Child," *Journal of Clinical Psychiatry*, vol. 47, no. 77, November 1986, pp. 566–567.

Page 42. Gabrielle Weiss's work on children's dislike of psychostimulants is quoted and cited in Alfie Kohn, "Suffer the Restless Children," *Atlantic*, November 1989, p. 98.

For Eleanor Sleator's research on children's dislike of psychostimulants, see Eleanor K. Sleator, Rina K. Ullmann, and Alice von Neumann, "How Do Hyperactive Children Feel About Taking Stimulants and Will They Tell the Doctor?" *Clinical Pediatrics*, vol. 21, no. 8, August 1982, pp. 474–479.

Page 43. For information on the media controversy surrounding the use of Ritalin, see "A Hyperactive Child's Parents Seek the Right to Say No to Drugs," *People*, August 8, 1988, pp. 59–60; and Virginia S. Cowart, "The Ritalin Controversy: What's Made This Drug's Opponents Hyperactive?" *Journal of the American Medical Association*, vol. 259, no. 17, May 6, 1988, pp. 2521–2523.

For information on the impact of the media controversy on sales of Ritalin, see Daniel J. Safer and John M. Krager, "Effect of a Media Blitz and a Threatened Lawsuit on Stimulant Treatment," *Journal of the American Medical Association*, vol. 268, no. 8, August 26, 1992, pp. 1004–1007.

For Ciba Geigy's report on the lack of information regarding long-term safety of Ritalin, see *Physicians' Desk Reference*, 1994 edition, p. 836.

Diane McGuinness is quoted from Diane McGuinness, "Attention Deficit Disorder: The Emperor's Clothes, Animal 'Pharm,' and Other Fiction," in Seymour Fisher and Roger P. Greenberg (eds.), *The Limits of Biological Treatments for Psychological Distress* (Hillsdale, NJ: Lawrence Erlbaum Associates, 1989), p. 171.

On cerebral atrophy in young males who took psychostimulants in childhood, see H. A. Nasrallah et al., "Cortical Atrophy in Young Adults with a History of Hyperactivity in Childhood," *Psychiatry Research*, vol. 17, no. 3, March 1986, pp. 241–246.

For the reference to drug dependence and Ritalin use in the *PDR*, see *Physicians' Desk Reference*, 1994 edition, p. 836.

For the use of Ritalin as an illicit drug in Canada and the United States, see Nora Underwood, "Questions About a Drug," *Maclean's*, April 11, 1988, pp. S10–S11, and Anita Manning, " '90s Teens Find a New High by Abusing Ritalin," *USA Today*, March 14, 1995, p. 1D.

Reports of drug hoarding appear in Carol K. Whalen and Barbara Henker, *Hyperactive Children: The Social Ecology of Identification and Treatment*, p. 44.

Page 44. The follow-up study reporting higher levels of drug abuse in men who had been diagnosed as hyperactive as children is found in Salvatore Mannuzza et al., "Adult Outcome of Hyperactive Boys," *Archives of General Psychiatry*, vol. 50, July 1993, pp. 565–576.

Carol K. Whalen and Barbara Henker are quoted from their book *Hyperactive Children: The Social Ecology of Identification and Treatment*, p. 34.

Jill Ireland's personal account is told in "Shattered for the Second Time: Jill Ireland Fights Cancer, Then a Family Drug Crisis," *Newsweek*, May 9, 1988, p. 66.

Pages 44–45. Peter Jensen's research was summarized in "Kids Talk About the 'Good Pill,'" *Science News*, vol. 135, no. 21, May 27, 1989, p. 332.

Page 45. Carol Whalen and Barbara Henker's statement on children crediting their pills for things that happened in their lives is quoted in Diane Divoky, "Ritalin: Education's Fix-It Drug?" *Phi Delta Kappan*, April 1989, p. 602

Carol Whalen and Barbara Henker's comment on the difficulties of reattributing drug-influenced actions to personal effort appears in their book *Hyperactive Children: The Social Ecology of Identification and Treatment*, p. 3.

The girl's account of how her drug use became known to her circle of peers is given in Carol K. Whalen and Barbara Henker, "Psychostimulants and Children: A Review and Analysis," *Psychological Bulletin*, vol. 83, no. 6, 1976, pp. 1113–1130.

For the impact of drug use in curtailing efforts at working on underlying academic problems, see P. Dianne Byrd and E. Keith Byrd, "Drugs, Academic Achievement, and Hyperactive Children," *The School Counselor*, May 1986, p. 327.

Jerry Weiner is quoted in Robin Marantz Henig, "Courts Enter the Hyperactivity Fray: The Drug Ritalin Helps Control Behavior, But Is It Prescribed Needlessly?" *Washington Post*, March 15, 1988, p. WH8.

Page 46. The Georgia parents' survey is cited in Eloise Salholz, "Behavior Pills: Disciplining Unruly Kids with a Potent Drug," *Newsweek*, April 20, 1987, p. 76.

The AAP's warning on the lack of adequate diagnostic work preceding the prescription of psychostimulants appears in The Committee on Children with Disabilities/Committee on Drugs, "Medication for Children with an Attention Deficit Disorder," *Pediatrics*, vol. 80, no. 5, November 1987, p. 758.

Julian Haber is quoted in Stefanie Weiss, "The Ritalin Controversy," *NEA Today*, September 1989, pp. 10–11.

The zip code check of drug shipments to Atlanta suburbs is cited in William E. Schmidt, "Sales of Drug Are Soaring for Treatment of Hyperactivity," *New York Times*, May 5, 1987, p. C3.

Utah's heavy Ritalin usage is noted in Stefanie Weiss, "The Ritalin Controversy," *NEA Today*, September 1989, p. 10.

Page 47. L. Alan Sroufe is quoted in Alfie Kohn, "Suffer the Restless Children," *Atlantic*, November 1989, p. 95.

Diane McGuinness is quoted from her article "Attention Deficit Disorder: The Emperor's Clothes, Animal 'Pharm,' and Other Fiction," in Seymour Fisher and Roger P. Greenberg (eds.) *The Limits of Biological Treatments for Psychological Distress* (Hillsdale, NJ: Lawrence Erlbaum Associates, 1989), p. 174.

Charles Cunningham and Russell Barkley's review is reported in Charles E. Cunningham and Russell A. Barkley, "The Role of Academic Failure in Hyperactive Behavior," *Journal of Learning Disabilities*, vol. 11, no. 5, May 1978, pp. 15–21.

Judith Rapoport's research is presented in P. O. Quinn and J. L. Rapoport, "One-Year Follow-up of Hyperactive Boys Treated with Imipramine and Methylphenidate," *American Journal of Psychiatry*, vol. 132, 1975, pp. 241–245; and D. Riddle and J. L. Rapoport, "A 2-Year Follow-up of 72 Hyperactive Boys," *Journal of Nervous and Mental Diseases*, vol. 126, 1976, pp. 126–134.

One four-year study showing no impact of Ritalin on academic achievement is L. Charles and R. Schain, "A Four-Year Follow-up Study of the Effects of Methylphenidate on the Behavior and Academic Achievement of Hyperactive Children," *Journal of Abnormal Child Psychology*, vol. 9, 1981, pp. 495–505.

Pages 47–48. On the impact of Ritalin dosage on learning and behavior, see R. Sprague and E. Sleator, "Methylphenidate in Hyperkinetic Children: Differences in Dose Effects on Learning and Social Behavior," *Science*, vol. 198, 1977, pp. 1274–1276.

Page 48. On non-responders to Ritalin, see John DiTraglia, "Methylphenidate Protocol: Feasibility in a Pediatric Practice," *Clinical Pediatrics*, vol. 30, no. 12, December 1991, pp. 656–660.

Sydney Walker is quoted from his article "Drugging the American Child: We're Too Cavalier About Hyperactivity," *Psychology Today*, December 1974, p. 43.

Diane McGuinness's estimates appear in her book *When Children Don't Learn*, p. 229.

Stanley Turecki is quoted from his book *The Difficult Child* (New York: Bantam, 1989), p. 231.

Pages 48–49. The AAP is quoted from Committee on Children with Disabilities/Committee on Drugs, "Medication for Children with an Attention Deficit Disorder," *Pediatrics*, vol. 80, no. 5, November 1987, p. 758.

Page 49. On the side effects accompanying abrupt termination of Ritalin, see *Physicians' Desk Reference*, 1994 edition, p. 836.

Martin Baren's recommendations appear in his article "The Case for Ritalin: A Fresh Look at the Controversy," *Contemporary Pediatrics*, vol. 6, January 1989, pp. 16–28.

William Pelham is quoted in Linda Williams, "Parents and Doctors Fear Growing Misuse of Drug Used to Treat Hyperactive Kids," *Wall Street Journal*, January 15, 1988, p. 21.

Chapter 5—To Control or to Empower: That Is the Question!

Pages 52–54. For examples of compliance-oriented behavior guides popular in the A.D.D. community, see Lee Canter with Marlene Canter, *Assertive Discipline for Parents*, rev. ed. (New York: Harper Perennial, 1988); Thomas W. Phelan, *1-2-3: Magic! Training Your Preschoolers and Preteens to Do What You Want* (Glen Ellyn, IL: Child Management, 1984); and Michael L. Bloomquist, *A Parent's*

Skills Training Guide for Children with Attention Deficits and Disruptive Behavior (Minneapolis: Division of Child and Adolescent Psychiatry, University of Minnesota, 1992), pp. 64–65.

Page 52. To see a wide range of A.D.D. products, consult the A.D.D. WareHouse 1994 catalog, available for no charge by writing to the A.D.D. WareHouse, 300 N.W. 70th Avenue, Suite 102, Plantation, FL 33317. See also Russell A. Barkley, *Attention Deficit Hyperactivity Disorder*, pp. 513–517.

Page 53. The Easter-bunny-removal technique is suggested in Robert A. Moss, *Why Johnny Can't Concentrate: Coping with Attention Deficit Problems* (New York: Bantam, 1990), p. 159.

A simple writing assignment is proposed as an example of an "unpleasant task" in Harvey C. Parker, *The ADD Hyperactivity Handbook for Schools* (Plantation, FL: Impact, 1992), p. 242.

The teacher's guidelines for "neatness" in written work is provided in Harvey C. Parker, *The ADD Hyperactivity Handbook for Schools*, pp. 222–223.

The advice to teachers to use short, simple sentences with "A.D.D. students" is provided in Harvey C. Parker, *The ADD Hyperactivity Handbook for Schools*, p. 138.

Page 54. An example of a guide that counsels student work to be broken up into shorter bits is Lauren Braswell, Michael Bloomquist, and Sheila Pederson, *ADHD: A Guide to Understanding and Helping Children with Attention Deficit Hyperactivity Disorder in School Settings* (Minneapolis: University of Minnesota, 1991), p. 72.

For information about the shortcomings of reward systems in schools, see Alfie Kohn, *Punished by Rewards: The Trouble with Gold Stars, Incentive Plans, A's, Praise, and Other Bribes* (Boston: Houghton Mifflin, 1993).

For a study demonstrating how rewards set people up as rivals, see James Garbarino, "The Impact of Anticipated Reward upon Cross-Age Tutoring," *Journal of Personality and Social Psychology*, vol. 32, 1975, pp. 421–428.

For research demonstrating the dampening impact rewards have on risk-taking, see Charles Pearlman, "The Effects of Level of Effectance Motivation, IQ, and a Penalty/Reward Contingency on the Choice of Problem Difficulty," *Child Development*, vol. 55, 1984, pp. 537–542.

To see how rewards negatively affect creativity, see Teresa M. Amabile, Beth Ann Hennessey, and Barbara S. Grossman, "Social Influences on Creativity: The Effects of Contracted-for Reward," *Journal of Personality and Social Psychology*, vol. 50, 1986, pp. 14–23.

For studies showing the negative impact of rewards upon the behavioral or academic performance of kids labeled A.D.D. or hyperactive, see Philip Firestone and Virginia Douglas, "The Effects of Reward and Punishment on Reaction Times and Autonomic Activity in Hyperactive and Normal Children," *Journal of Abnormal Child Psychology*, vol. 3, 1975, pp. 201–215; Virginia I. Douglas and Penny A. Parry, "Effects of Reward on Delayed Reaction Time Task Performance of Hyperactive

Children," *Journal of Abnormal Child Psychology*, vol. 11, 1983, pp. 313–326; Janet A. Kistner, "Attention Deficits of Learning-Disabled Children: Effects of Rewards and Practice," *Journal of Abnormal Child Psychology*, vol. 13, 1985, pp. 19–31; and Virginia I. Douglas and Penny A. Parry, "Effects of Reward and Nonreward on Frustration and Attention in Attention Deficit Disorder," *Journal of Abnormal Child Psychology*, vol. 22, no. 3, 1994, pp. 281–302.

Kohn is quoted from his book *Punished by Rewards*, p. 71.

Page 55. For an excellent review of research supporting the need of children to engage in active project-centered and problem-solving learning settings, see Howard Gardner, *The Unschooled Mind* (New York: Basic Books, 1992).

For information on children's "other ways of knowing" see Howard Gardner, *Frames of Mind* (New York: Basic Books, 1987); and Howard Gardner, *Multiple Intelligences* (New York: Basic Books, 1993).

Zentall's work supporting the need of "hyperactive children" for novelty and high stimulation includes Sydney Zentall, "Environmental Stimulation Model," *Exceptional Children*, vol. 43, 1977, pp. 502–510; and Sydney Zentall and Thomas R. Zentall, "Optimal Stimulation: A Model of Disordered Activity and Performance ,in Normal and Deviant Children," *Psychological Bulletin*, vol. 94, no. 3, 1983, pp. 446–471.

For studies demonstrating the importance of self-regulation in the lives of children identified as hyperactive, see Donald H. Sykes, Virginia I. Douglas, and Gert Morgenstern, "Sustained Attention in Hyperactive Children," *Journal of Child Psychology and Psychiatry*, vol. 14, 1973, pp. 213–220; and Rolf G. Jacob, K. Daniel O'Leary, and Carl Rosenblad, "Formal and Informal Classroom Settings: Effects on Hyperactivity," *Journal of Abnormal Child Psychology*, vol. 6, no. 1, 1978, pp. 47–59.

For research on "hyperactive children" resenting being excluded from decision-making processes, see Gary A. Williamson and Robert Anderson, "The Ecological Treatment of Hyperkinesis," *Psychology in the Schools*, vol. 17, no. 2, April 1980, p. 252.

"Effective" treatments for A.D.D. are reviewed in Barbara D. Ingersoll and Sam Goldstein, *Attention Deficit Disorder and Learning Disabilities: Realities, Myths, and Controversial Treatments*.

Pages 55–56. The "turning flash cards" technique is suggested in Barbara D. Ingersoll and Sam Goldstein, *Attention Deficit Disorder and Learning Disabilities: Realities, Myths, and Controversial Treatments* (New York: Doubleday, 1993), p. 104.

Page 56. Ingersoll and Goldstein say that double-blind placebo-controlled studies can take years in Sam Goldstein and Barbara Ingersoll, "Controversial Treatments for Children with Attention Deficit Hyperactivity Disorder," *Chadder Box*, vol. 6, no. 2, Fall/Winter 1992, p. 19.

For a review of several alternative research paradigms, see Mary Simpson Poplin, "Self-Imposed Blindness: The Scientific Method in Education," *Remedial and Special Education*, vol. 8, no. 6, November/December 1987, pp. 31–37.

Page 57. Linus Pauling is quoted in Ray Wunderlich and Dwight K. Kalita, *Nourishing Your Child: A Bioecologic Approach* (New Canaan, CT: Keats, 1984), pp. 93–94.

Beverly Rubik is quoted in Leslie Miller, "Getting to the Heart of Healing and the Mind," *USA Today,* October 26, 1993, p. 4D.

Pages 57–58. The recommendation for clearly defined expectations for kids identified as A.D.D. is included in Christine Hunter, *Creative Approaches to ADHD: Myths and Reality* (Minneapolis: University of Minnesota, 1991), p. 4.

#1—Provide a Balanced Breakfast

Pages 68–69. The George Washington University study was reported in *Science News,* vol. 132, no. 11, September 12, 1987, p. 168.

Page 70. Richard Morriss's guidelines for monitoring behavioral effects of a balanced breakfast are included in his article "Children with Attention Disorders in School: A Descriptive Guide for Parents and Teachers," ERIC Document ED 329 061/EC 300 055.

Lendon Smith is quoted in Jane Kinderlehrer, "Wake Up Your Life with a Healthy Breakfast," *Prevention,* February 1984, p. 50.

The *New England Journal of Medicine* study is reported in the January 24, 1991, issue (vol. 324, no. 4, p. 232).

#2—Consider the Feingold Diet

Page 73. The Food Research Institute study was published in J. Preston Harley et al., "Hyperkinesis and Food Additives: Testing the Feingold Hypothesis," *Pediatrics,* vol. 61, no. 6, June 1978, pp. 818–828.

For the pro-Feingold-diet study which appeared in the same issue as the Food Research Institute study, see J. Ivan Williams et al., "Relative Effects of Drugs and Diet on Hyperactive Behaviors: An Experimental Study," *Pediatrics,* vol. 61, no. 6, June 1978, pp. 811–817.

For the study that found two out of twenty-two kids displaying negative reactions to food additives, see Bernard Weiss et al., "Behavioral Responses to Artificial Food Colors," *Science,* vol. 207, no. 28, March 1980, pp. 1487–1489. See also Katherine S. Rowe and Kenneth J. Rowe, "Synthetic Food Coloring and Behavior: A Dose Response Effect in a Double-Blind, Placebo-Controlled, Repeated Measures Study," *Journal of Pediatrics,* vol. 125, 1994, pp. 691–698.

The governmental panel assembled to evaluate diets like the Feingold diet reported its findings in Lloyd W. Denny et al., "NIH Consensus Development Conference: Defined Diets and Childhood Hyperactivity," *Clinical Pediatrics,* vol. 21, no. 10, October 1982, pp. 627–630. It should be noted that it is also difficult to tell in advance whether specific children will benefit from medications such as psychostimulants and antidepressants.

#3—Limit Television and Video Games

Page 75. For John Rosemond's perspective on television, children, and A.D.D. write him at P.O. Box 4171, Gastonia, NC 28054-0020.

Pages 75–76. Matthew Dumont is quoted in Marie Winn, *The Plug-In Drug* (New York: Penguin, 1985), p. 15.

Page 76. Jane Healy's views on the role of television and video in modifying children's attentional mechanisms are presented in her book *Endangered Minds: Why Our Children Don't Think* (New York: Simon & Schuster, 1990), pp. 199–200.

The experiment using the Bobo dolls is presented in Albert Bandura, "Influence of Models' Reinforcement Contingencies on the Acquisition of Imitative Responses," *Journal of Personality and Social Psychology*, vol. 1, 1965, pp. 589–595.

The study done with two groups of boys watching violent and non-violent films is presented in J. P. Leyens et al., "Effects of Movie Violence on Aggression in a Field Setting as a Function of Group Dominance and Cohesion," *Journal of Personality and Social Psychology*, vol. 32, 1975, pp. 346–360.

Page 77. APA figures on TV murders and brutality taken from Tori DeAngelis, "It's Baaack: TV Violence Concern for Kid Viewers," *APA Monitor*, August 1993, p. 16.

Jerry Mander is quoted from his book *Four Arguments for the Elimination of Television* (New York: Morrow Quill, 1978), p. 168.

For research on the ability of children identified as A.D.D. to split their attention between TV and other activities, see Steven Landau, Elizabeth Pugzles Lorch, and Richard Milich, "Visual Attention to and Comprehension of Television in Attention-Deficit Hyperactivity Disordered and Normal Boys," *Child Development*, vol. 63, 1992, pp. 928–937.

For some of the benefits of TV watching (and video games) for children, see Patricia Marks Greenfield, *Mind and Media: The Effects of Television, Video Games, and Computers* (Cambridge, MA: Harvard University Press, 1984).

#4—Teach Self-Talk Skills

Page 79. One of the first studies to document the benefits of self-talk with "hyperactive children" was done by Donald H. Meichenbaum and Joseph Goodman. See Meichenbaum and Goodman, "Training Impulsive Children to Talk to Themselves: A Means of Developing Self-Control," *Journal of Abnormal Psychology*, vol. 77, no. 2, 1971, pp. 115–126.

Page 80. The University of Montana study is reported in Philip H. Bornstein and Randal P. Quevillon, "The Effects of a Self-Instructional Package on Overactive Preschool Boys," *Journal of Applied Behavior Analysis*, vol. 9, 1976, pp. 179–188.

The report on the private speech of children labeled A.D.D. is presented in Laura Berk and Steven Landau, "Private Speech of Learning Disabled and Normally Achieving Children in Classroom Academic and Laboratory Contexts," *Child Development*, vol. 61, no. 2, April 1993, pp. 555–571.

For a description of visual and haptic types of learners, see Viktor Lowenfeld and W. Lambert Brittain, *Creative and Mental Growth*, 5th ed. (New York: Macmillan, 1971), p. 234.

Zentall's research is presented in Sydney Zentall, "Production Deficiencies in Elicited Language but Not in the Spontaneous Verbalizations of Hyperactive Children," *Journal of Abnormal Child Psychology*, vol. 16, 1988, pp. 657–673.

#5—*Find Out What Interests Your Child*

Page 82. Russell Barkley presents the view on motivational deficits in his book *Attention Deficit Hyperactivity Disorder: A Handbook for Diagnosis and Treatment*, pp. 26–27.

Page 84. David's teacher reports on her work with him in Nadine Markowitz, "David Was Always On the Move," *Learning*, October 1986, pp. 53–54.

Page 85. The story of the "weepals" is reported in Thomas Armstrong, "Sparking Creativity in Your Child," *Ladies' Home Journal*, October 1993, pp. 122–124.

#6—*Promote a Strong Physical Education Program in Your Child's School*

Page 86. The report on PE classes in Texas schools appears in *The American Journal of Public Health*, vol. 82, no. 2, February 1993, p. 262.

Figures on the nation's PE requirements are presented in Jessica Portner, "46 States Mandate P.E., But Only Four Found to Require Classes in All Grades," *Education Week*, November 3, 1993, p. 10.

The Kellogg Foundation study is cited in Stephen J. Virgilio and Gerald S. Berenson, "Super Kids—Superfit: A Comprehensive Fitness Intervention Model for Elementary Schools," *Journal of Physical Education, Recreation, and Dance* (*JOPERD*), vol. 59, no. 8, October 1988, p. 20.

Page 87. On the Galindo Elementary School program, see Vern Seefeldt and Paul Vogel, "What Can We Do About Physical Education?" *Principal*, vol. 70, November 1990, pp. 12–14.

The Bogalusa, Louisiana, program is described in Stephen J. Virgilio and Gerald S. Berenson, "Super Kids—Superfit," pp. 20–25.

The Bettendorf, Iowa, program is described in Richard L. Marsh, "Physical Fitness Can Be Fun," *Principal*, January 1987, p. 41.

Hugh Stevenson is quoted in T. Coat, "Can Running Help Troubled Kids?" *San Diego Tribune*, January 13, 1982.

NASPE recommendations for PE appear in Jessica Portner, "46 States Mandate P.E., But Only Four Found to Require Classes in All Grades," *Education Week*, November 3, 1993, p. 10.

Jeffrey Alexander is quoted from his article "Hyperactive Children: Which Sports Have the Right Stuff?" *The Physician and Sportsmedicine*, vol. 18, no. 4, April 1990, p. 106.

For other ideas about getting involved as a parent in the improvement of your child's PE program, see Stephen J. Virgilio, "A model for Parental Involvement in Physical Education," *JOPERD*, October 1990, pp. 66–70.

#7—Enroll Your Child in a Martial Arts Class

Page 89. Jeffrey Alexander is quoted from his article "Hyperactive Children: Which Sports Have the Right Stuff?" *The Physician and Sports Medicine*, vol. 18, no. 4, April 1990, p. 106.

#8—Discover Your Child's Personal Learning Style

Page 92. My own research on the strengths of children with school difficulties is presented in Thomas Armstrong, "Describing Strengths in Children Labeled 'Learning Disabled,' Using Howard Gardner's Theory of Multiple Intelligences as an Organizing Framework" (Ann Arbor, MI: University Microfilms, 1985).

Pages 92-93. Howard Gardner's theory of multiple intelligences is presented in his book *Frames of Mind: The Theory of Multiple Intelligences* (New York: Basic Books, 1987). See also Howard Gardner, *Multiple Intelligences: The Theory in Practice* (New York: Basic Books, 1993).

Recent articles on the theory of multiple intelligences include the following: "Seven Ways of Knowing, Not One," *Education Week*, January 27, 1988, p. 19; Marie Winn, "New Views of Human Intelligence," *New York Times Magazine*, April 29, 1990, p. 16; David Stipp, "New Intelligence Tests Emphasize Abilities Overlooked by IQ Exams," *Wall Street Journal*, March 12, 1987, p. 35; Art Levine, "Getting Smart About IQ," *U.S. News and World Report*, November 23, 1987, pp. 53–55; and "A Lot to Learn," *Life*, vol. 13, no 7, Spring 1990, pp. 56–60.

#9—Use Background Music to Focus and Calm

Pages 97-98. For the Oregon Health Sciences University study, see Frances F. Cripe, "Rock Music as Therapy for Children with Attention Deficit Disorder: An Exploratory Study," *Journal of Music Therapy*, vol. XXIII, no. 1, 1986, pp. 30–37.

On the focusing effect of Beatles' music on children identified as hyperactive, see Thomas J. Scott, "The Use of Music to Reduce Hyperactivity in Children," *American Journal of Orthopsychiatry*, vol. 40, no. 4, 1969, pp. 677–680.

Page 98. The Eastern Kentucky University study is presented in Sydney S. Zentall and Jandira H. Shaw, "Effects of Classroom Noise on Performance and Activity of Second-Grade Hyperactive and Control Children," *Journal of Educational Psychology*, vol. 72, no. 6, 1980, pp. 830–840.

For the study conducted near Los Angeles International Airport, see S. Cohen et al., "Aircraft Noise and Children: Longitudinal and Cross-Sectional Evidence on

Adaptation to Noise and the Effectiveness of Noise Abatement," *Journal of Personality and Social Psychology*, vol. 40, 1981, pp. 331–345.

Page 99. To learn more about the use of music as a healing or integrating force in the past or in other cultures, see Don Campbell (ed.), *Music: Physician for Times to Come* (Wheaton, IL: Quest, 1991); and E. May, *Musics of Many Cultures* (Berkeley, CA: University of California Press, 1980).

#10—Use Color to Highlight Information

Pages 101–102. For Zentall's work on the impact of color with children labeled A.D.D., see Sydney S. Zentall and Theresa Kruczek, "The Attraction of Color for Active Attention-Problem Children," *Exceptional Children*, vol. 54, no. 4, 1988, pp. 357–362; Sydney S. Zentall, Steven D. Falkenburg, and Linda B. Smith, "Effects of Color Stimulation and Information on the Copying Performance of Attention-Problem Adolescents," *Journal of Abnormal Child Psychology*, vol. 13, no. 4, 1985, pp. 501–511; and Sydney S. Zentall, "Effects of Color Stimulation on Performance and Activity of Hyperactive and Nonhyperactive Children," *Journal of Educational Psychology*, vol. 78, no. 2, 1986, pp. 159–165.

Page 102. Barbara Meister Vitale is quoted from her book *Unicorns Are Real: A Right-Brained Approach to Learning* (Rolling Hills Estates, CA: Jalmar, 1982), p. 67.

#11—Teach Your Child to Visualize

Pages 104–105. For examples of eminent individuals throughout history who used their imaginations to advance their ideas, see Stanley Krippner and William Hughes, "Genius at Work," *Psychology Today*, vol. 4, no. 1, June 1970, pp. 40–43.

Page 105. Robert A. Moss is quoted from his book *Why Johnny Can't Concentrate: Coping with Attention Deficit Problems* (New York: Bantam, 1990), p. 59.

Pages 105–106. The Turtle Technique is presented in Arthur Robin, Marlene Schneider, and Michelle Dolnick, "The Turtle Technique: An Extended Case Study of Self-Control in the Classroom," *Psychology in the Schools*, vol. 13, no. 4, October 1976, pp. 449–453.

Page 106. The girl's fantasy of the wild horse is presented in Thomas D. Schneidler, "Application of Psychosynthesis Techniques to Child Psychotherapy" (paper presented at the International Conference on Psychosynthesis, Val Morin, Quebec, August 1973).

#12—Remove Allergens from the Diet

Page 108. The University of Calgary study is published in Bonnie J. Kaplan et al., "Dietary Replacement in Preschool-Aged Hyperactive Boys," *Pediatrics*, vol. 83, no. 7, January 1989, pp. 7–17.

Page 109. The 1985 British study is presented in J. Egger et al., "Controlled Trial of Oligoantigenic Treatment in the Hyperkinetic Syndrome," *Lancet*, March 9, 1985, pp. 540–545.

For a pro-link perspective on the relationship between allergies and A.D.D., see Norbert Roth et al., "Coincidence of Attention Deficit Disorder and Atopic Disorders in Children: Empirical Findings and Hypothetical Background," *Journal of Abnormal Child Psychology*, vol. 19, no. 1, 1991, pp. 1–13; for an opposing view, see Rob McGee et al., "Allergic Disorders and Attention Deficit Disorder in Children," *Journal of Abnormal Child Psychology*, vol. 21, no. 1, 1993, pp. 79–88.

Pages 109–110. For more specific information on procedures and foods involved in an allergy-free diet, see William Crook, *Solving the Puzzle of Your Hard-to-Raise Child* (New York: Random House, 1987), pp. 96–105.

#13—Provide Opportunities for Physical Movement

Page 111. Tony's story is told in Maureen Murdock, *Spinning Inward: Using Guided Imagery with Children* (Culver City, CA: Peace Press, 1982, pp. 37–38).

Page 112. The story of Otto and the Mechanic is presented in Matthew Galvin, *Otto Learns About His Medicine: A Story About Medication for Hyperactive Children* (New York: Brunner/Mazel, 1988).

Pages 112–113. On the CH.A.D.D. education guidelines, see The Education Committee of CH.A.D.D., "Attention Deficit Disorders: A Guide for Teachers" (Plantation, FL: CH.A.D.D., 1988). Available by contacting CH.A.D.D. at 499 NW 70th Avenue, Suite 109, Plantation, FL 33317; 305-587-3700.

Page 113. A teacher's account of building David's special desk is provided in Nadine Markowitz, "David Was Always On the Move," *Learning*, October 1986, pp. 53–54.

#14—Enhance Your Child's Self-Esteem

Page 115. The child's story of going to school is from a lecture given by Robert Brooks entitled "Fostering the Self-Esteem of Children with ADD: The Search for Islands of Competence," at the fourth annual CH.A.D.D. conference, October 1992, in Chicago.

Pages 115–116. On A.D.D.-identified kids and self-esteem: Jill A. Walters-Pace, David B. Baker, and Susan L. Anderson, "Evaluations of Self-Perception in ADHD Children" (paper presented at the annual convention of the American Psychological Association, San Francisco, August 1992).

Page 116. On Jan Loney's research showing low self-esteem in "hyperactive children," see Jan Loney, "The Intellectual Functioning of Hyperactive Elementary School Boys," *American Journal of Orthopsychiatry*, vol. 44, no. 4, October 1974, pp. 754–762.

#15—Find Your Child's Best Times of Alertness

Pages 119–120. Timothy Monk's findings are reported in Edward Dolnick, "Snap out of It!" *San Francisco Chronicle*, April 19, 1992, p. 9 (suppl.).

Page 120. The results of the Northwestern study are presented in Robert Zagar and Norman D. Bowers, "The Effect of Time of Day on Problem Solving and Classroom Behavior," *Psychology in the Schools*, vol. 20, July 1983, pp. 337–345.

For the National Institute of Mental Health study, see Linda J. Porrino et al., "A Naturalistic Assessment of the Motor Activity of Hyperactive Boys," *Archives of General Psychiatry*, vol. 40, June 1983, pp. 681–687.

Robert Sylwester and Joo-Yun Cho are quoted from their article "What Brain Research Says About Paying Attention," *Educational Leadership*, December 1992–January 1993, p. 74.

#16—Give Instructions in Attention-Grabbing Ways

Page 122. The educator's guide that recommends stating specific, ten-words-or-less instructions is Lauren Braswell, Michael Bloomquist, and Sheila Pederson, *ADHD: A Guide to Understanding and Helping Children with Attention Deficit Hyperactivity Disorder in School Settings* (Minneapolis: University of Minnesota, 1991), p. 52.

Pages 122–123. Ellen Gellerstedt is quoted in Sid Kirchheimer, *The Doctors Book of Home Remedies II* (Emmaus, PA: Rodale, 1993), p. 295.

Page 123. Tony Buzan's suggestions for making information compelling are presented in his book *Use Both Sides of Your Brain* (New York: Dutton, 1976), p. 63.

Robert Sylwester and Joo-Yun Cho are quoted in their article "What Brain Research Says About Paying Attention," *Educational Leadership*, December 1992–January 1993, p. 71.

Sydney Zentall's comments on novelty and the use of music to present instructions are contained in Sydney Zentall, "Outcomes of ADD: Academic and Social Performance and Their Related School and Home Treatments," *Proceedings of the CH.A.D.D. Fourth Annual Conference* (Fairfax, VA: Caset Associates, 1993), p. 17.

#17—Provide a Variety of Stimulating Learning Activities

Page 126. For a description and justification (as well as several illustrations) of the "Cruickshank classroom," see William M. Cruickshank, "The Learning Environment," in William M. Cruickshank and Daniel P. Hallahan (eds.), *Perceptual and Learning Disabilities in Children, Vol. 1, Psychoeducational Practices* (Syracuse, NY: Syracuse University Press, 1975).

Pages 126–127. Zentall's ideas on optimal stimulation and hyperactivity are presented in Sydney S. Zentall and Thomas R. Zentall, "Optimal Stimulation: A model of Disordered Activity and Performance in Normal and Deviant Children," *Psychological Bulletin*, vol. 94, no. 3, 1983, pp. 446–471; and Sydney Zentall, "Optimal Stimulation as a Theoretical Basis of Hyperactivity," *American Journal of Orthopsychiatry*, vol. 45, no. 4, July 1975, pp. 549–563.

Page 127. Zentall's high-stimulation/low-stimulation experiment is summarized in Sydney S. Zentall and Thomas R. Zentall, "Activity and Task Performance of

Hyperactive Children as a Function of Environmental Stimulation," *Journal of Consulting and Clinical Psychology*, vol. 44, no. 5, 1976, pp. 693–697.

Zentall's study on the effect of loud talking as a distractor in the classroom is presented in Sydney S. Zentall and Jandira H. Shaw, "Effects of Classroom Noise on Performance and Activity of Second-Grade Hyperactive and Control Children," *Journal of Educational Psychology*, vol. 72, no. 6, 1980, pp. 830–840.

Page 128. Zentall is quoted from Sydney Zentall, "Outcomes of ADD: Academic and Social Performance and Their Related School and Home Treatments," *Proceedings of the CH.A.D.D. Fourth Annual Conference*, p. 17.

A description of the Underwood Elementary School curriculum is given in "At Schools," *Instructor*, May 1986, pp. 24–26.

The accomplishments of South Medford (Oregon) High School students are reported in "No More Business As Usual," *NEA Today*, February 1989, pp. 4–5.

#18—Consider Biofeedback Training

Page 133. Joel Lubar is quoted from Joel Lubar and Russell A. Barkley, "Point/Counterpoint: Is EEG Neurofeedback an Effective Treatment for ADHD?" *Proceedings of the CH.A.D.D. Fourth Annual Conference*, p. 209.

For the review of the literature and evaluation of the effectiveness of biofeedback, see Steven W. Lee, "Biofeedback as a Treatment for Childhood Hyperactivity: A Critical Review of the Literature," *Psychological Reports*, vol. 68, 1991, pp. 163–192.

#19—Activate Positive Career Aspirations

Page 136. For long-term studies of individuals identified in childhood as hyperactive, see Gabrielle Weiss et al., "Psychiatric Status of Hyperactives as Adults: A Controlled Prospective 15-Year Follow-up of 63 Hyperactive Children," *Journal of the American Academy of Child Psychiatry*, vol. 23, 1985, pp. 211–220; and Salvatore Mannuzza et al., "Adult Outcome of Hyperactive Boys," *Archives of General Psychiatry*, vol. 50, July 1993, pp. 565–576.

The McGill study comparing teacher and employer reports is presented in G. Weiss, L. Hechtman, and T. Perlman, "Hyperactives as Young Adults: School, Employer and Self-Rating Scales Obtained During Ten-Year Follow-Up Evaluation," *American Journal of Orthopsychiatry*, vol. 48, 1978, pp. 439–445.

For the study that showed higher levels of the self-employed among individuals who were identified as hyperactive in childhood, see Mannuzza et al., 1993.

#20—Teach Your Child Physical-Relaxation Techniques

Page 139. For a review of the literature on relaxation training for "hyperactive children," see Neil C. Richter, "The Efficacy of Relaxation Training with Children," *Journal of Abnormal Child Psychology*, vol. 12, no. 2, 1984, pp. 319–344. See also,

Dvora Zipkin, "Relaxation Techniques for Handicapped Children: A Review of the Literature," *The Journal of Special Education*, vol. 19, no. 3, 1985, pp. 283–289.

Page 140. For the study that used progressive relaxation tapes with children identified as hyperactive, see L. Braud, "The Effects of Frontal EMG Biofeedback and Progressive Relaxation upon Hyperactivity and Its Behavioral Concomitants," *Biofeedback and Self-Regulation*, vol. 3, 1978, pp. 69–89.

On the importance of self-pacing and multiple sessions in progressive relaxation training, see T. D. Borkovec and J. K. Sides, "Critical Procedural Variables Related to the Psychological Effects of Progressive Relaxation: A review," *Behaviour Research and Therapy*, vol. 17, 1979, pp. 119–125.

Page 141. T. Berry Brazelton is quoted from his article "How Active Is Hyperactive?" *Family Circle*, May 12, 1992, p. 47.

#21—*Use Incidental Learning to Teach*

Page 143. For studies that point to the capacity of "A.D.D. and LD children" to diffuse their attention over a wide spectrum of activity, see Stephen J. Ceci and Jayne Tishman, "Hyperactivity and Incidental Memory: Evidence for Attentional Diffusion," *Child Development*, vol. 55, no. 6, December 1984, pp. 2192–2203; and William E. Pelham and Alan O. Ross, "Selective Attention in Children with Reading Problems: A Developmental Study of Incidental Learning," *Journal of Abnormal Child Psychology*, vol. 5, no. 1, 1977, pp. 1–8.

Page 145. For information about superlearning or suggestopedia applied to special education, see Lyelle L. Palmer, "Suggestive Accelerative Learning and Teaching (SALT) with Learning Disabled and Other Special Needs Students: A Literature Review and Meta-analysis," *Journal of the Society for Accelerative Learning and Teaching*, vol. 10, no. 2, 1985, pp. 99–127; and Fran Lehr, "ERIC/RCS Report: Suggestopedia," *Language Arts*, vol. 64, no. 7, November 1987, pp. 778–781.

#22—*Support Full Inclusion of Your Child in a Regular Classroom*

Page 147. To learn more about the full-inclusion movement, see Susan Stainback, William Stainback, and Marsha Forest (eds.), *Educating All Students in the Mainstream of Regular Education* (Baltimore: Paul H. Brookes, 1989); C. Beth Schaffner and Barbara Buswell, *Opening Doors: Strategies for Including All Students in Regular Education* (Colorado Springs, CO: Peak Parent Center, 1991), Peak Parent Center, 6055 Lehman, Colorado Springs, CO 80918; and Douglas Biklen, *Schooling Without Labels: Parents, Educators, and Inclusive Education* (Philadelphia: Temple University Press, 1992).

Wade Horn is quoted from *Chadder Box*, January 1994, p. 1.

Page 148. On the problems connected with special education programs that exclude students from the mainstream, see Denny Taylor, *Learning Denied* (Portsmouth, NH: Heinemann, 1991); Bill and Lori Granger, *The Magic Feather: The*

Truth About "Special Education" (New York: Dutton, 1986); Hugh Mehan, *Handicapping the Handicapped: Decision Making in Students' Educational Careers* (Stanford, CA: Stanford University Press, 1986); Alan Gartner and Dorothy Kerzner Lipsky, "Beyond Special Education: Toward a Quality System for All Students," *Harvard Educational Review*, vol. 57, no. 4, November 1987, pp. 367–395; Anne Martin, "Screening, Early Intervention, and Remediation: Obscuring Children's Potential," *Harvard Educational Review*, vol. 58, 1988, pp. 488–501; and Todd Silberman et al., "Left Out: The Special Education Stigma," *The Raleigh* (N.C.) *News and Observer*, March 7, 1993, Section J (special suppl.). This latter piece won Grand Prize in the 1993 Benjamin Fine Journalism Awards sponsored by the National Association of Secondary School Principals.

Page 149. For a critique of the underlying ethos of special education programs, see Mary Poplin, "The Reductionistic Fallacy in Learning Disabilities: Replicating the Past by Reducing the Present," *Journal of Learning Disabilities*, vol. 21, pp. 389–400; and Scott Sigmon, *Radical Analysis of Special Education* (London: Falmer, 1987).

Page 150. On problems connected with retention of students, see Mary Lee Smith and Lorrie A. Shepard, "What Doesn't Work: Explaining Policies of Retention in the Early Grades," *Phi Delta Kappan*, October 1987, pp. 129–134.

On problems associated with tracking systems, see Jeannie Oakes, *Keeping Track: How Schools Structure Inequality* (New Haven, CT: Yale University Press, 1985).

#23—Provide Positive Role Models

Page 152. Edison's biographer was Robert Conot, who was quoted from his book *A Streak of Luck* (New York: Seaview, 1979), p. 6.

Pages 152–153. Victor Goertzel and Mildred G. Goertzel's comments about Winston Churchill are quoted from *Cradles of Eminence* (Boston: Little, Brown, 1962), pp. 262–266.

Pages 153–154. The brief anecdotes about eminent individuals with behavioral difficulties are from the Goertzels' study (see above) and from R. S. Illingworth and C. M. Illingworth, *Lessons from Childhood: Some Aspects of the Early Life of Unusual Men and Women* (London: E & S Livingstone, 1966).

Page 154. The boy being introduced to the recreational leader is quoted from Dorothea M. Ross and Sheila A. Ross, *Hyperactivity: Current Issues, Research, and Theory* (New York: Wiley, 1982), frontispiece.

James Evans is quoted in Thomas G. West, *In the Mind's Eye: Visual Thinkers, Gifted People with Learning Difficulties, Computer Images, and the Ironies of Creativity* (Buffalo, NY: Prometheus, 1991), p. 63.

#25—Channel Creative Energy into the Arts

Page 160. On the study showing "A.D.D. kids" tell more novel stories than so-called normals, see Sydney S. Zentall, "Production Deficiencies in Elicited Language but Not in the Spontaneous Verbalizations of Hyperactive Children," *Journal of Abnormal Child Psychology*, vol. 16, no. 6, 1988, pp. 657–673.

The general article and three studies on creativity and "giftedness" in kids labeled A.D.D. are the following: James T. Webb and Diane Latimer, "ADHD and Children Who Are Gifted," *Exceptional Children*, vol. 60, no. 2, October-November 1993, pp. 183–184; Geraldine A. Shaw, "Hyperactivity and Creativity: The Tacit Dimension," *Bulletin of the Psychonomic Society*, vol. 30, no. 2, 1992, pp. 157–160; Geraldine A. Shaw and Geoffrey Brown, "Laterality, Implicit Memory, and Attention Disorder," *Educational Studies*, vol. 17, no. 1, 1991, pp. 15–23; and Geraldine A. Shaw and Geoffrey Brown, "Laterality and Creativity Concomitants of Attention Problems," *Developmental Neuropsychology*, vol. 6, no. 1, 1990, pp. 39–56.

Page 161. Cynthia Swope's observations about the creativity of children labeled A.D.D. were presented in John O'Neil, "Looking at Art Through New Eyes," *Curriculum Update*, January 1994, p. 1. *Curriculum Update* is the monthly newsletter of the Association for Supervision and Curriculum Development.

The story of the "A.D.D. boy" who saved the school's music program was told by Evelyn Berlin in *Ladies' Home Journal*, October 1989, p. 108.

For an account of the national trend toward budget cuts in the schools' arts programs, see Debra Viadero, "Music and Arts Courses Disappearing from Curriculum, Commission Warns" *Education Week*, March 13, 1991, p. 4.

#26—Provide Hands-on Activities

Page 165. For a description of Piaget's attitude toward hands-on learning, see John H. Flavell, *The Developmental Psychology of Jean Piaget* (New York: Van Nostrand, 1963), pp. 365–368.

Viktor Lowenfeld is quoted from Viktor Lowenfeld and W. Lambert Brittain, *Creative and Mental Growth*, 5th ed. (London: Macmillan, 1970), p. 234.

Robert McKim is quoted from his book *Experiences in Visual Thinking*, 2nd ed. (Boston: PWS Engineering, 1980), p. 46.

Violet Oaklander is quoted from her book *Windows to Our Children* (Moab, UT: Real People, 1978), p. 228.

#27—Spend Positive Times Together

Page 169. Zig Ziglar was quoted from his book *Raising Positive Kids in a Negative World* (New York: Ballantine, 1989), p. 130.

For the study on the preference of "A.D.D. children" for time with parents as a reward, see Robert D. Hill et al., "A Comparison of Preference for Familial, Social, and Material Rewards Between Hyperactive and Non-hyperactive Boys," *School Psychology International*, vol. 12, no. 3, August 1991, pp. 225–229.

The Hawaii study is presented in E. E. Werner, J. M. Bierman, F. E. French, *The Children of Kauai* (Honolulu: University of Hawaii Press, 1971).

For the study linking positive contact in mothers with fewer commands and more praise, see Robert W. Chamberlin, "Parent Use of 'Positive Contact' in Child-Rearing: Its Relationship to Child Behavior Patterns and Other Variables," *Pediatrics*, vol. 56, no. 5, November 5, 1975, pp. 768–773.

For a description of "invulnerable" or resilient children, see Helen Bee, *The Developing Child*, 4th ed. (New York: Harper & Row, 1985), p. 506; and Michael Rutter, "Resilient Children," *Psychology Today*, March 1984, pp. 57–65.

On the importance of parental involvement in school success, see Michael Marriott, "The Home's Link to School Success," *New York Times*, June 13, 1990, p. A1+.

#28—Provide Appropriate Spaces for Learning

Page 172. For a description of animal behavior under crowded conditions, see Edward T. Hall, *The Hidden Dimension* (Garden City, NY: Anchor Doubleday, 1969), pp. 23–40.

Carol S. Weinstein is quoted from her article "The Physical Environment of the School: A Review of the Research," *Review of Educational Research*, vol. 49, no. 4, Fall 1979, p. 585. See also Joachim F. Wohlwill and Willem van Vliet (eds.), *Habitats for Children: The Impacts of Density* (Hillsdale, NJ: Lawrence Erlbaum, 1985), pp. 107–108.

Pages 172–173. For the impact of crowding in housing projects on hyperactivity, see Alexander Thomas et al., "Cross-Cultural Study of Behavior in Children with Special Vulnerabilities to Stress," in *Life History Research in Psychopathology*, vol. 3, edited by D. Ricks et al. (Minneapolis: University of Minnesota Press, 1974), p. 61.

Page 173. Anita R. Olds is quoted from her article "Designing Developmentally Optimal Classrooms for Children with Special Needs," in Samuel J. Meisels (ed.), *Special Education and Development* (Baltimore: University Park Press, 1979), p. 95.

Page 174. For information about Rita Dunn's model of learning styles, see Rita Dunn and Ken Dunn, *Teaching Elementary Students Through Their Individual Learning Styles* (Boston: Allyn & Bacon, 1992).

#29—Consider Individual Psychotherapy

Pages 175–176. Dorothea Ross and Sheila Ross are quoted from their book *Hyperactivity: Current Issues, Research, and Theory* (New York: Wiley, 1982), p. 7.

Page 176. Barbara Ingersoll is quoted from her book *Your Hyperactive Child: A Parent's Guide to Coping with Attention Deficit Disorder* (New York: Doubleday, 1988), p. 92.

For research on the presence of anxiety and depression in children identified as A.D.D., see Joseph Biederman, Jeffrey Newcorn, and Susan Sprich, "Comorbidity of Attention Deficit Hyperactivity Disorder with Conduct, Depressive, Anxiety, and Other Disorders," *American Journal of Psychiatry*, vol. 148, no. 5, May 1991, pp. 564–575.

James Satterfield's research is presented in James Satterfield, Brenda Satterfield, and Ann Schell, "Therapeutic Interventions to Prevent Delinquency in Hyperactive Boys," *Academy of Child and Adolescent Psychiatry*, vol. 26, 1987, pp. 56–64.

Page 177. Erik Erikson is quoted from his book *Toys and Reasons* (New York: W. W. Norton, 1977), pp. 33–34.

#30—Use Touch to Soothe and Calm

Page 179. Ashley Montagu's views on the value of human touch can be found in his book *Touching: The Human Significance of the Skin* (New York: Harper & Row, 1986).

Page 180. T. Berry Brazelton is quoted from his article "Living with a Hyperactive Child," *San Francisco Chronicle*, July 16, 1991, p. D5.

On the pediatrician group's study of therapeutic holding with "hyperactive children," see Arvin T. Henderson et al., "A Hypothesis on the Etiology of Hyperactivity, with a Pilot Study Report of Related Nondrug Therapy," *Pediatrics*, vol. 52, no. 4, October 1973, p. 625.

#32—Help Your Child Appreciate the Value of Personal Effort

Page 186. The experiment with rats is described in A. Altenor, E. Kay, and M. Richter, "The Generality of Learned Helplessness in the Rat," *Learning and Motivation*, vol. 8, 1977, pp. 54–61.

Page 187. For research linking learned helplessness with children labeled A.D.D., see Richard Milich and Mimi Okazaki, "An Examination of Learned Helplessness Among Attention-Deficit Hyperactivity Disordered Boys," *Journal of Abnormal Child Psychology*, vol. 19, no. 5, 1991, pp. 607–623.

On "hyperactive children" seeing events as beyond their control, see Richard T. Linn and Gordon K. Hodge, "Locus of Control in Childhood Hyperactivity," *Journal of Consulting and Clinical Psychology*, vol. 50, no. 4, 1982, pp. 592–593.

For an examination of the differences between Asian and U.S. students regarding effort and native ability, see Harold Stevenson and James Stigler, *The Learning Gap: Why Our Schools Are Failing and What We Can Learn from Japanese and Chinese Education* (New York: Summit, 1992), pp. 94–112.

For an account of Jaime Escalante's use of *ganas* as a motivating tool, see Jay Matthews, *Escalante: The Best Teacher in America* (New York: Henry Holt, 1988), p. 191.

Pages 187–188. For the study in which "hyperactive students" improved after receiving attribution training, see Molly K. Reid and John G. Borkowski, "Casual

Attributions of Hyperactive Children: Implications for Teaching Strategies and Self-Control," *Journal of Educational Psychology*, vol. 79, no. 3, 1987, pp. 296–307.

Page 188. The study cited by Dorothy Rich is included in her book *MegaSkills* (Boston: Houghton Mifflin, 1992), p. 54.

#33—Take Care of Yourself

Page 189. For high levels of reported stress among parents of children identified as A.D.D., see Mariellen Fischer, "Parenting Stress and the Child with Attention Deficit Hyperactivity Disorder," *Journal of Clinical Child Psychology*, vol. 19, no. 4, 1990, pp. 337–346.

Pages 189–190. For reports of depression and anxiety in parents of A.D.D.-diagnosed kids, see Bruce Bower, "Hyperactivity: The Family Factor," *Science News*, June 18, 1988, p. 399.

Page 190. On parents of "A.D.D. kids" with greater social support finding the most behavioral improvements in their children, see Wade F. Horn et al., "Behavioral Parent Training and Cognitive-Behavioral Self-Control Therapy with ADD-H Children: Comparative and Combined Effects," *Journal of Clinical Child Psychology*, vol. 16, no. 1, 1987, pp. 57–68.

#34—Teach Your Child Focusing Techniques

Pages 193–195. For a comprehensive bibliographic review of the physiological and psychological benefits of meditation (including its role in enhancing concentration and attention), see Michael Murphy and Steven Donavan, *The Physical and Psychological Effects of Meditation* (San Rafael, CA: Esalen Institute Study of Exceptional Functioning, 1988).

Pages 194–195. For the use of meditation techniques with children labeled A.D.D., see Jonathan Kratter and John D. Hogan, "The Use of Meditation in the Treatment of Attention Deficit Disorder with Hyperactivity," ERIC files: ED 232–787. The approach used in this study was similar to that developed by Harvard Medical School researcher Herbert Benson (who used the word "one" as a focus). See Herbert Benson, *The Relaxation Response* (New York: William Morrow, 1975). See also D. Simpson and A. Nelson, "Attention Training Through Breathing Control to Modify Hyperactivity," *Journal of Learning Disabilities*, vol. 7, 1974, pp. 274–283.

Page 195. Violet Oaklander's approach to helping "hyperactive children" focus is presented in her book *Windows to Our Children* (Moab, UT: Real People, 1978), pp. 226–227.

#36—Provide Your Child with Access to a Computer

Page 199. For a popular description of hypermedia, see Michael Rogers, "Here Comes Hypermedia," *Newsweek*, October 3, 1988, pp. 44–45.

The example of the man mowing the lawn is taken from Robert A. Moss, *Why Johnny Can't Concentrate* (New York: Bantam, 1990), p. 166.

Page 200. For the story of Alan Kay's life, see Frank Rose, "Pied Piper of the Computer," *New York Times Magazine*, November 8, 1987, pp. 56+.

For the study that suggests children labeled A.D.D. prefer computer software in the form of games, see Mary Jane Ford, Virginia Poe, and Juanita Cox, "Attending Behaviors of ADHD Children in Math and Reading Using Various Types of Software," *Journal of Computing in Childhood Education*, vol. 4, no. 2, 1993, pp. 183–196.

Pages 200–201. For the study that shows "A.D.D. children" spend more time with computers than with paper-and-pencil tasks, see P. G. Millman, "The Effects of Computer-Assisted Instruction on Attention Deficits, Achievement, and Attitudes of Learning-Disabled Children" (doctoral dissertation, University of Virginia, 1984); abstract in *Dissertation Abstracts International*, vol. 45, p. 3114A.

#37—Consider Family Therapy

Page 203. Alan Zametkin was quoted in Philip Elmer-DeWitt, "Why Junior Won't Sit Still," *Time*, November 26, 1990, p. 59.

Sandra F. Thomas was quoted in Debra Viadero, "Biological Study May Fuel Debate over Hyperactivity," *Education Week*, November 28, 1990, p. 10.

Page 204. Murray Bowen was quoted in James F. Framo, "Family Theory and Therapy," *American Psychologist*, vol. 34, no. 10, October 1979, pp. 988–992.

Pages 204–205. Evidence for greater misbehavior of "hyperactive children" with mothers than fathers is presented in J. Tallmadge and R. A. Barkley, "The Interactions of Hyperactive and Normal Boys with their Mothers and Fathers," *Journal of Abnormal Child Psychology*, vol. 11, 1983, pp. 565–579.

Page 205. For the study linking marital discord with child behavior, see Andrew Christensen et al., "Parental Characteristics and Interactional Dysfunction in Families with Child Behavior Problems: A Preliminary Investigation," *Journal of Abnormal Child Psychology*, vol. 11, no. 1, 1983, pp. 153–166.

On the study linking parental moderation of a difficult child's temperament with fewer later childhood behavior disturbances, see James R. Cameron, "Parental Temperament, Children's Temperament, and the Risk of Childhood Behavioral Problems," *American Journal of Orthopsychiatry*, vol. 48, no. 1, January 1978, pp. 140–141.

For the impact of different family structures on outcomes for children labeled A.D.D., see Robert Ziegler and Lynn Holden, "Family Therapy for Learning Disabled and Attention-Deficit Disordered Children," *American Journal of Orthopsychiatry*, vol. 58, no. 2, April 1988, pp. 196–210.

For a review of family therapy programs, see Russell A. Barkley et al., "A Comparison of Three Family Therapy Programs for Treating Family Conflicts in Adolescents with Attention-Deficit Hyperactivity Disorder," *Journal of Consulting and Clinical Psychology*, vol. 60, no. 3, 1992, pp. 450–462; and Eugene Arnold,

Katherine Sheridan, and Donna Estreicher, "Multifamily Parent-Child Group Therapy for Behavior and Learning Disorders," *Journal of Child and Adolescent Psychotherapy*, vol. 3, no. 4, 1986, pp. 279–284.

#38—Teach Problem-Solving Skills

Page 208. The study at Toronto's Hospital for Sick Children is reported in Darcy L. Fehlings, Wendy Roberts, Tom Humphries, and Gigi Dawe, "Attention Deficit Hyperactivity Disorder: Does Cognitive Behavioral Therapy Improve Home Behavior?" *Journal of Developmental and Behavioral Pediatrics*, vol. 12, no. 4, August 1991, pp. 223–228.

Betty Youngs' problem-solving method is presented in her book *Stress in Children* (New York: Avon, 1986), pp. 160–162.

#39—Offer Your Child Real-Life Tasks to Do

Page 209. Robert Brooks's story was told in his talk "Fostering the Self-Esteem of Children with ADD: The Search for Islands of Competence," presented at the Fourth Annual Conference of CH.A.D.D., October 1992, in Chicago.

Page 211. For a description of Erikson's "industry-versus-inferiority" stage of human development, see Erik H. Erikson, *Childhood and Society* (New York: W. W. Norton, 1963), pp. 258–261.

On children labeled A.D.D. performing better when they are paid, see Diane McGuinness, *When Children Don't Learn*, pp. 203, 205; and Russell A. Barkley, *Attention Deficit Hyperactivity Disorder*, p. 58.

#40—Use "Time Out" in a Positive Way

Pages 215–216. The dialogue illustrating how to use a 1 . . . 2 . . . 3 . . . time-out procedure is taken from Thomas Phelan, *1-2-3: Magic! Training Your Preschoolers and Preteens to Do What You Want* (Glen Ellyn, IL: Child Management, 1984).

Page 216. On punitive time out's adverse impact on children identified as hyperactive, see Sydney S. Zentall and Thomas R. Zentall, "Optimal Stimulation: A Model of Disordered Activity and Performance in Normal and Deviant Children," *Psychological Bulletin*, vol. 94, no. 3, 1983, pp. 446–471.

Mary Kurcinka is quoted from her book *The Spirited Child* (New York: HarperCollins, 1991), p. 82.

Jane Nelsen and H. Stephen Glenn are quoted from their book *Time Out* (Fair Oaks, CA: Sunrise Press, 1991), p. 13.

#41—Help Your Child Develop Social Skills

Page 219. The 50 to 60 percent figure for social rejection of "A.D.D. youngsters" was taken from David Guevremont, "Social Skills and Peer Relationship Training," in *Attention Deficit Disorder: A Handbook for Diagnosis and Treatment,* edited by Russell A. Barkley (New York: Guilford Press, 1990), p. 540.

Page 220. The University of Pittsburgh study was reported in David J. Kolko, Linda L. Loarr, and Diane Sturnick, "Inpatient Social-Cognitive Skills Training Groups with Conduct Disordered and Attention Deficit Disordered Children," *Journal of Child Psychology and Psychiatry,* vol. 31, no. 5, 1990, pp. 737–748.

#43—Use Effective Communication Skills

Page 225. On the negative communication patterns used by parents of children labeled A.D.D., see C. E. Cunningham and R. A. Barkley, "The Interactions of Hyperactive and Normal Children with Their Mothers During Free Play and Structured Task," *Child Development,* vol. 50, 1979, pp. 217–224.

Pages 226–227. The five communication "barriers" and "builders" are described in more detail in H. Stephen Glenn and Jane Nelsen, *Raising Self-Reliant Children in a Self-Indulgent World* (Rocklin, CA: Prima, 1989), pp. 72–93.

Page 228. The formula for giving "I" messages is presented in Don Dinkmeyer and Gary D. McKay, *S.T.E.P.: The Parent's Handbook* (Circle Pines, MN: American Guidance Service, 1989), pp. 64–65. The "I" message procedure originated in the 1970s with Thomas Gordon. See his book *Parent Effectiveness Training* (New York: Plume, 1991).

#44—Give Your Child Choices

Page 231. The "Johnny look at me! You have a choice!" ultimatum is quoted from Harvey Parker, *The A.D.D. Hyperactivity Workbook for Parents, Teachers, and Kids,* p. 53.

On improvements in motivation in children with behavior problems who are given a voice in decision making: Howard S. Adelman et al., "Motivational Readiness and the Participation of Children with Learning and Behavior Problems in Psychoeducational Decision Making," *Journal of Learning Disabilities,* vol. 23, no. 3, March 1990, pp. 171–176.

On the Purdue study linking higher attentional rates with active involvement in advancing slides, See Sydney S. Zentall and Martha J. Meyer, "Self-Regulation of Stimulation for ADD-H Children During Reading and Vigilance Task Performance," *Journal of Abnormal Child Psychology,* vol. 15, no. 4, 1987, pp. 519–536.

Pages 231–232. Violet Oaklander is quoted from her book *Windows to Our Children* (Moab, UT: Real People, 1978), p. 230.

#45—Discover and Treat the Four Types of Misbehavior

Page 234. Kahlil Gibran's poem is quoted from his book *The Prophet* (New York: Alfred A. Knopf, 1964), p. 17.

Page 237. Mr. Gilbert is quoted in Jane Nelsen, *Time Out* (Fair Oaks, CA: Sunrise, 1992), pp. 37–38.

#46—Establish Consistent Rules, Routines, and Transitions

Pages 238–239. Diana Baumrind's model of parenting styles is described in Helen Bee, *The Developing Child* (4th ed.), (New York: Harper & Row, 1985), pp. 464–465.

#47—Hold Family Meetings

Page 242. Rudolf Dreikurs is quoted from Rudolf Dreikurs and Vicki Soltz, *Children: The Challenge* (New York: Hawthorn, 1964), p. 305.

#48—Have Your Child Teach a Younger Child

Page 246. The program involving high school students teaching children labeled mentally retarded is cited in Helen Featherstone, "Big Kids Teach Little Kids: What We Know About Cross-Age Tutoring," *The Harvard Education Letter*, vol. III, no. 2, p. 1.

Page 247. The Fernald Child Study Center research is summarized in Duane Burhmester et al., "Prosocial Behavior in Hyperactive Boys: Effects of Stimulant Medication and Comparison with Normal Boys," *Journal of Abnormal Child Psychology*, vol. 20, no. 1, 1992, pp. 103–121.

The Utah tutoring project is cited in Featherstone, p. 2.

The program that matched "behaviorally disabled" with "gifted" students is cited in Russell T. Osguthorpe, "Trading Places: Why Disabled Students Should Tutor Non-disabled Students," *The Exceptional Parent*, September 1985, p. 45.

#50—Hold a Positive Image of Your Child

Page 253. Linda S. Budd is quoted from her book *Living with the Active Alert Child* (New York: Prentice-Hall, 1990), pp. 34–35. Her position and the A.D.D. issue is presented on page 225.

Pages 253–254. Mary Sheedy Kurcinka's position on A.D.D. is presented in her book *Raising Your Spirited Child* (New York: HarperCollins, 1991), p. 38.

Page 254. Thom Hartmann is quoted in his book *Attention Deficit Disorder: A Different Perception* (Lancaster, PA: Underwood-Miller, 1993), p. 13.

Pages 254–255. For background on the maturational lag hypothesis for hyperactivity, see Dorothea M. Ross and Sheila A. Ross, *Hyperactivity: Current Issues, Research, and Theory*, 2nd ed. (New York: Wiley, 1982), pp. 103–106.

Page 255. Ashley Montagu's views on neotony are presented in his book *Growing Young* (New York: McGraw-Hill, 1983). A wonderful example of neotony at work in adulthood can be seen in the life of perhaps the world's best example of a genius, Albert Einstein, who wrote: "How did it come to pass that I was the one to develop the theory of relativity? The reason, I think, is that a normal adult never stops to think about problems of space and time. These are things which he has thought of as a child. But my intellectual development was retarded, as a result of which I began to wonder about space and time only when I had already grown up. Naturally, I could go deeper into the problem than a child with normal abilities." Quoted in Howard Gardner, *Creating Minds* (New York: Basic Books, 1993), p. 89. I sometimes think Einstein's fabled absent-mindedness might have even qualified him for the label "attention deficit disorder without hyperactivity" had he grown up in today's world and gone to a specialist for his daydreaming (and what might Ritalin have done to his creative mental ramblings?).

See Also Bonnie Cramond, "Attention-Deficit Hyperactivity Disorder and Creativity: What Is the Connection?" *Journal of Creative Behavior*, 1994, vol. 28, no. 3, pp. 193–210.

Paul Cooper, "Attention Deficit Hyperactivity Disorder and the Strange Case of Vincent van Gogh," *Therapeutic Care Education*, Summer 1994, vol. 3, no. 2, pp. 86–95.

Index

Index

Wisconsin Card Sort Test, 17
WKRP in Cincinnati (TV series),
    172
Wordsworth, William, 153
Wright, Orville, 153

Yoga, 139
Youngs, Betty B., 208

Your Hyperactive Child (Ingersoll),
    176

Zajonc, Robert, 62
Zametkin, A. J., 20–21, 203
Zentall, Sydney, 55, 80, 101–2, 123,
    126–28
Ziglar, Zig, 169